INVISIBLE CAREERS

Women in Culture and Society
A series edited by Catharine R. Stimpson

INVISIBLE

Women Civic Leaders
from the Volunteer World

CAREERS

Arlene Kaplan Daniels

The University of Chicago Press
Chicago and London

Arlene Kaplan Daniels, professor of sociology at Northwestern University, is the
co-author of *Working in Foundations: Career Patterns of Women and Men* and co-editor
of *Women and Work: Problems and Perspectives*.

The University of Chicago Press, Chicago 60637
The University of Chicago Press, Ltd., London
© 1988 by The University of Chicago
All rights reserved. Published 1988
Printed in the United States of America

97 96 95 94 93 92 91 90 89 88   5 4 3 2 1

Library of Congress Cataloging-in-Publication Data

Daniels, Arlene Kaplan, 1930–
  Invisible careers.

  (Women in culture and society)
  Bibliography: p. 285.
  Includes index.
    1. Women volunteers in social service—United
States.   2. Voluntarism—United States.   3. Women in
community organization—United States.   I. Title.
II. Series.
HV40.42.D36   1988   361.3'7'088042   87–25515
ISBN 0–226–13610–8

In memory of
Caroline Charles
a gallant citizen and a great lady

Contents

Series Editor's Foreword

In the boffo Marx Brothers comedy *Duck Soup*, Margaret Dumont plays Mrs. Teasdale, a society matron of a certain age and girth. At the end of the film, after her country has won a war, she bursts into song, "Hail, Freedonia." Undaunted by either her patriotism or her position, the Marx Brothers pelt her with fruit.

The tweaking of Mrs. Teasdale is one of the responses, at once envious and hostile, that democratic cultures have to wealthy, well-born women. Now *Invisible Careers* asks us to regard them more dispassionately. Arlene Kaplan Daniels gives us a group of seventy upper-middle class and upper-class women in "Pacific City," a major urban center in the Northwest. About sixty percent of them are Protestants; the rest are Catholics and Jews. Not surprisingly, given the iniquities of race and class in the United States, only one is black. The rest are white.

These women dislike two images of their peers: ". . . the woman as a senseless, if ornamental, appendage and the woman as a directionless, problem child." They have made a mature choice to work for society. They devote themselves to better schools and parks; museums and music; conservation and preservation; hospitals and shelters; good government and civic causes. They are philanthropists and volunteers. They do not file a W-2 or a W-4 form. Their rewards are, instead, prestige, experience, "psychic income," some civic power, and a sense of virtue. In brief, they work for free.

Free things still extract a price. Because the women of Pacific City contribute their labor, and because they are women, their work is invisible. Like glue, it cannot be seen—even as it holds things together. Yet, as Arlene Kaplan Daniels insists, their voluntarism is work. Daniels persuasively and originally renders voluntarism visible as an occupation, as a career. It has its entry points, career

ix

paths, mentors, specialized tasks, and criteria of success—such as membership on a prestigious board. As volunteers move up through the ranks, they will first co-operate with, and then govern, professional staffs. Daniels carefully maps the social relationships between those who get a paycheck and those who do not. However, the latter determine the amount of the paycheck. Daniels permits the women of Pacific City to speak for themselves. Their language, like their lives, is serviceable. Brought up to obey the laws of decorum, the women of Pacific City seem to adjure both the dangerous depths of introspection and the wild flights of lyricism. They are pleasant, clear, well spoken, polite, often self-deprecating. Yet, that very self-deprecation is one sign of the stresses, tensions, and conflicts that their careers embody.

For, in the United States, careers demand commitment. The women of Pacific City claim that their first duty is to their family, not to their career. Caring for their husbands and children is their primary job. Indeed, their first volunteer activity is often with schools or programs for children. Careers ask for a sense of autonomy; yet, the women of Pacific City praise self-sacrifice. Careers demand public performance; yet, the women of Pacific City confess that performing in public often scares them. Careers are inseparable from the market. Many feminists believe that women's traditionally unpaid labor, whether at home or in philanthropy, is exploited labor; yet, the women of Pacific City believe that unpaid labor is a good. Altruism is necessary for "the community."

Daniels ruefully and shrewdly comments that the word "community" glosses over and denies the reality of Pacific City. For it is a number of communities, each with a different rank and status. It has a class structure. The women of Pacific City represent, even if they do not recognize, the interlocking of our structures of class and gender. Because of their wealth and family, elite women have power over men and other women; because they are women, they have less power than their fathers, brothers, husbands, and sons.

The upbringing of the women of Pacific City to be ladies leads them to downplay conflicts among the classes and between the genders. So doing, they have two precarious, mutually reinforcing tasks. First, they must do to class what gender has done to their work—render it invisible. Next, they must maintain the same class structure they have struggled to veil. They support their husbands in the male roles of being social leaders and managers. They raise their sons to be like their fathers, daughters to be like themselves.

They offer their goodness as proof of the system's benevolence. Their hands weave safety nets.

Since the 1960s, more and more women have entered the public labor force. The well-bred volunteer's daughter is more apt to go to law school than her mother was. This intelligent book hardly laments the disapperance of the economically dependent women. It is far too aware, and wary of, the inequitable structures that have produced her. *Invisible Careers* does remind us, however, that caring for others is a mark of a virtuous person and of the virtuous society. In the United States, volunteer work and these invisible careers blend good intentions with bad consequences, high principles with divisions between persons of high and low status. *Invisible Careers* suggests the possibility of a bleak future in which we have not a partial and partially self-serving altruism, but no altruism at all. Mrs. Teasdale may disappear, except as an image on a screen, but so may a pressure toward fruitful giving. As *Invisible Careers* asks us to expand our descriptions of work, so, too, does it demand that we expand our concept of active benevolence.

Catharine R. Stimpson

Preface

The main difficulty in writing this book was one of adopting a consistent tone and style toward the women of this study and forming a stable opinion or judgment about them. At first I was guided by the ordinary stereotype of "society ladies," and I accepted the somewhat negative stereotypes of women volunteers.

Social commentaries often disparage both the motivation for women to engage in volunteering and what they accomplish. One interpretation of their motives suggests that most women are "really" interested in venal rather than altruistic ends in their charitable works. They only wish to meet celebrities, parade in fancy clothes, or push themselves and their families up a social ladder—all under the guise of charity and community concern. Satiric sketches of such women, appearing in novels and plays about the nouveaux riches in this country and abroad, are taken as representative of women in the volunteer world. The novels of Sinclair Lewis, Henry James, Edith Wharton, and Marcel Proust offer many examples of these women. Some American actresses became famous for their comic characterizations of such women: Margaret Dumont in the Marx Brothers movies and Billie Burke in films like *Topper* and *Dinner at Eight* are examples.

Comic characterizations of women at their volunteer efforts also stress incompetence. Whatever their purpose, women are aimless or even silly in their volunteer activity, merely wasting time. The club movement and the efforts of club women to engage both in self-improvement and community improvement have been dogged by this characterization (Blair 1980).

While some of the club women undoubtedly deserved to be labeled as weak or dilettantish participants, others used the opportunity presented through these contacts to develop important reform projects and to become community leaders (Degler 1980: 300–303). But these distinctions are not made in the popular stereotype. The club women and their leaders have been lumped together and the consequent image is overlaid with that of someone like the dear Helen Hokinson lady of the cartoons: sweet, but slightly dotty. Serious people have no time for the worlds inhabited by such women, whether they are considered with fondness or with derision. Serious people are *paid* workers; their own concerns are pressing and urgent, and the work they do is hard. This evaluation stands in contrast to the leisurely, ladylike work on the periphery of important matters that the volunteer stereotype embodies. Rohatyn (1982:27) makes this distinction clear in his plea for volunteers to help bail New York City out of its miseries: "Volunteers will have to do often demanding work, as opposed to genteel fundraising on Park Avenue." The implication is clear. If these women really want to help the society, they will have to change, shape up. What they are already doing is not good enough. Those who make a career of volunteering and become civic leaders in the process rise to prominence against this background of expectations—and stereotypes—attached to volunteers in this society.

The stereotype is particularly hard on well-to-do women who are often seen as mere ornaments for their husbands. Ironic commentaries on conspicuous consumption have been popular since Veblen used the term to describe the public display of wealth that captains of industry delegate to their wives as a symbol of male success and power. Women are expected to show, through their conspicuous consumption of the leisure required to become artistically cultivated, the vast quantities of vicarious leisure available to their husbands (Veblen 1953). But the activity loses something in the delegation. Business and professional men disparage both the activity and those who organize it once it is seen as predominantly feminine (Potter 1964:65–84). It is men who gain status from women's activity, not the women themselves.

My first draft of the study reflected these views. It was easy to find ways, even while adhering to my original plan of showing how seriously these volunteer leaders work and what important community benefits they provide, to mock some of the ladylike ways and the genteel condescensions to people of the lower classes that were sometimes revealed through interviews. My informants helped me see the error of my ways. For example, one woman pointed out how condescending it was on my part to call this group of women "ladies;" so I went over the copy to remove the term wherever it appeared.

As I came to know these women better, I gained perspective and so repented my earlier, flippant ways. I rewrote the study, adding new material that showed their work in a more serious and respectful light. This time, perhaps, I went too far in the other direction. As my sociology colleagues pointed out, I was listening so carefully to my informants that I neglected my duties as a sociologist to analyze their position and place it in perspective. For example, they rarely mentioned class and, if the subject was mentioned, they generally downplayed the importance of their privileged status in becoming a volunteer civic leader. Accordingly, in my second draft I also ignored the importance of class. For example, I accepted their use of the term "community service" without sufficient consideration of the limitations of the term. These women saw themselves serving the entire city as their community, but they usually represented special communities within it. I came to realize that in my effort to redress the condescension of the first draft, I had gone too far in accepting their views of how women volunteer leaders ought to be presented.

These efforts have taken considerable time. More than ten years have passed since the initial draft was prepared. I comfort myself about my slowness in coming to a reasonable assessment of the data with the belief that these women present a difficult problem for study.

Even social scientists, trained to study behavior and assess it within a larger perspective, cannot separate stereotype from observed behavior when asked to consider some of the unique qualities these women possess. When two academic colleagues and their wives visited my home area at the same time as a prominent volunteer leader and her husband, I invited all three couples to my home for dinner; for I wanted friends from these two worlds to meet one another. Before this meeting, I had explained to these two colleagues what I was doing in the study, and I had also told them something of the signal importance of this woman as a leader in her city, how she helped shape social services there, what her political influence was, and how she had trained and inspired several generations of volunteer leaders. Despite this preparation, I was disappointed to discover, after the dinner party, that my colleagues had not "seen it." They saw only a conventional upper middle-class dowager and were more intrigued with her husband, who represented class interests and values they might wish to study. Interestingly enough, the wives of these social scientists did see what I tried to show them. Both women thanked me for the opportunity I had offered to meet a truly remarkable woman. They called it a privilege to see a woman of such spirit who had made so remarkable a career for herself.

Perhaps it is not surprising that women would be receptive to a woman developed and trained through women's worlds. But it is curious that male friends, sharing my professional training, sympathies, and even special interests within the discipline could not see what their female colleague pointed out to them. And yet, in all fairness to them, it is difficult to learn how to evaluate the world of nonsalaried work and the demeanor of various types of workers in it. Certainly my own perceptions were much closer to these male colleagues when I began to study volunteers.

Whatever the evaluation, in the final analysis the data must stand as support for the positions taken and the judgments reached. This book is an effort to redress the balance of ignorance or condescension often shown about the activities of women in volunteer leadership positions. I hope readers will be able to see these activities—whatever their limitations—as important systematic and incremental contributions to society and community, worthy of the term "career."

Acknowledgments

The data for this study were collected under the auspices of a larger study of women volunteers sponsored by the National Institute of Mental Health (MH 21929, 1972–74) and by a Ford Foundation Faculty Fellowship (1975–76). I am grateful to the grant administrators, particularly Mariam Chamberlain of the Ford Foundation, for their faith in this project.

My special thanks go to the staff in the sociology department for their assistance in typing the many drafts. Under the direction of June Weatherly, I enjoyed the help of Leyla Gungor, Nancy Klein, Elizabeth Pereyra, Jean Mitchell, and Barbara Williamson. During my year as a Fellow at the Center for Research on Women (now the Institute for Research on Women and Gender) at Stanford in Palo Alto, I was aided by Bethany Alley and Frances Bertetta.

I am grateful to Gabrielle Morris and Willa Baum at the Regional History Office of the Baucroft Library at the University of California, Berkeley, for making documents available for study.

Throughout the course of this work I have been fortunate to have the advice and encouragement of the women who participated in this study. Although their names must be kept confidential, I wish to offer them my heartfelt gratitude for both their enthusiasm and patience with this project.

It sometimes feels as though my friends and colleagues have dragged me through the project—either by reading draft after draft or by helping me with particular chapters. In the early phases of writing I benefited from the reviews of Erwin Linn, Gaye Tuchman, and Lillian Rubin. I was helped with discussions of women's activity in the board room by Paul Hirsch, Edward Zajack, and Meyer Zald. Kathryn Pyne Addelson, James Benét, Arlie Hochschild, and Robert Weiss offered detailed comments when I needed them in the intermediate stages of writing. My colleagues at Northwestern, Janet Abu-Lughod and Howard Becker—as well as my dear friend and mentor Jessie Bernard—read drafts and kept prodding me along when I slowed to a snail's pace. Marjorie DeVault, Nona Glaser, John Kitsuse, Teresa Odendahl, and Kathleen McCarthy offered encouragement and finishing touches when I was almost done. Joan Emerson, Eliot Freidson, Barbara Laslett, and Barrie Thorne gave me detailed criticism on the final draft that helped me finally see the major direction and shape of the book.

All these people offered invaluable help; but I would never have completed this work without the constant prodding, critiques, and suggestions for revision after revision that I received from Rachel Kahn-Hut, the best editor I have ever known and a treasured friend and colleague with whom I have worked—and argued—for the greater part of my professional career.

Introduction

It is impressive when a volunteer comes willingly to
work to make a slave of herself.

The woman who made this remark is a prominent volunteer and
civic leader in her city. She points to the apparently anomalous behavior of many dedicated women in American society who work
without salary. In a society where "the pursuit of the almighty dollar" is given so high a value, how can the paradox of people willing
to work for nothing be explained? The commitment from well-to-do
women, like the woman just quoted, is especially noteworthy. If
women are well-off and don't have to work, why should they want
to do it?

This book focuses on the women of "Pacific City"—a large metropolis in the northwestern United States—who are active in the
service of their city. The seventy civic leaders who were interviewed stand at the intersection of philanthropy and "Society" in
their city. They use their position as members of influential families
to gain a hearing for their causes among the politically powerful or
to raise money among the wealthy. They also use their credibility as
seasoned, experienced volunteers in the city to persuade businessmen, professionals, local politicians, the general public, community welfare recipients, and agency workers to work together on
civic problems.

It is in this process that the women of Pacific City become "civic
leaders." They are known by the accumulated honors and deference they receive in their communities and cities. Sometimes they
rise to eminence in their regions or become known nationwide.
They are recognized with woman-of-the-year awards, testimonial
banquets in their honor commemorating their contributions to
health, education, culture, and general welfare. Their celebrity
status is indicated by frequent news coverage of their activities;
their opinions about community events, issues, and problems are
sought by media representatives, local officials, and major political
figures. Occasionally, public buildings or environmental preserves

are named after them when they die—or even while they are still living. Yet the record of their accomplishments is not easily retrievable (although local newspapers record some of their achievements in their obituaries).[1]

These women fund, organize, and manage school, church, and neighborhood services. They work on boards of organizations to set policy and raise funds for worthwhile causes. They support cultural projects, participate on advisory boards to develop new services (a new way to develop experimental education projects in the schools, for example), and sit on local, regional, and federal commissions to review issues in education, housing, aging, and family planning. Sometimes they spearhead political campaigns and work for local reforms or political candidates who support a particular cause (for example, ecology, historical preservation, protection of children). All these efforts focus on two major lines of interest: voluntary activities in social reform and community welfare and cultural interests, community beautification, or "uplift."

The Pacific City leaders have both the advantages and disadvantages of their class position. Their political and social connections offer both relatively easy entry to important networks and then experience in working with the local power structure. Their relative affluence affords the opportunity to use a wider range of strategies than many women (without a car, money for transportation and lunches, a big home in which to hold meetings, for example) can manage. However, they face disadvantages connected to their affluence and class position. Women are limited in the scope of their activity by their understanding of the proprieties: what behavior is acceptable for women in their position, what aspirations seem reasonable, what tactics may be used to achieve desired ends. Generally, the way these women conceptualize social issues or problems is limited by their basic acceptance of a status quo in which they, after all, are very privileged. They do not make explicit or discuss at any length the conditions under which they work because many wish to avoid the implicit issues: the use of volunteering to acquire status or privilege in the community; the importance of volunteer-

---

1. *The New York Times Obituary Index* collects political and community service obituaries together in one category which includes mainly paid careerists whose community service is part of or additional to their regular employment. Most other newspaper obituaries are indexed only alphabetically. Considerable knowledge of the community, as well as persistence and diligence, are required to transform these uncategorized materials into unobtrusive measures (Webb et al. 1966) of accomplishment by local volunteer women.

ing as an avenue for conspicuous consumption; the use of philanthropy to ameliorate social conditions and therefore avoid more
drastic social changes; and, most important, the place of money
and power in the work of successful volunteers.

Whether or not they are willing to face this aspect of their work,
its importance in the support of a class system has been recognized
by others. Domhoff (1971:34) describes the efforts of women volunteer leaders from the leisure class as combining three functions: (1)
providing the introductions and socialization for suitable entrants
to the upper-class world from other classes as well as the social setting for contacts leading to suitable marriages for their own children; (2) developing social and cultural standards for others; (3)
participating in welfare movements to improve the lot of the general population. In all these endeavors, upper-middle-class and
upper-class women represent upper-class perspectives in areas
where their male counterparts have neither time nor inclination to
participate.

The work these women do, however, is complicated by their own
resistance to any class analysis of it. They prefer to view their service
as being in the interests of the entire community rather than a special segment within it. They ignore—or deny—any suggestion that
their privileged position may be part of the problems they wish to
solve. Such a view assumes that a city can be seen as a more or less
unified community and that these women know how to serve all—
or the major—interests in it. This view also minimizes the amount of
work in constructing class that is part of their volunteering. They
consider as community service their work in maintaining private
schools and social gathering places where children, as well as other
members of their class, meet appropriate peers; but it is specialized
for a particular segment—and class—in that community.

Understanding their activity as work is difficult for the women
because they do not consider explicitly all the consequences of
these agendas. The hidden work of constructing class is part of
their responsibility as family members and wives, but it is mixed in
with their own understandings and aspirations concerning the
value of community service. Part of that value is the reassurance
that service provides: it justifies a feeling of participation in and
contribution to society that can generate a sense of superiority and
a rationale for class privilege. At the same time, some of that work
may become antagonistic to their own class interests. Women who
become advocates of reforms may find themselves fighting the local
establishment—and some people in their own family or friendship

networks. From that perspective, an analysis of their function, such as Domhoff has made, may not entirely cover what they actually do.

Domhoff's concern is with locating these women in the class structure. In this view, the work these women do is part of a functional division of labor in the upper classes. Women provide the legitimation of and even, where possible, some mitigation for the inequalities in our society. This view stresses the class impetus behind their volunteer work and minimizes the independence or initiative women may show in that work. Such a picture of women's work as civic leaders, although it may suggest that women are only the assistants of the male power elite (see Ostrander 1984 for a statement of this position), does show women's activities as serious work. We learn little, however, about how they conduct this work and what it is they accomplish.

Civic Leadership as a Career

One difficulty in describing, much less assessing, women's community service arises from the particular difficulty of seeing any individual woman's service as a systematic program of endeavor. No generally accepted vocabulary exists for the systematic, detailed discussion of a lifetime of volunteer service, and so there is no language to discuss self-development and augmented skill. This omission combines with the general philosophy of community work (nobody does it alone) to obscure specific authorship or leadership in projects, both for the community at large and for the women themselves, so there is no way to focus on personal accomplishments.

The difficulty of disentangling the web of authority and responsibility is exacerbated by the conventional belief systems of women volunteers, some of whom believe men should hold the leadership positions. In consequence, these women do not challenge the picture of totally male-dominated community power structures. At the same time women do see their own work as important and some women civic leaders take credit for major community improvements. It is not really possible for an outside observer to specify whether they over- or underestimate their exact contribution and their power in the community. But it *is* possible to learn how they work and what *they* learn from a lifetime of experience in community service.

This understanding provides a way to expand our thinking about achievement beyond the limitations suggested by the usual criteria in evaluating work and career. If we consider the characteristic organizational form in modern society to be bureaucracy (Weber 1946), we see how this form pervades major modes of organization. The central principle of the form, as exemplified in governmental bureaucracy, is efficiency assured through the right pattern of education and certification for workers and their accountability for appropriate performance by a system of records. In entrepreneurial activities, the issue of efficiency is primarily judged by profit maximization. In either governmental or business bureaucracy, organizational efficiency requires segregation of roles to avoid mixing family and business, personal and public or business interests. We take these usual expectations so much for granted that we easily forget that they do not describe all workers, even in modern society. Women who rise to leadership positions through volunteer work do not fit these conceptions. In studying them, we see how people can create a livelihood or career outside these general expectations of how work is organized. We also learn how these careers are related to the more visible kind. The structure of bureaucracy and even social class may look different, for example, when these careers, developed in the interstices of the work world, are analyzed.

Significance of the Formulation of Volunteer Careers for Women

Some women focus on the concept of career as a way to distinguish the professional, nonsalaried volunteer from two other groups: the nonsalaried dilettantes who are part-time workers and the salaried workers who donate some of their time to volunteering (Lyman 1982). But the concept of career is not widely used by civic leaders. This formulation needs explanation, for the concept of career has usually been associated with (salaried) occupations. Typically it includes some idea of sequentially ordered activities occurring in predictable stages of one's work life. Hughes (1958:129) described career as: "A sort of running adjustment between a man [sic] and the various facts of life and his professional world [including] . . . projections of himself into the future and the course of events."

Other definitions of career (Wilensky 1961:523) stress the hierarchical nature of a succession of related jobs, so that the concept involves the opportunity to estimate one's own progress through graduated stages. Van Maanen (1977) and his colleagues focus on the idea of careers in organizations. Roth's (1963:94) use of the concept of career is broader for he uses the concept to analyze conditions outside of work life like patienthood and child development. His concept also includes the idea of related and definable stages with some idea of progress through them.

This progress is either up or down, as in the careers of successful or failed achievers at some metier. Sometimes the notion of progress is paradoxical, as in the careers of school dropouts, juvenile delinquents, or felons where the culmination of stages in a career is a socially derogated title or even an institutional record. Or, on occasion, the idea of progress may be ambiguous: people may feel they are successful achievers although in the eyes of many they are not; alternatively, some may feel they have failed to achieve their aims although apparently they have been very successful in their society.

Such considerations suggest that the concept of career should stress the notion of legitimation or validation. Recognition appears in the form of a salary or occupational titles, indicating acceptance or even acclaim for someone in a working career. Pejorative labels—from institutions, neighborhood, or family—suggest socially disapproved categories. The mix of inner and external pressures may differ for different persons and various careers, but it is always a part of the equation.

The concept of career is important for understanding those who embrace the notion of direction or control in their working lives. It permits the analyst to examine the interplay between self-direction, external pressures, and the ensuing status which marks the events of a career. Such a formulation of the concept of career contains the implicit understanding that career is an individual phenomenon that stands for or sums up something about personal history and achievements.

The problem for many of the Pacific City women is that the concept of career, with its connotations of individualistic progress through stages, is difficult to adapt to their circumstances without also suggesting an unattractive element of striving: either social climbing or what might be seen as too great an interest in personal success. As a result, the limitations on this career are set, not only by the difficulties of working without salary in a society that places high value on economic worth, but by traditional women's understandings of how ambitious they should be.

An additional problem for these women is their response to class issues: Is there class conflict in our society? Is there a ruling class to which they, perhaps, belong? How would their concept of career fit in with such assumptions? Are these women agents of a ruling class, whether or not they themselves are members? After all, they clearly have privileges—financial resources, access to the power elite in their community—not so readily available to just anyone. Does the informal sponsorship and training they receive in their work show a systematic class influence? These are questions which complicate their attitude toward striving and ambitiousness. They wish to see their career development as affected by experience, talents, and chance encounters as much or more than by special patronage. Further, if we live in a democratic society, free of class distinctions, patronage and social striving can have little meaning, for we are all equals. These questions also raise difficulties in explaining the public served through a volunteer career; is it the disadvantaged or the peers of the volunteers themselves (who are so clearly among the privileged)? If the public served is the former, the activity takes on overtones of benevolent charity toward a lower class. If it is the latter, the activity has overtones of being self-serving: partying with or improving the lot of those who are already well-off. The following chapters show that these themes appear but are downplayed in the women's own conceptions of career. Instead, women focus on the sense of vision (something needs to be done) and the sense of community (the city is or can be united behind a common sense of purpose—improvement of the life of all citizens) that spurs the most motivated. Despite the troubled events of the sixties and seventies in this country—calling attention to increasing social inequality rather than a greater democratization of society—the women in this study remain committed to the picture of a democratic American society painted by de Tocqueville.[2] Consequently, class is not an important part of their own analysis. They believe merit is recognized and individual achievers are "accepted"

2. The admiring words of de Tocqueville ([1840] 1954:114–18) after his visits to America have become part of the ideology of those who speak for volunteerism. De Tocqueville praised Americans for their ability to set a common project and induce other citizens to participate in it enthusiastically. He also praised them for the variety of their volunteer associations, available to meet the needs of all ages, conditions, and dispositions. He saw these associations as a vital and necessary complement to government that made the citizenry stronger—through self-help—than would be the case if all problems were solved by government action. His ideas are also used to support the picture of the United States as an essentially classless society where individual initiative and ability will be rewarded regardless of one's origins.

wherever they "wish" to go. It is not class but personal friendships and preferences which create groupings and cliques of the like-minded.

There are, however, some further limitations on the concept of career for these women; the place of women within the family is a priority for them. Women should dedicate themselves to altruistic work for their families and, secondarily, their community. For some conventional women who espouse traditional values the concept of a career is too individualistic; it suggests too great a focus on personal striving. A woman should not wish to place career above family, for example. Nor should she wish to shine apart from (or above) her colleagues in volunteer work; for it is collective endeavor and collaboration rather than independent achievement that should be emphasized. If women do this work properly, it leaves no time for a personal career. In any case, can women aspire any higher than to be good wives and mothers? Why should it matter if they receive personal recognition for efforts outside the family? The women in this study wrestle with this dilemma in various ways. Some ignore it and accept traditional perspectives on women's aspirations. For such women, the problem of career is relatively unimportant. Some embrace feminist perspectives and see autonomy and an individual identity as important enough to ask family to make sacrifices for it. And there is a spectrum of sometimes mutually contradictory views in between these alternatives, complicated by a growing desire on the part of some of these women for paid employment.

These formulations develop and change over time, making, as Hughes says, a career through the running adjustment between a man, his life, and his professional world. Only in this book the topic is women, and they are professionals with no generally recognized metier or portfolio, nor do they have a legitimated or institutionalized collegial community or workplace; they are community service professionals with invisible careers. Some part of their activity is recognized—the associations or organizations they serve, the results of their efforts; other elements—including the overall structure or framework within which their work occurs—remain unnoticed. Some of their work problems are very like those of other professionals, entrepreneurs, and business executives. Still other problems are similar to those of any woman in the middle and upper classes who tries to coordinate family and work obligations. But these women have a strong enough work commitment to have developed what we may call substantial unsalaried careers. They want more than a limited volunteer job that serves as a change of scenery and an opportunity for sociability outside the home.

Yet their ambitions are hampered by the invisibility of their careers. Their work can be seen as just the service women traditionally do to support and maintain the society. In that sense, the work is only part of the gender tasks that women do by virtue of their position as wives and mothers. At the same time, they are privileged women; their service includes the construction and re-creation of their class through provision of educational and recreational projects for their own circle. Work for the more general community also serves to justify their privileged position. Thus their gender tasks support the status quo both materially and ideologically. These underlying themes of gender and class create contradictions that make it difficult for women themselves to recognize their work as a career. Insisting on credit for their service as "real" work would require acknowledging not only its basis in gender but also its class elements. Both would be unwelcome because they question the ideas of classlessness and disinterested service these women formally espouse. Consequently, seeing their work as a career is difficult for these women. The concept of career is given a new dimension by studying the problems associated with recognition as well as the development of this commitment, the directions it takes, and the resources which support it.

The study which follows is thus an occupational analysis. Part 1 presents the context for career development. It begins with a description of why a life in volunteering seems valuable to women and how they are recruited into it, and the study continues in the second chapter with an analysis of the value system and life style which reinforce this choice of work. Part 2 shows how careers are discovered and adapted to personal tastes. In this section, chapter three presents the development of skills and interests that keep women motivated to work, and chapter four describes the substantive areas for and general approaches to work. Part 3 shows how work-related specialties develop. Chapters five and six present the specialties (such as fund-raising and public relations) that women must learn, whatever their particular interest or style. In Part 4, the rewards and limitations of the career are analyzed. Chapter seven shows what satisfactions women believe their work provides and chapter eight explains the limitations their work sets for them. Part 5 presents the career site. Chapter nine analyzes the context for work: the nonprofit board as both organizing structure and workplace. The conclusion considers the paradoxes this working area reveals, focusing on the central issue of how nonsalaried work can be understood as an occupational career and what we may learn from the study of invisible work. For this occupational analysis of volunteer work tells us not only about the construction of entrepreneurial areas but also about invisible (taken-for-granted) careers in society. Further, it shows us what forces in society keep this work invisible.

Women civic leaders organize support for existing community services and sometimes serve as the catalysts for change by developing new services and agencies to meet new problems. Their work in local communities is frequently unnoticed, though it is essential. When their work is noticed, it is often misunderstood and lumped with that of less productive women, sometimes under the pejorative stereotypes of idle and socialite volunteers. Sometimes it is dismissed as merely the class-maintaining activity of the women of the leisure class; or it is understood only as part of the work that women do for their families. Yet the significance of volunteer effort in America is widely acclaimed as something unique and praiseworthy about our country. Only it is the "citizenry" that volunteers and creates the associations that strengthen democracy. The special contributions of women are, again, invisible.

The Context for Career Development

1

Pathways into the Volunteer Career

The Privileged Volunteer

The data for this study come from systematic interviews with seventy women in their homes or offices and additional interview-observations of them and their friends during a five year period (1971–76) at luncheons, social gatherings, and philanthropic events. After that period, and continuing through 1987, I have seen or phoned some of them, and gathered news of the rest, in occasional visits back to Pacific City, at least twice yearly. These are women who know each other through family and friendship connections, through community service, or through both. They are volunteer workers who have risen to leadership in a major metropolitan area to be called Pacific City, a large and relatively old, established city in the northwestern section of the United States.

These women present a mix of the upper and middle classes in Pacific City. Some of them come from old families in this or other communities; some are from newly prosperous families (new rich or solely dependent upon professional men's income for their affluence); and some are from ordinary middle-class homes where they are financially secure but not notably prosperous. This estimation of class position within a social stratification system resembles that of Davis et al. (1941) in their study of the Deep South. Davis and the Gardners (1941:63–64) formulated their classifications through observations and by asking people about their own and other's class position. The upper-upper class were accorded deference; people were anxious to associate with them; they belonged to exclusive churches; their names were sought for patron's lists; they lived in imposing mansions. The lower-upper class were the "people with

3

whom the 'old aristocracy' is willing to participate in informal relationships, whom they know intimately and recognize as fundamentally no different from themselves. . . . But they are not 'old
aristocracy.'" Such criteria as wealth, fame, and power do not assure upper-upper class status; the kind of wealth and how old it is,
a particular life-style and relationship to power are more important. Baltzell (1958:7) sees this life-style and relationship developing out of intimate and informal interactions among families at the
top of the social class hierarchy.

Warner and Lunt (1941) used the term upper-upper class for the
aristocracy who combined birth and wealth to distinguish them
from the newer rich. The women in this sample come predominantly from this latter group, with a few from the upper-upper
class and a few from the upper-middle class as well.

These distinctions are somewhat amorphous and difficult to re-
fine, for movements between the ranks of upper-middle class and
the lower-upper class membership are never without some questions or disputes over their legitimacy, as Kerbo (1983:188) notes.
"Differences in occupational, bureaucratic, and property positions,
as well as income and educational level, may all be important dimensions to people; but they do not always correspond." The com-
plexities of assigning class in America are often noted by satirists
who delight in showing how life-style can reveal class distinctions
(Fussell 1983). Implicit in these observations is the idea that knowledge of the fine points will enable individuals to appear to have a
class standing they might otherwise not possess.

The problem of ranking is further complicated by the ambiguous
place of women in the stratification system (Acker 1973; 1980). To
date, research has been inconclusive on the relation of achieved
and derived status in the social standing of married women. The
social status added to the social standing of a family through the
successes a woman achieves in a volunteer career is particularly
difficult to assess. Difficulties of assessment are compounded when
informants are reluctant to see their work in these terms—as well
as too genteel to state financial worth or to boast of family background. The rankings presented here are based on a combination
of women's own assessments and those of others about them, as
well as on my own observation of their life-style.

The seventy women who form the nucleus of the study are an
economically privileged group, raised in a time when traditional
careers as homemakers, mothers, and spouses were the primary
choices available to women in their positions (see table 1.1). By the

Table 1.1 Age of Volunteer Civic Leaders

Class	Under 40	40–50	51–60	61–70	71 and over	Total
Upper and lower-upper	1	18	13	12	4	48
Upper-middle and middle	0	10	4	5	3	22
Total	1	28	17	7	7	70

time they had risen to the status of community leaders, many were more than fifty years of age. Those under forty are just getting there, those in their forties are in mid career, those in their fifties are at the peak of their career, those in their sixties are retiring or getting ready to retire, and those in their seventies and beyond are generally (with a few exceptions) no longer active. This career pattern reflects the life cycle commitments of traditional women with families. The great career opportunities come a bit late and last a shorter time than would be the case for men in comparable positions.

These women are well educated: eighteen have had some college, forty-seven hold bachelor's degrees, and fifteen of these have advanced degrees as well. They exhibit the life-style of the upper-middle or upper classes—living in comfortable or even opulent surroundings. Most (62) have household help, second homes, travel widely in the United States and abroad, and live in the best part of the city. One of the women is black; the rest are white. Most (48) have never held a salaried job or have worked only for a year or two before marriage, although a few (5) have begun to work for pay after a long volunteer career. Only six women in this group have worked for a major portion of their lives at salaried positions, and an additional eleven have had paid careers in addition to their volunteer experience—after a husband's illness, widowhood, or divorce. Of course, the more upper-class women are far more likely to have never worked than are the more middle-class women. The remaining differences, however, do not provide a consistent pattern. Here (as in the following discussions where class differences within the group of women are not shown) distinctions between the more upper-class and the more middle-class groups do not appear to make much difference in experience (see table 1.2).

Acceptance of traditional values in the establishment, as sug-

Table 1.2 Salaried Careers

	Upper and Lower-Upper Class	Upper-Middle and Middle Class	Total
Never worked	30	5	35
Before marriage only	5	8	13
After family difficulties:			
illness, widowhood, divorce	7	4	11
After volunteer career	4	1	5
Throughout adult life	2	4	6
Total	48	22	70

gested by these characteristics, is supported by other aspects of life-style. Virtually all (65) have either attended private schools themselves or have sent their children to private schools. And about half (34) are listed in the Social Register. (Another ten belong to wealthy and prominent Jewish families who are not listed in the register but who show their exclusivity by membership in a variety of other important social clubs.)

Every woman in the study has been married; thirteen are divorced and twenty-one have been widowed (six of these twenty-one have remarried). Most of these women (63) have had children, ranging in number from one to ten, with the average at about three. The husbands of these women are mainly businessmen of various sorts: seven are brokers in stock, insurance, food and merchandise; five are investment analysts or counselors; thirty-three are in business firms—generally the family company and often as chairmen ·of the board. But substantial numbers of them are doctors (14) and lawyers (11). The women are predominantly Protestant (40), but there are a number of Jews (18) and Catholics (12) among them.

In sum, these volunteers come from the most privileged sectors of the community. Many are related to the (male) community power structure and to the great "social" families of the city. Their special distinction among other women in their position is that they devote much of their time to philanthropic activities.

Family and Class Expectations

This group of women engages in charitable works as part of the noblesse oblige practiced by an elite, for even when they are not wealthy, they consider themselves "fortunate." They are fortunate not to have to work and to have been well provided for by husbands when widowed.

The upper-class women in this sample, like those described by Ostrander (1980a; 1980b), prepare their children for a place in the privileged class and are themselves active participants in upper-class society. In addition to the traditional social expectations that women should take responsibility for the care and socialization of children, these women uphold class expectations by sponsoring and actively supporting private schools and exclusive dancing classes where their children can socialize with appropriate peers (Daniels 1987). Some informants see to it that their daughters "come out" as debutantes in Pacific City's exclusive cotillion. Those who are not of the upper class reaffirm the importance of "society" and the social scene through their acceptance of its importance by setting the stage for benefits and attracting potential contributors. A drive to provide scholarships for college students majoring in science, for example, will be more successful if the initial fundraising dinner is given at a prominent socialite's home and attended by some of her friends.

These women meet both class and family expectations for their behavior when they attend to the wishes of their own and their husbands' families in accepting the obligation to be beautifully groomed themselves and to spend time on decorating their homes and entertaining in them. They are, of course, also available as assistants when this background is a useful adjunct to their husbands' careers. The background is also useful in their own volunteer careers. Thus, these expectations are all connected; for family responsibilities involve both philanthropic work and participation in status- and class-maintaining activities.

This mix of expectations means that women develop careers against a background of understandings that are reflected in a mix of activities. They engage in the leisure-class behavior appropriate to subordinate and ornamental wives while constructing the particular form of family that their social status requires. At the same time, they pursue their own volunteer careers, engaging in some activities that might appear to involve social climbing or personal ambition but that also produce important services for various communities.

From a woman's own perspective, latent strains are always present and are recognized from the moment of entry. If women become too absorbed in their volunteer work, children may complain or husbands may resist and even show jealousy. Women undertaking volunteer activities that depart from traditional philanthropy and involve social reforms may face conflict with family members over expectations of appropriate womanly behavior; but even in family-approved charitable work, women face limitations on their personal ambitions or individual maneuverability that are set by their place in the traditional family structure. The responsibilities (even when eased by servants) of mothers with small children limit women's opportunities early in the adult life cycle. And family responsibilities to parents, husbands, and children affect women's flexibility throughout their lives.

Thus, women develop their patterns of community service within the framework of such traditional family relations. They work within and around their husbands' requirements and their own childcare responsibilities. Where husbands are busy with their own careers and childcare burdens are eased by household help, women can create almost independent lives. They may have to. Paradoxically, husbands may demand that their wives become independent. As early as the 1850s, commentators on the American scene reported that women were often neglected by their men who, "immersed in a whirl of business, spent only short periods with their families" (Isabelle Bird, quoted in Douglas 1977:61). In modern day professional families, this neglect may mean the entire burden of household management falls to the woman (Fowlkes 1980). Yet it can also provide the opportunity for a career of one's own, independent of a husband's name or fame. Further impetus comes from the social expectation that those with some free time should contribute their time and effort for the community welfare. This expectation has developed around the ideology of domesticity. As Sklar (1973) argues, the development of American middle-class culture in the nineteenth century increasingly polarized separate ideals for men and women. Many well-to-do Americans also accepted the idea that males were to experience self-realization in independent activity while females were to accept self-sacrifice in service to others as the female equivalent of self-fulfillment. The desire to serve could be expressed in the activities involved in promoting community as well as family welfare, as long as family service came first. A career in service, then, is built in the interstices of family life.

The ability that women show in their community service fulfills family obligations to represent the family and maintain social class position, develop social connections, and show some individual initiative (Davidoff 1973; Coser 1975). For personally ambitious women in this social milieu, community service is the best compromise with class and family demands and the best channel for their energies.

However, the limitations of this choice for an ambitious woman should be noted: this career is not a formally recognized one. The separation of women's work from the visible, income-producing sector of the society that accompanied the separation of the home and workplace in the nineteenth century changed the work that women did (Kessler-Harris 1981); it also lowered the estimation of that work. Women's work was visible when it had a direct relationship to the production of family support and maintenance. Without that relationship, the social value of women's activities was no longer apparent. The distinguishing characteristic of women became their use of leisure. They were expected to stay home to beautify and ennoble their surroundings. Husbands and family considered this activity to be part of a woman's nature and therefore not really work. When considered as work, it, as well as the work of volunteer women who become community leaders, has a faintly pejorative image. This pejorative image is dominated by the assumption that the work is mainly trivial or nonessential; it is marginal in comparison with the main productive work in the profit economy. The women who make homemaking and volunteering their life's work are also considered marginal by the primary actors in that economy. These women are useful only as agents who display, by life-style, the wealth and culture that husbands and fathers can afford (Veblen 1953).

The ability to maintain women in leisure was an important asset for the middle-class as well as the upper-class family. As Douglas (1977:55) says of the lady in mid-nineteenth century America, even when she was not idle, her leisure became the most interesting and significant thing about her. This assessment hangs over the twentieth century equivalent of that lady. Much of the work that women volunteers do is seen as part of leisure activity. Some of their own comments suggest that they may accept this view. They say, for example, that they do the work because they enjoy it, not because they have to. Or they regard the expenses of volunteering as part of something they *like* to do and therefore part of their amusement rather than a work expense. Yet for many, the way they learn to be disciplined at their volunteer work, and to define it *as* work, is part of an effort to resist the stereotypic definition of the society matron with its connotations of idleness and inconsequentiality. The resistance suggests that these women create their careers against cultural counterpressures.

The stereotype, however, does reflect some aspects of their work, such as display of class or family status and conspicuous consumption of leisure (Veblen 1953), even while it entirely neglects other aspects—such as community building and performing important services that would otherwise be neglected. Women's resistance to the pejorative overtones of the stereotype may make it difficult for them to acknowledge their class-maintaining activities or to see the tensions between these and their service activities for the larger community.

Middle-class volunteers have many of the same problems in both avoiding the pejorative overtones of the stereotype of their work and in recognizing the various aspects of that work. They resist some aspects of the stereotype by trying to avoid the label of being "just" a housewife (Lopata 1971). Women of either class try to resolve some of the latent problems or conflicts about whom they serve and escape some of the ambiguity of the catchall title volunteer by calling themselves citizen participants. Some use the terms career and professional volunteer (Lyman 1982) to suggest the seriousness of their commitment.

The sensitivity to what they are called reflects the problems women volunteers have in explaining or justifying their choice of volunteer work as a career. The following sections show how women frame their choice of career: they point to the need for their services and the necessity for professional quality work while strongly resisting pejorative images of volunteer work. The women receive moral support in this endeavor from their sense of the contribution people with their resources and training ought to offer their communities. This background infuses the patterns of entry and ascent described in the closing section.

Developing the Rationale for a Volunteer Career

Women in this study resist those aspects of the volunteer concept that lead toward the "Lady Bountiful" stereotype. They dislike the connotations of both the class and gender stereotypes implicit in the lady bountiful image and regret that many in the larger society see their work as merely that. These women are caught up in the problem of defining their own activity as important against the indifference or even pejorative stereotypes they see in the world around them. They formulate their argument around two major themes: the need for their services and the professional quality of their performance.

THE NEED FOR VOLUNTARISM

For the unsalaried middle-class or upper-class woman, the ideology of voluntarism combines ideas about the unsuitability or impracticality of paid employment for women like themselves with the desire to find interesting or challenging employment. In addition, ideas about the necessity for altruism and unpaid community service combine with ideas about the selfishness of seeking paid work when many others really need those jobs. Thus, most women come to accept a collective rationale for what volunteer tasks are involved, how they might be done, who ought to do them, and why they are necessary. This view is colored by some defensiveness and some disappointments caused by public indifference or misunderstanding. To the extent that this defensiveness does exist, statements about voluntarism have the characteristic of an ideology: a theory to justify conduct rather than to reveal its origins in the conditions of their existence (Mannheim 1961, chapter 2).

The defensive component in the ideology becomes more pronounced as more women find alternative uses for their time in paid work. Many women who once gave all their working time to the cause of voluntarism, now enter salaried employment. They are part of the growing number of married women in the labor force.[1] There are two sources for this trend. Often, women have to work to support themselves and their families. Second, changing values, whether or not they are seen as desirable, permit or even encourage women to have salaried careers. Understandings of these changes, combined with defensive responses to charges that volunteers take jobs away from those who need them, lead to further assertions about the value of volunteer work—that it can provide the experience and opportunity to find salaried work. These ideas are sometimes added to justify voluntarism despite the ambiguities they may raise and the uncertainty they may reflect about the value of a full-time permanent volunteer career.

The ideology of voluntarism, then, cannot entirely protect adherents from moments of doubt about whether they could or should

---

1. "Between 1947 and 1978, married women's rate [of participation in the labor force] increased from 20 percent to 48 percent" (Smith 1979:4).

work for pay. These doubts center on the value of work that has no financial return. But they have also been exacerbated by the feminist attacks on volunteering in recent years. The early position of the National Organization of Women (later modified somewhat) strongly denounced volunteer work as exploitation—both of women doing it and, indirectly, of the workers denied paid jobs when volunteers would do them. Critics like Eriksson-Joslyn (1973–74) and Gold (1971) argued that all classes of women are exploited when some offer their services without expectation of payment. Kaminer (1984) wrestled with this problem in explaining how a feminist position permits a positive view of volunteering, even though social services are provided at less than their actual costs when women offer regular, free labor. The rationale for the system ultimately accepted by Kaminer and others is that such services would simply be unavailable without this free labor; social policies would not be adopted to provide funds to pay people to perform the services. In accepting this rationale, volunteer women support the status quo—and the social priorities that permit insufficient tax revenues for various community services.

The most general statement women in this study offer about the importance of their service encompasses three major themes: volunteers knit the community together in ways that other institutions do not; volunteers search out and pioneer necessary services that other institutions overlook or neglect; volunteers provide service that the community needs but cannot afford.

In elaborating these themes, women point to the necessity for volunteer initiative in the organization of political, cultural, and educational activities. These women recognize that the major institutions of the society do not fulfill many human needs. Many bits and pieces of necessary activities are left dangling, as it were, requiring integration and coordination by concerned volunteers. Although they do not see a pattern in capitalist society of people neglecting general welfare while pursuing profitable business ventures, these women do see education, culture, health and welfare as areas where major institutions are lacking. They see themselves as intermediaries between existing institutions and newly developing requirements. They argue that they do the promotion and development that eventually produces new agencies and institutions to meet human needs. They do not, of course, emphasize how class divisions are maintained and even strengthened when both publicly and privately sponsored institutions depend upon free or underpaid service from women to survive (Saraceno 1984b). Instead they focus on what they as individual women can do within the limits of the existing system.

Changing problems in the society at large and new crises in specific communities assure that the need for volunteer efforts is never ending; extant institutions always require some modifications and assistance from other sources. The ability to use volunteer services gives a society greater flexibility in adapting to changing conditions; voluntarism is viewed with pride by these women as "the great strength of our country."

The careers of the women in this study show how these ideas appear in daily practices. But informants also generalize from their experience to explain the significance of voluntarism. They talk, for example, of how communities benefit from volunteer "ambassadors" who move between institutions and organizations to coordinate, mediate, and negotiate.

> Volunteerism . . . gives strength to the community and opportunity . . . to establish ties with various segments of the larger community [as, in this informant's experience, between Jewish and non-Jewish groups] that would not otherwise be possible.

These proponents of the volunteer philosophy also note how their efforts complement the existing division of labor by finding neglected areas where they can work. "If you eliminate the volunteer, you eliminate those extra touches to the institutions which make them much more human." The concern for the community reflected in this commitment becomes a woman's responsibility, especially for the privileged women of the community. They accept the assignment to watch out for matters that go untended in the formulation of social policies. The sick, the elderly, the homeless children who are neither publicly valued nor part of a profitable industry are traditionally regarded as the concerns of women (Saraceno, 1984a). These concerns form the nucleus of the areas women are expected to care about.

Proclaiming the Professional Character of Volunteer Work

The successful accomplishment of their wish to provide service is possible because the work is done in a professional manner. These women deny that their work is peripheral to the main concerns of society or that their working pattern is less committed than that of professionals. They are angry with salaried staff who condescend to or patronize volunteers; and they strongly assert that nonsalaried workers perform as well or better than their salaried colleagues. This mixture of assertion and denial, however, is complicated for these women by some ambivalence about the social value of unpaid work and by a consciousness of their own special privileged position.

One way to show the significance of volunteer work is to explain how it can benefit from the independence of workers. In support of their role, women point to the fact that "no one can shut you up." For those who wish to take advocacy roles, the independence attached to the volunteer's position offers advantages most paid work cannot equal.

Women also note the commitment and the discipline that many volunteer jobs require. They point out that the dedicated volunteer is very professional in the way she conceives of and undertakes her work. Yet some elements of the defensive character of the rationale emerge when they talk of this aspect of the work. Volunteers are quick to point out that this work can be performed *just as if* it were a recognized profession. As one woman put it, "It is a tremendous advantage if you can turn out a job as though you were a professional." Another woman declared, "Contrary to what most people believe . . . volunteers can be as reliable and devoted as persons in paid employment." And another insisted that "volunteers often work longer and harder than paid workers." The motivation that fuels such commitment is suggested by the following woman:

> A volunteer can be a great deal less disciplined. If you don't feel like doing it, there's no way they can make you do it. . . . The other side of the coin is that . . . it takes more discipline, because you have to discipline yourself. And this is a great value for women like me and [my friends]. Because we wanted to be disciplined. We wanted to get out of the lower level jobs [to become leaders].

This stress on dedicated work and self-improvement accompanies assertions about the professional performance of volunteers. Women point to the opinions of others to verify their judgment. "The girls [holding salaried jobs] during the political era [when this woman had been active] used to say that you [volunteers] are just as good as we are."

Some women see an improved future for the image of volunteer work simply through insistence on the terms of professionalism. "I have told professional members [salaried women who also do volunteer work] of the Junior League that they are no different from the other members because [they are, like me], professional volunteers." Others are not so sanguine, but hope that professionalization will help. In this regard they resemble members of any occupation seeking to upgrade its status to a profession through training (Hughes 1958). "You have to professionalize the volunteer's role. I don't mean requiring credentials and degrees, but demonstrated ability. You have to set up a criterion: in-service training like professional training [where] you have continuing education."

The foregoing statement by a lifelong volunteer presents a number of the elements contributing to the ambiguous public image of the volunteer. The social worth of and respect for volunteering is or should be attached to the levels of demonstrated skill. Volunteering can be professional and should receive professional status.

COMBATING NEGATIVE IMAGES OF VOLUNTARY WORK

These women must define their own activity against the array of negative images (lady bountiful, social butterfly or social climber, do-gooder) that attach to the volunteer activities of well-to-do women. The negative image combines both class and gender stereotypes of idle or nonproductive activity.

The women in this study are successful volunteers. Nonetheless they are well aware of their ambiguous position and the mixed views that others hold of their work. "I wish that the volunteer was treated with more respect," said one woman. "It's incredible to me that [some] consider volunteer work demeaning," said another.

In addition to the general, public view, volunteer women contend with the sometimes pejorative estimates of their contributions from other, paid, professionals. Some women are cowed by that estimate ("I find myself rather intimidated by this group"). Descriptions by these women of how they see paid professionals treating volunteers as "slapping their hand and putting them down" explains how even the very self-confident might be dampened—if not entirely cowed.

While some women express more bitterness and resentment than others, a common issue for grousing is the lack of respect shown to the volunteer. The connotations of patronizing condescension attached to "the lady bountiful" image are particularly grating—as are ideas that the work done by volunteers is unnecessary and that the workers are frivolous. While the organization of volunteer effort inevitably creates what one woman deplored as "wasted motion," these women argue that the real volunteer contribution to the community should not be dismissed.

A few women just accept their subordinate status as volunteer women and so try harder to win the approval of men and salaried professionals.

> On the women's committee I'm afraid I'm known as the late Mrs. Lathrop. But I'm careful [to be on time] when there are men on the committee. When you work with businessmen and women [remember] they have to be as efficient as possible in the time allotted.

The difficulties of maintaining professional status as a volunteer are always exacerbated by the lack of a salary to assert one's value. Some doubts are managed by an almost fierce denial of the importance of dollar-based evaluation. Here is how one community leader, who had worked as a volunteer and as a salaried semiprofessional until she married and had children, put it.

> I tell you one thing I disagree with is that women who volunteer are taken advantage of. There is nothing more untrue than [that] pay is the only thing that is worthwhile. . . . Particularly if you don't have to work and like your community. You are fortunate to be able to give something back to the community.

While the woman just quoted explicitly denies the need for pay, many see the problems of volunteers resulting from the difficulty in setting an agreed upon dollar value to the work of the volunteers. One response is to entertain the possibility of salaried work:

> I want to see the non-dollar sign working woman receive the same respect [as the salaried woman]. I thought to myself so many times, maybe I should go to work for pay in order to get the satisfactions that I want . . . or can I receive them volunteering?

Whatever the satisfactions of volunteer work, some doubts about its value remain. Two of the women in this little group of doubters are both in their late fifties and have never worked for pay themselves. One of them remarks upon what she sees as her ambiguous position. "If I'd taken all the time or energy in a [salaried] specialty, would it have been as satisfying? Many people could say [what I do as a volunteer] is just busy work. What are you *really* doing?" And the other comments, a little sadly, on the drawback of never working for pay. "There is not the satisfaction of being paid and knowing you have done a job others thought really worth X number of dollars. . . . Sometimes I wonder if I'm working just to fill my life. I'm certain that if I were a young woman now, I would work." Whatever their doubts, most women in this sample are bolstered in their convictions about the significance of a volunteer career by their belief in community service.

Noblesse Oblige

Despite the pejorative overtones to the idea of the volunteer as leisured dilettante, these women give full support to idea of noblesse oblige as expressed in the volunteer spirit. For them, the term noblesse oblige refers to the altruistic service performed by those who have the resources for those who don't. McCarthy (1982) uses the term this way to cover the benevolence shown in reform movements and in the charity and cultural philanthropy of Chicago at the turn of the century. Implicit in the term is also the idea of noblesse as what the better classes owe the less fortunate. From that perspective, the volunteer spirit is required for upper-class and privileged middle-class women who are rich in resources of time, money, and connections; but they help, rather than share in the fate of, the less fortunate. The limitation of this perspective is that it has no systematic, corrective device for incorporating the responses of those helped. The services provided may not be the desired ones; the tone or style of service may be perceived as offensive and patronizing. Further, the notion that the haves *should* help the have nots is an indirect legitimation of inequality and an acceptance of a fundamentally unjust system. A sharp picture of how this behavior can look to others appears in Coles (1977:306–17), who shows how the problems and limitations of noblesse oblige, as practiced by the very wealthy, appear to their children. Children, for example, see that parents may urge public compliance with school desegregation yet expect their own children to attend private schools. Or they see that parents require their children to be kind and polite to domestics yet discourage the development of friendships with those domestics or their children.

The dimension of gender, added to class stereotypes, encourages the public image of the Lady Bountiful that these women wish to dissociate from their own notions of noblesse. This aura of noblesse oblige does not permeate the charitable work of poorer members of the society (Kaminer 1984). Working-class members and welfare recipients help their peers with the understanding that the donor today may be the recipient tomorrow. Helping one another knits together a community network of resources. Stack (1974), for example, shows how this interdependence is created by black mothers on welfare as a strategy for survival.

These distinctions are not always easy to keep clear, for both upper-class and middle-class women see their work as contributing to the good of their community at large. Just how far this community stretches can be variably interpreted. Some of the work is indirectly or even directly for the benefit of their own class—as when women do volunteer work to support the private schools and churches their family attends. Some of the work is rationalized as benefiting a wider community—as when members of any class can enjoy the public parks and museums for which these women work. But some of the work is primarily altruistic, as when women work for the orphanages, hospitals, and social services to aid those in the working class and those on welfare. The spirit of volunteering, then, is somewhat different for the work of privileged women compared with that of the working-class volunteers and welfare recipients who help one another.

The combination of ideas about altruism and noblesse oblige provide a special motivation for these volunteer women. They respond to the notion of altruistic service as an appropriate framework for their own actions and goals. They learn to care about altruism through early socialization. The desire to conform to a pattern, set by admired and respected parents, is reinforced by the sense of responsibility internalized at the same time. "I was brought up to feel guilty" expresses the sentiment of many who are taught that they are specially privileged and must work for others accordingly. Such ideas fit well with the notion that women who are comfortably placed should not compete with those who need to earn their living. If you don't need a job, you shouldn't take one; indeed, you have no right to one.

These ideas are complemented by the training traditional women receive in ingratiating manners; noblesse oblige can also include the idea of making special efforts for others. "I like to please people," said one woman. And this statement expresses a general tendency or desire to smooth over interpersonal difficulties and to avoid unpleasantness. The proscriptions on how one ought to act and what one ought to do are reinforced by traditional notions about the dependence and subordination of women. Pleasing and serving are more important than independence and equality. For women of the upper-middle and upper classes, the rewards of the traditional sys-

tem can be great enough to make gender equality seem super-
fluous. As one woman said, "I'm of the old school. It wasn't necessary to have equality."

The Volunteer Calling

The themes of primacy of service to family, the desire to produce
professional-quality work, noblesse oblige, and the unmet needs of
society combine in the traditional upbringing of privileged women
to provide the impetus for their concern for community. They wish
to avoid competition in the world of employed work and to suit
their own work to a pattern that will not inconvenience their husbands and children, and they wish to be useful members of society.
These wishes make work for community welfare a natural choice.
And women talk about this work as intrinsic to their way of life.
"[There is] a Talmudic saying that you should try to change things a
little bit while you are here. I want my children to feel that way
too." The "concept of service is distinctive and important" and
those who hold it "contribute to the betterment" of their city.
Those who serve can see the results of their efforts, "knowing . . .
the community is a little better off."

The expression of concern for community welfare can also offer a
sense of independent choice and freedom in volunteer work. "Nobody and nothing owed me a thing. I did it because I wanted to."
The sense of choice might, from a different perspective, seem unrealistic when expressed by women who appear constrained by
their class position. Women in traditional upper-middle-class and
upper-class marriages with limited experience in the world of paid
employment might find any employment other than volunteer
work extremely difficult. However, the advent of the women's movement and the growing acceptance of ideas about women's rights to
their own independent careers have popularized the notion that
other choices are possible.

Still, for many, and especially for these women, volunteer work
is an appropriate and honorable activity for women in the community. From this perspective, middle-class women volunteer as home
and childcare responsibilities permit, hiring baby-sitters if they can
or waiting until children enter school. Wealthier women, with
regular full-time support from paid household assistants, have
greater freedom for a fully developed career outside the home earlier in their domestic careers. Not all women use this opportunity

to become leaders, of course. Many who volunteer stay in the rank
and file. But all those who do develop into leaders begin with volunteer service.

Entry and Ascent

The precise nature of an individual's interest in volunteer work is
often hard to assess, particularly since so many diverse activities (a
donation, voting, precinct work, block soliciting for charity, attendance at a meeting—as well as the sustained activity of daily,
weekly, or monthly volunteer work throughout the year) are encompassed by the general notion of volunteering. Some people
make an occasional effort while others develop serious commitments. These women are, of course, in this second category. They
entered because of the encouragement of their parents, their husbands and in-laws, or because of their own determination to rise in
the volunteer world, even without assistance.

Parental Influence

Perhaps the most effective introduction to the volunteer career
comes from intimates: parents, other relations, the social circle approved by parents, close friends. Such influences are reinforced in
private schools and sororities where well-to-do parents can place
their children. At least forty-one women were recruited in this way.

For the most privileged, this kind of entry meant following in a
well-established family pattern where their role was preordained.
That role was to be a civic leader (38 out of the 41 mentioned above
showed this pattern). Some women, when speaking of their early
background, commented, "It is expected, if you had the time, that
you would get out and do something . . . I just learned through the
pores. My mother and father were very much for public service.
My mother was a dedicated volunteer. My father . . . was a very
strong influence when I was young . . . how you live and what you
did. Noblesse oblige and how he must give back to the community." Parents led by example. Sometimes family examples extended more than one generation: "My grandmothers always did
volunteer work; they were both very strong and dedicated women."
For some the guidance—or pressure—to enter upon a volunteer
career was more direct. "When I was a senior in college I joined the
Junior League . . . it was really the determination of my mother.
I went to work for the Opera Auxiliary. My mother got me in when I

was invited to join the Junior League." Other parents provided avenues of access to desired opportunities. "The summer I graduated from college I worked in the Senate Foreign Relations Committee for six months . . . only because my father knew [a senator] and . . . asked him to help me get out of the house." Jewish women in this study often talked about family guidance (or pressure) toward volunteer work within the context of the philanthropic tradition in their culture.

> My grandfather was president of the hospital. The Jewish tradition is such that philanthropy is better than religion.
> My father taught us . . . this little city was pretty good to all of us and it should continue to help others. And we [in the well-to-do Jewish community] have a responsibility to others . . .

The foregoing comments suggest how parents provide both opportunities (through their connections) and direction (through their insistence) to guide girls and young women into volunteer activity. In addition, both boys and girls (Coles 1977) learn about their responsibilities for charitable work through observation, as well as through direction.

One woman offered an insight into how children may observe their parents' activity and then strive to emulate them. This woman—an extremely successful volunteer—is influential in politics and a variety of artistic and liberal causes in Pacific City. "I remember I was president of my high school sorority. And when I came home I put my gavel next to that of my mother and father."

This type of parental influence is not, of course, limited to the upper class. The women studied by Gittell and Naples (1981:18) come from a socialist, union, politically active family background in the working class; or they grew up in supportive, "liberal-minded" families or were encouraged by that type of spouse. Kaminer (1984) notes that community service is an important part of life for many women, even when busy with family and salaried employment. Some of the women Kaminer interviewed came from a welfare background and from inner city ghettos where they learned to help others. Through family example, and their own developing interests, they began a lifelong commitment to improving their community and helping their neighbors in volunteer efforts. Implicit in both studies is the idea that the desire to express altruism is not just found in noblesse oblige but in community activism. The sense of necessity that anyone capable of offering help should contribute to the community welfare may be the same across class lines.

However, in the upper classes, the sense of responsibility to the family is as important as a sense of responsibility to community or society (Ostrander 1984). Davis et al. (1941:91) note that "the upper-class child is taught that he must behave in a certain way not so much to maintain his own social status as because he had an obligation to his whole extended family group to do so, and thus to the entire upper class." These teachings, of course, apply to the upper-class female children as well. These ideas are not overtly expressed but still have currency in Pacific City. Women place their children in the "right" schools, supervise the recreational activities of their children, take children along on volunteer projects, and teach them how to become involved in appropriate projects of their own (Daniels 1987).

These women seemed to accept the responsibilities—and their implications—without objection. Not all of them, however, get the same indoctrination so early in their lives. Like the women with "liberal-minded" spouses cited by Gittell and Naples above, women who marry into families with a tradition of philanthropy in Pacific City pick up the guidance from their new families.

Influence of Husband and In-laws

Some women found their greatest impetus to begin a volunteer career coming from their husbands. (Husbands could provide the standing to a volunteer that references and a record of past employment offer the outside applicant in salaried careers.) Six women married men who opened doors for them through some combination of wealth, social standing, and political prominence. While most minimize the significance of a husband's status in doing more than promoting entry, they still needed a powerful sponsor to replace the normal accretion of friendships in a social network that encourages recruitment into volunteer work. These women were all attractive and capable, but didn't have the previous training (such as finishing school, Junior League) or social credentials (listing in the social register, membership in prestigious social clubs) to move into prestigious and interesting positions potentially available to them as wives of influential men.

Women spoke of the specific encouragement or urging from husbands—beyond the doors opened and resources offered to become a community leader. "My husband said I cannot spend my life being interested in Chinese art and poetry. 'Do something for your community,' he said. I was being asked to do things and refusing them [until then]." If husbands were insistent, so were in-laws. They provided direction to their new relation. Sometimes they also provided the resources (and respite) for a volunteer career. "I was rather occupied with small energetic boys. . . . It was probably not more than a couple of years, because my nice mother-in-law thought I needed full-time help and so a black lady came and gave me breathing room." Or else they provided the contacts for young married women who moved to their husbands' hometown where the women knew no one. "I was put up by my husband's cousin—sort of family. Junior League was a godsend to me because I was happy with my marriage and friends but I desperately wanted to make more friends in this community."

In all, fifteen women described how husbands and in-laws started them on the pathway to volunteer leadership. Their remarks focus on the provision of resources and on the encouragement and direction offered. If there are any profits from volunteering for family or husband in business contacts or improved public relations, these possibilities are left unspecified. As we shall see, the relation between self-interest and altruistic interest is always a difficult one for women in this study to face directly. However, asides by women, particularly doctors' wives, about their efforts to help their husbands or husbands' colleagues in the preparation of convention activities do suggest that sometimes, at least, husbands put their wives' skills to use for some personal or professional advantage.

Whatever the mix of motives pointing a woman toward volunteer work, the help or encouragement from the new family provides a suitable rationale for women who do not wish to appear overly aggressive or ambitious. Some women, however, did not have the advantages of family sponsorship and rose to leadership in volunteer work without it. They were forced to make explicit some of the issues involved in rising.

Working Up without Connections

It is impossible to say exactly how many among those interviewed had created their own entry. Some women are not eager to advertise their humble social origins—nor are they willing to explain just how difficult the climb to their current prominence was. One of the problems is that many avenues to civic leadership (through invitation-only organizations, for example) are only open to women of social position—whether their own or their husband's—and to the women *they* select as suitable for inclusion. Other openings can, under some circumstances, become available after great persistence and the display of extraordinary talents. Where no family assistance or friendship connection is possible, this persistence or display is often associated with social climbing. Distinctions among these types of opportunity would be very difficult except that, fortunately, some women wanted to talk about how their own initial interest in social climbing had influenced the shape and direction of their later careers. Others stated very firmly that they were interested in community service, but not in social prominence.

From a group of fourteen women, not assisted by their own or their husband's family, a few could talk about entry without assistance. In the upper-middle class, all of these women are comfortably placed in life and have handsome homes; some have household help and second homes as well. Married, widowed or divorced, they live well and have the resources to volunteer if they wish. Five are currently employed in professional or otherwise prestigious occupations in addition to their volunteering. These employed women promoted their paid careers as well as their leadership status in the volunteer world through volunteer work done earlier in their lives. They found alternatives open to "self-made" women without any clear help up the rungs of the volunteer career ladder from family, husband, or husband's family.

For those whose main interest is strictly community work, opportunities to become trained and then eligible as candidates for appointment to prestigious and policy-setting boards and commissions arise through participation in traditionally acceptable avenues for women's activities: nursery school administration; Parent Teachers Association; League of Women Voters; and the political parties. Some women, even without prior interests in community welfare, become concerned as they learn of problems in their city through another traditional women's activity: efforts to help their own youngsters progress through the local school system. Such interests can lead some women into the political arena, where they discover how interconnected their own special concerns are with the local and regional political structures. In this study, there were at least eight such women: three whose concern with preserving public schools led them into the politics of integration and busing; four who became well-known citizen's advocates on the basis of specific concerns in health and child welfare; and one who became politically prominent through earlier conservation interests. Although at least three were from the upper class, these women have different interests from those with "social" volunteer interests.

The women who combine philanthropic and "social" interests are a little more difficult to describe, for "social climbing" is a delicate and painful subject to many. It is a label often attached to the cultural activities associated with "society" and social interests. Consequently, participation in social events can give one the reputation of too great an interest in society and its activities. Fortunately, two women were willing to explain their own method of entry into this precarious mix of community leadership and entrance into upper-class society. Here is the analysis of one middle-class woman from another geographic area who has successfully breached the barriers against unsponsored newcomers.

> [I knew I had to join the Junior League in order to begin social climbing . . .] You make it known. I was in a house tour for the Heart Fund and I met a gal there who went to bat for me. And there was Mimsy Cooper—I met her at the volunteer bureau. Every time I'd meet somebody [in the course of doing volunteer work], I'd go through the Junior League roster to see if they were there [in a search for potential sponsors]. A funny thing, I asked [a past Junior League president] "How do you get into the League?" And she said, "Serena, that is one question you never ask."

Serena was successful in acquiring the necessary sponsors for nomination to the League and continued from there to mix a distinguished career of social and philanthropic activity. The woman in the following illustration was not so fortunate, perhaps because of her working-class origins in the city. Carmen Del Gado is an older woman eminent in her own ethnic community as well as in Pacific City more generally. Now in her sixties, she has been prominent in the worlds of culture for many years; she is an acknowledged master at producing benefits. Unfortunately, the ambition and determination which have made her known beyond her local ethnic community are associated with a combative and challenging manner that many find abrasive. She is known for a quarrelsome, confrontational approach which other respondents said they (or others) resented. And so, although she has had an important career in philanthropic work, she has never achieved any close, personal friendships with those from upper-class society with whom she mixes in her daily volunteer work. Yet all the other rewards of civic leadership are hers (commemorative medals, directorships on major boards, governmental commissions, reports of her activities in the news and society pages).

In describing her career, Carmen Del Gado explained how she began, and how she reached her prominence as a civic leader.

> Well, let's start out with the church. From the church I followed my daughter's schooling . . . in private school . . . I did parties for the school functions. I was always a leader and seems as though I was the one who started things. You start getting experience—one promotion leads to another—the prestigious schools and the better communities to work in. I research everything when I start. I want to be the best. . . . When you feel you have done it all, you look outside. What's my next move? Then I got into the International Center. When you are in a private school, you get to know a certain kind of people, you hear about the different organizations they belong to. Then I thought it was time to join a club. You are sponsored, you have to have friends. . . . All this wasn't easy because [of my ethnic background]. I could not make it through the Junior League. You have to have a college education for that group. They are very clannish; you have to be known by some of them.
>
> I was outspoken, yet very much in demand because of . . . business acumen and . . . artistic . . . talent. So I went on the Museum Council and used my business ability giving rummage sales or supervising students who would do the decorating for parties. Then I did the Jonquil Ball. That made my reputation because it is a citywide affair and the most influential people in the city are connected with it. . . . When you work there, you have gotten known.

The developing career in the preceding report suggests how obstacles of ethnicity and the lack of a college education (as well as the lack of finesse or tact reported by others) can be overcome in becoming a civic leader. Some of the prerequisites for leadership, belonging to organizations that indicate one's membership in a network of civic leaders, for example, are obtainable through effort. Others, such as participation in some invitational exclusive clubs, are not. But one can develop enough contacts, experience, and skills in other associations to compensate for that omission. If one is sufficiently determined, resourceful, talented and persistent, the lack of an acceptable social manner and first-class social contacts are not sufficient barriers to a career as a civic leader, even in the intersection of society and philanthrophy where the woman in this account has made her place. Furthermore, as other studies of social mobility have shown, if one's own place in a desired world is in some respects tenuous, one can construct a more secure place for one's offspring. This woman was able to arrange matters so that her daughter entered many exclusive clubs closed to the mother.

The preceding account is also interesting in what it shows about the ability to see a career in stages. An explicit concern for progression—here, perhaps a form of social climbing—shows that women can formulate their notions of their work in career terms. The two women discussed above were willing to attribute social climbing interests to their earlier endeavors, but explicitly disavowed these interests in their later work. They now espoused goals more similar to their colleagues in this study: disinterested concern for the community welfare. Interests and ambitions suitable for expression at entry point, then, may be discarded as a career progresses. Hughes' remarks, quoted earlier, about running adjustments between a man, his life and his professional world, seem particularly appropriate to this type of adjustment in changing patterns of the motives women explicitly avow for their entry and ascent in the volunteer career.

2
Values and Perspectives
of Civic Leaders

The profile of civic leaders and the description of pathways into the volunteer career suggest how privileged and accepting of conventional understandings about gender stereotypes this group of women are. They have the resources of money and connections; and they have an understanding of their place as women in the system that produces these resources. They are not rebels; they try to work within the system to find appropriate activities and goals for themselves. However, even within these limits the women show a diverse mix of liberal (in support of social reforms and in political advocacy) and conservative (in support of status quo and fashionable causes) attitudes. This chapter presents their descriptions of how they coordinate and give priority to family and volunteer work responsibilities. These descriptions also reveal just how they see themselves embedded in the social world around them—in their relationships to their families and the volunteer organizations they serve. Their perspectives shape and delimit both the direction and the kinds of commitment in their volunteer careers.

The women interviewed hold many traditional values: they say their families are central to their lives; that women should be willing to assume subordinate and gender-stereotyped roles. Yet, they also exhibit a capacity for and interest in leadership; and sometimes they show ambivalence about the traditional role and a complementary willingness to espouse some nontraditional views. In the main, however, volunteer work is the old-fashioned response, institutionalized in Junior League or League of Women Voters or Volunteer Agency training programs, to the desires of energetic and able women to do interesting work. And it is a safety-valve substitute for the professional career in paid work that is not possible given the boundaries of a traditional woman's role in the upper classes. Those who do want an independent and autonomous life face family and social pressures not to move too far from traditional expectations. Generally, they acquiesce to these pressures in return for all the advantages provided women in the privileged classes. Sometimes however, they show the costs of their acceptance of a role which can leave them feeling somehow disregarded, subordinate, or inadequate.

Their understanding of their place in the world defines or delimits the types of careers these women choose. For values give life meaning and direction. They are important in constructing any plan of action, showing why some choices are possible and others distasteful (Miller, Galanter, and Pribram 1960). The course of action suggested by our own value system often seems so natural as to be inevitable. It is easier to see how the realities of life are socially constructed (Berger and Luckmann 1967) when examining the lives of people different from ourselves. The women in this study see the world from the perspectives of rich or comfortably settled women who have been raised to take a traditional and privileged role in the society. This background offers the "vocabulary of motives" (Burke 1954) that explains their actions to themselves in choosing one path or another, in praising or deploring ambition, authority, and other leadership qualities that are attributed to themselves and other community leaders.

Setting Priorities and Formulating Rationales about Work

The best overview of the traditional notion of priorities comes from a woman who finished our interview with this spontaneous observation: "The nicest volunteer job of all is making a happy marriage and seeing five reasonably happy children. . . . A close family is something." When I asked a sample of fifty of these women what accomplishment they were proudest of in their careers, a fourth (12) ignored their volunteer work and mentioned their families. Although the question was asked in the context of volunteer work, these women focused on the health and attractiveness of their children and the longevity of their marriages (e.g., "Most proud of having thin [i.e., visibly acceptable] normal grown-up children and thirty-one years with a husband and a grand life"; "My ten children, and my husband still loves me"). When they discussed their early careers, twenty (of the total sample of 70) told me their volunteer work was limited by home responsibilities when children were young. Even women with household help felt these constraints. They were "always home by three when the children were small" or they said they could only do volunteer work irregularly when their children were young. Some women in this study explained how they have always organized their volunteer work so that it will not interfere with family life.

> One of my favorite hobbies or interests has been my family. I try to be home when they get home. The first thing [about accepting volunteer responsibilities] was never to neglect my family. And my home, I have always loved my house. And I always put my husband first.

Some women see this pattern not only as usual or expected, but obligatory. Four women told me that women *should* be with their children when they are young. One used her influence as a civic leader to restrict the volunteer activities of mothers with young children.

> If there are any young people on a committee and they have . . . a new baby, I say to them "Don't do anything to take you from your child. I nursed both of my babies for ten months. If you've brought someone into the world, you owe them that." So I would say, "You can't be on the committee." Certain things people can do at home, like telephoning and addressing, . . . [though] that's not glamorous.

As the preceding quote suggests, work can be found to fit around home duties. It is suitable for early stages in the volunteer career; but it is not so likely to lead to upward mobility, because it is "foot soldier" work that is repetitive and time consuming. One has no chance to show (or develop) skills beyond reliability and efficiency in easily performed tasks. Here, as in the world of paid employment, decisions to focus on work that can be conveniently adjusted to family schedules postpone the development of skills and experience in jobs that help build careers in challenging and prestigious work.

Those who don't have to work and yet choose to do so are particularly vulnerable to criticism. One woman explains the philosophy behind the critique in some detail. Her feelings about paid work also reflect on the mother who volunteers too seriously.

> I feel very strongly about women taking jobs unless they need to. [There are] many women I know—salesladies and hairdressers—that would rather be out working and [think]

it is more fun at the office. If they are lucky there is a grandma to take care of the children. . . . I wish there was some way of getting housekeeping a better status; it is not the drudgery it used to be. It is almost fun to do domestic work because of the gadgets to play with.

This woman seems to overestimate the number of women who have a real choice in seeking salaried employment. More important, she downplays her own privileged position to argue that most women, like her, can be virtuous, put family first, and enjoy it. She also has strong views on the importance of women staying home even when they really need employment. "I would rather see the government subsidize women. . . . Better than for them to earn a tiny bit net and never be home when their kids come home from school." This civic leader presents an odd mixture of liberal political and conservative gender stereotypes. It is interesting to see how a traditional focus on homemaking and parenting can lead a political conservative (as this woman is) to contemplate a liberal or even radical position: her husband subsidizes her, so why not government subsidies for mothers to raise their children?

The privileged women in this study have not had the "excuse" of needing paid work when their children were young. But many found outlets for their energy in family-centered volunteer work. Every woman with children worked for the schools attended by her children. The majority (55) worked for private schools, and the others worked for the public schools or some mix of public and private. In addition, a few directed scout troops and boys' or girls' clubs or organized dancing classes so that their own children could participate. For many, this family-oriented work became the first step on the career ladder. All these activities were justifiable as part of family responsibility; for women are expected to negotiate for their children and mediate childrens' introduction to the society beyond the home. Whatever interest or work experience this activity provides for mothers, it is seen as part of the priority of family.

Most of the women in this group took it for granted that salaried work was not a real option. As one women put it, "I should say that very early I realized that Chester could never stand for me to have a job. We were perfectly well off . . . so there really wasn't any need for it." Her remarks suggest one rationale for putting their families first. These women are in well-off families with generous rewards. These rewards also make it easier to accept the value system where families should come first. There is always an added rationale for a

few: that it would be wrong to take a job from one who really needs
it. (None, however, take the next step to consider that their husbands might be overcompensated while other men don't make as
much as they should.)

The traditional woman's view of family priorities includes some
limitation on their ambitions as well as their hours of work; these
priorities shape the scope of their career ladders. At least four of
these community leaders were asked to run for political office but
refused on grounds of family responsibility. As one of them put it,
"I received several requests to run for Congress. But I couldn't see
how I could do that. How could I stay home with my husband and
go to Washington?" Several other women refused the presidency
of local organizations, preferring the vice-presidency or a lesser
office.

> I was offered the presidency (of a major civic organization)
> . . . but I felt my loyalties were with my family. And I don't
> think I am qualified. I have never had labor relations expe-
> rience, for example. And I couldn't sit up until four in the
> morning in negotiations. You have to know your limitations.

These refusals show a mixture of family responsibilities and fear of
jobs too far beyond traditional conceptions of a woman's role. The
older woman just quoted might not feel she had the stamina for all
night negotiations, yet she has often managed all-night benefit parties for her favorite charities and civic improvements.

Despite the prevailing ideology about the importance of family,
many of these women began their volunteer careers when they still
had young children at home. Women tackle the problem of finding
an excuse or rationale for active community involvement along
with family responsibilities in various ways. In the course of this
work, women also developed an ideology of how working might fit
with a husband's own wishes. This view reinforces the picture of
the husband as dominant and provides additional pressure to
make the work less visible. Women maintain a low profile to avoid
any appearance of competition with their husbands. Although
many husbands could not tolerate a wife in paid employment, and
the families do not need the money from a wife's earnings, her unpaid work can be acceptable. However, women still have to develop
some rationale for career commitment. One commonly recognized
reason is mental health. "I told [my husband]: either I was active or
I would sit home and eat candy and get fat. I am in a better state of

mind if I am active and involved." But the pact to allow activity implies that home responsibilities will not suffer and that the priority of family is recognized. It is not only a husband's wishes which act as a limitation on career aspirations but also a woman's sense of the time she wants to spend on marital well-being.

> If I had to stay home and change diapers all day it would have hacked up our marriage. I was fortunate to have help. And I was careful not to abuse [the privilege] of volunteer activity. I would be content to come home at five and be with Mac . . . just turn off the phone and say "Very sorry, I'm busy with family now." . . . I didn't want my relationship with Mac threatened. He pays the bills and backs me up and in return I owe that to him.

The wheedling tone in which negotiations with husbands are reported suggests how the ideology that husbands will want their wives to be active is developed. For example, the following community leader is known to have been a tough and efficient manager when she was president of one of Pacific City's most prestigious boards in the field of health, education, and welfare. Yet she presents herself as one who coaxes and is commanded at home.

> I seem to be a driver, somewhat. And big John is quite easygoing. I had a little talk with him and I explained if I didn't take time from him or from the house or from the children, can I please find something to do? And he said "Out!" [i.e., Go out and find something to do.]

When women cannot resolve their desires for a work commitment—and the consequent pile of responsibilities they acquire—with their own notions of how family responsibilities should be met, they see themselves as inadequate in some way. The result is guilt. Feelings of guilt at not meeting family responsibility are sometimes assuaged by ritual preparations—setting the table and arranging flowers—even if the husband is left to prepare hot dogs for the dinner he will eat alone. Or women will not "count" the time spent on the phone contacting committee members and organizing events as time spent away from family because it is time spent in the home. Yet two of these women reported their children's resentment of the phone because it took their mother's time away from them.

Community leaders, like other busy working women, often worry about whether it is ever right to give their own interests priority over parental responsibilities. One strategy is for women to try to be supermom.

> I remember the telephone calls on projects for the League. It was a full-time job and I'd wear myself out—buzzing home with those big binders and [then] have all those materials to read. And I would feel I had to get my phone calls done before dinner. Now I think I should have been taking a hot bath and reading to my children. I did all that too, of course (laughs).

Whatever the negotiations, most of these women work out a satisfactory compromise between their traditional responsibilities and their wish for an independent career. Their work, after all, is a benefit to the community; sometimes the work offers some benefits to the family as well.

> The kids needed help too, and I felt I was gypping them [by going back to school]. One way that I subsequently used the degree was suggested by the needs my kids had [for special educational programs in career counseling]. But [it did cost] the family. One concept is to plough all education and training into the next generation. And I did proceed that way when we were not so well-off. Now I feel I can realize my own potential [and risk not] doing as much for the children as I should.

Since childhood these women expected that they would play a traditional—and subordinate—role in the family. These expectations make it easier to accept a system of priorities where the family comes before one's career. For example, they have accepted parental decisions limiting their career opportunities with fortitude and resignation.

> I grew up in a political family but that is one place where I don't seem to have my own identity. Although all the children were bright in my family, the message was somehow different to the girls than the boys. I knew I was expected to be something like a nurse or a social worker or a wife. In a different time I would have gone to law school.

In addition to career restrictions, women may discover how restricted they have been in social interactions by their own sense of family responsibility. When events free them—through widowhood, divorce, or children's departure—as happened for this widow—they experience a sense of their earlier confinement.

"After his death, there was no one to consider first before my wishes. I could decide what I wanted to do. For example, I could go out for drinks after a meeting. I never had done that in all those years because of the family."

While most women accept these restrictions as natural, some resist or become angry at what they see as the unfairness of priorities that offer them so little. A few women began to have misgivings in later life, after the resurgence of the women's movement in the sixties. One woman recognizes that she substituted an important role as a civic leader for opportunity missed. "I could have done a number of things. My brothers are in the business. There was never any question that I could be involved and I just accepted it. Now I feel it was a mistake. Now, very late in my life, I am saying, 'Why not me?'" Another woman changed her volunteer status to salaried professional in response to increasing resentment over the limitations placed on women. She returned to school when her children were grown and then went to work.

> I worked for my father until I had a baby. It was the lowest kind of employment. I look back and it makes me angry that I was never considered someone who could be taken into the family business, that I was expected to make sacrifices for my brother.

The early training that cuts off opportunities is often reinforced by husbands who don't want their wives to work. In all, about ten women see a husband's wishes as the stumbling block.

Even though these women have built impressive careers as civic leaders, the clear message is that wife and mother are their most important roles. Almost all the women interviewed said as much (and sixty of them said so quite explicitly; see table 2.1).

Of course, asserting the priority of husband and family is made easier when women can choose from an array of strategies in deciding how to meet all of their commitments. Conflicts between burgeoning volunteer careers and home responsibilities were mitigated through family resources (housekeepers, plenty of money for transportation and other costs of participation) and family support. These resources are placed at the disposal of women, particularly those with responsibilities to maintain family position in the upper class. As Ostrander (1984) and Rapp note (1982:183), upper-class women represent and further class interests when they work for high culture, education, social welfare, and charity. All these

Table 2.1 Setting Priorities: The Family Comes First

Family most important accomplishment in career	12
Volunteer work limited when children were young	20
Always organized volunteer work not to interfere with family life	10
Husband permitted entry into—and continuity in— volunteer career	8
Husband's wishes a barrier to paid employment	10
Total	60

institutions are, in a sense, created by their own class and maintain those class interests. It is not surprising, then, that parents, in-laws, and husbands initially accepted and even encouraged community effort.

As careers grow and take shape, however, they require more and more time and effort. Such commitments require an explanation which permits these efforts to be seen as compatible with the priority on family. Pointing to the support and encouragement husbands offer is one way to do it. If husbands see career volunteering as suitable for their wives, then it must be an appropriate part of—or does not intrude upon—family responsibilities. This approval is important when husbands are seen as what Lipman-Blumen (1984:50) calls "strong, wise, and especially . . . benevolent despot(s)." Accepting this notion leads women to transfer responsibility for their lives to "moral and ethical rulers." The women in this study lend support to this view when they stress the importance of a husband's encouragement in their decision to build a career. Husbands as moral and ethical rulers become a further constraint/support in the construction of a career ladder.

In reviewing all the interviews, it was clear that women wanted to stress their husband's support, and even pride, in their accomplishments. In all, thirty-four women mentioned a husband's pleasure in some aspect of his wife's achievement. For the traditionally oriented women, a husband's support is the sign of having the best of both worlds. The support is a credential to show that one is in a happy, co-operative marriage and that one is *not* one of those overly ambitious, striving women who want to seek personal aggrandizement at the cost of domestic harmony.

The women in this study minimize the importance of their work to their husband's career, giving little attention to, for example, the usefulness of their community experience in organizing business or professional conventions and parties at a husband's request.[1] In general, their focus of interest is on describing volunteer work as their own turf, as it were; they do not wish to dwell on those aspects of the work that suggest they are only working at the bidding of another. These women also resist the instrumental or opportunistic cast given to their work by the idea of its usefulness in advancing careers. Nonetheless, from the traditional perspective, they do need a rationale for explaining the development of a career independent of wife and homemaker roles, even, occasionally, suggesting how that work is useful to their husbands.

One way to develop this rationale is to stress the advantages of volunteering to marriage. Activities encouraged by one's husband, partnership with a husband who also takes on civic leader roles, community work which then makes a wife more interesting to her husband at the dinner table are all positive advantages within a traditional view of what a good wife should do or be. From this perspective, the basic spheres of activity for husbands and wives are separate but complementary. Complementary, however, does not necessarily mean equal. The husband is still the head of the family. The wife requires his support and, sometimes, his active guidance.

Whatever the ambition, celebrity, or mastery of a highly successful community leader, the public stance she takes is that her husband wants her to do it, or even helps her to do it. Women can turn to a husband, as superordinate and expert, for advice even in areas outside his own field. When women were asked "Who do you turn to in a bind?" most discussed other men and women civic leaders, but twenty-four mentioned their husbands specifically (another five mentioned family without specifying the person). Some of these women use their husbands as a sounding board, an agent of catharsis ("If I need to blow off steam"), an instructive critic ("more coldblooded and objective than I am able to be"), a general resource ("total help, emotional, financial support in every way," "if I'm in trouble he has a good perspective, maturity"). Or they may stress their dependence upon his superior abilities: "He is terribly wise. He understands me very well and listens and occasionally slows me down a little bit."

This dependence may include a need for personal validation as

1. Expressions of class position and responsibility in working with or for husbands to maintain that position appear more clearly in the work of Susan Ostrander (1984). Her respondents speak more openly of the importance of maintaining their own class through acts of charity and philanthropy.

well as advice. "My husband always supports me in shoring up my self-worth and understanding how to deal with problems—putting the problem into focus." Sometimes a husband's support includes specific assistance to accomplish a project. "I had to speak in the legislature and I was petrified. So my husband drove [my committee] up to [the state Capitol]." This assistance may be combined with pressure to take on greater responsibilities, with some possible advantages accruing to husbands.

> I was asked to be president and I think it is one of the super boards of the city; I was flattered to be asked. My husband was anxious for me to be the president. He was absolutely great at helping me—listening to my speeches and [helping me do] my letters.

This assignment is on a very powerful and prestigious board in Pacific City. There are professional advantages to, in this case, a lawyer, from the entry provided by his wife. This woman does not acknowledge these benefits here. In fact, she only emphasizes the help that *he* gives her. Yet her husband can make professional contacts and acquire "insider" information about future changes in community organizations that can affect his practice.

A doctor's wife explicitly mentioned the helpful ambience that she could create for her husband. "I loathed being president of the auxiliary; but I was a doctor's wife. I did it for my husband, of course. It wasn't unimportant, really, that men have the women create social connections." One woman was quite explicit about how a wife's honors are a credit to her husband. "My husband wanted me to be in volunteering. He felt it accrued to his prestige to have me [be] president of the Junior League." This last example suggests another element of benefit to be derived from a wife's volunteer work: the conspicuous consumption available to the husband who can afford so active a consort. In addition, there is always the possibility that a wife can improve the social status of her husband through her participation in prestigious community welfare activity.

Some assignments undertaken specifically at a husband's request occur only when he—and his wife—are already in leadership positions. Prom 'nent physicians asked to host the convention of their professional society, for example, need their wives and their wives' friends and connections to produce the social arrangements that add lustre to the substantive program. But the generally supportive behavior of husbands—and any rewards received for it—are mentioned as possibilities throughout all the stages of a woman's career. A husband's willingness to support or encourage his wife in her career as a community leader, then, is reinforced by the interest this career adds to his own life.

Some women stressed the Scheherazade-like aspect of their accomplishment: it helped them hold their man. And it contributed to family welfare when they could offer a perspective on new ideas to everyone. Six women said their work made them more interesting conversation partners at the dinner table. "If I come home and say (what a Nobel prize winner) said to me at lunch . . . everybody sits up."

One woman presented a blend of "mental health" and "more interesting" arguments for justifying a volunteer career.

> When I first arrived here as a young woman, I became very close with James' sister and spent a lot of time at her house cooking up messes together and giving joint parties. Then she went to Europe for a long time. I didn't know what was the matter with me; but my weight went down to ninety pounds and I had very bad stomachaches all the time. I went to my internist and he gave a long talk about my life and said he would not recommend a psychiatrist but that I should do something. I said I didn't need a psychiatrist— just something done about my stomachaches. The internist gave me some tranquilizers to use when I needed them. . . . James and I talked and I asked if it would be all right if I went into the community. He agreed that I should get busy. And after a time, he asked me not to take the pills anymore because he liked me better when I went up and down; I was more exciting company. And I decided I didn't need them.

A theme running throughout this discussion of support from husbands is that work is a privilege and not a right these women can take for granted. Just as husbands are given credit for permitting their wives to begin a volunteer career, many express happiness at the magnanimity shown by husbands or family in permitting these women to continue. Women commented on the generosity their husbands showed in permitting them to have male friends in the course of their work. They also spoke of the "bargain" they have struck with their husbands in exchange for their tolerance.

> My husband really liked it when governors and vice-presidents and other important people came to our house. He

was not so hot on the precinct workers. But I have to say if you allow your wife to give her whole life to volunteering, if those things are rewards, it is cheap enough.

A few spoke of the generosity of men who can't fend for themselves; the price of their tolerance is some extra pressure on the wife to manage—or pick up later. Although the passivity or helplessness of these men presents problems, the men are willing to wait patiently until the women find solutions.

> My husband is very understanding. If I am late home and there is no dinner, he understands. I can remember one evening, phoning and saying I would be late. I told my husband to do a few things. But then I got worried about trying to explain the pressure cooker and this good friend [who was also phoning her husband about the delay] said "I should phone my husband back and tell him to go over and help yours!"

In all, about eight women speak explicitly of the "favor" accorded by husbands who let their wives pursue careers. They epitomize the acceptance of traditional roles for women in marriage and the family: opportunity for self-development in a personal career outside the family is not a right but a privilege. Women can take advantage of this privilege when they meet all their other familial obligations and when they have especially kind or indulgent spouses. While the benevolent direction of husbands may help integrate ambitions and traditional expectations for feminine behavior, not all husbands and families are supportive—and not all ambitions can be realized within conventional expectations.

A group of nine women say they did not have that good fortune. And five in this group are now divorced, partly, they say, because of their resistance to a husband's wish for a submissive wife. Many women speak of the strain involved in juggling these two careers; but only these few show any special bitterness about the way conflicts at home impeded or diminished pleasure in a career outside the home. Some (who were not divorced) successfully ignore their husband's disinterest. ("My husband couldn't care less about all of my activities.") They pursue their own interests while leaving a husband to his own devices.

> My husband thought it was utterly mad to have causes. After our vacation in the East . . . I said, "You can fly home if you want." But I stopped at other cities to learn how their

officials got redevelopment plans through when our city couldn't.

One way around the problem is to keep arguing with family in an effort to gain acceptance for an expanded role outside the home.

> My son, in his heart of hearts, knows it is better this way. But he would like to see me in an apron with the house smelling of bread. I specially asked him to come to a concert not only because I thought he would enjoy it but because I had arranged it and was very proud of it. I now feel able to say something in reproach when he didn't do it. He said he was sorry he hadn't come but was doing something he liked better at the moment. But I pointed out how many times I had to drop things I wanted to do in order to see him play in a basketball game. When I go outside the home I would like more support and praise within my family than I feel I get. It's exhausting sometimes.

The divorced women in this group saw their conflict over their volunteer career as part of growing rupture in the overall marital relationship. "My ex-husband felt it accrued to his prestige to have me president of the museum board. But it became a source of irritation to him that it filled my life—a vacuum because it was not a rich full life with him." One woman felt literally imprisoned by the conflict. "I was never allowed out after 5:00 P.M. when I was married. Ira used to try to break my spirit."

The conflicts described thus far concern the disposal of a wife's time and her availability for familial duties. But one woman described the conflict as one of open competition between herself and her husband.

> He was pretty jealous. And it threatened him because more people were getting to know me [rather] than him. I suggested it would be useful for him in his profession [to have me so prominent] but he didn't see it that way. But I helped him through two political campaigns. Maybe the marriage could have lasted if he had won.

It is not surprising, then, that five of the nine women in this group are divorced. Their sense of oppression and thwarted individuality is expressed by the following woman who pursued her career despite opposition from her husband.

> My husband didn't want me to have any further education [after we married]. He wanted an appendage, someone to

take care of him and type his grad school notes. "Your gratification has to come through me," he said when we were
first married. I tried to do it and I slowly went right under
the carpet. That wasn't enough of a life—iron shirts and
type notes. I didn't want to do it so I did them horribly.
That's when I went to a psychiatrist. As the psychiatrist
helped me, I developed my own career. And I became more
and more of a threat to my husband.

These women who do not find the roles of traditional women
compatible with their volunteer careers are the minority. But they
highlight the problematic aspects of that role: without a benevolent
superordinate, the conflicts between household and career responsibilities—even for a volunteer career—create difficulties, exacer-
bating whatever tensions already exist between a couple. The question of just how these women should set family priorities and
when their own careers can be given consideration is not resolved
to mutual satisfaction.

However, for most of these women, as we have seen, the priorities
of family and the development of a volunteer career can be made
compatible. And they see the value system within which these priorities seem appropriate as basically beneficial to everyone.

Acceptance of Traditional Gender Stereotypes
at Home and at Work

These women show how their traditional roles in the family can
be organized around careers when they explain how they see the
world around them. They have a comfortable niche in society and,
in general, accept the social conditions that produced it. The feminine characteristics of conciliation, indirection, and modesty have
worked well in the development of a volunteer career. The opportunity for that career did not require great assertiveness (or else the
pushing for their advancement came from others) and so a career
evolved naturally.

While some women in this study see the way traditional sex roles
give men power over women as unfair and, after divorce, express
bitterness at their fate, many of the women I interviewed spoke
quite frankly about appreciating the advantages that benevolent
paternalism provided them. They like the status quo and find it
easy to function within it.

Most generally, they expressed acceptance of men's and women's
places in the traditional scheme of things. For example, they expect
to socialize boys and girls differently.

> I was a den mother and we did a lot of the usual scout projects. I tried to gear crafts more to boy-oriented crafts because boys get awfully bored with painting and pasting which maybe girls can stick with. So I had the boys doing a decathlon and mosaics. That was a natural for them because it was rough and heavy. Boys enjoyed making stepping stones—so visible and more mannish a product to show for their effort.

They see nothing wrong with sex segregation in restaurants. "I think that if restaurants are closed to women at lunchtime it makes it more exciting at night. I don't see what all the fuss is about. And I wouldn't care to go to a restaurant if it were closed to women."

They accept a sexual division of labor in their civic leaders' tasks as well.

> The women's board of the Orphanage ran the establishment and the men's board invested the money and argued with the women about the budget. . . . The committee to merge the women's and men's boards [has bogged down]. But I don't like to do the finance and none of the other women on the board do either.

They may also protest strongly if the distinctions show signs of breaking down, developing a rationale for the belief that women should stick to their own field.

> We had a very fine men's board for the Halfway House and there was a tendency for the women to take on too much of the financial activities and not enough of the activities they were more efficient in such as housekeeping. This is the great danger of women getting in too far. We lost some of the men's board because of trying to interfere and not doing the proper work we were qualified to do. I left the board for that reason.

Whether they see the status quo as proper or unfair, a further limitation on careers is that these women work within the general understanding that, in our society, men are superordinate and focus on practical matters. Women accept this order of things to get their work done.

One expression of this view is belief in the primacy of strategies of negotiation and indirection to gain desired ends. As noted, many community leaders are known for their abilities at conciliation or mediation. These abilities are learned in the traditional role of family peacemaker. These women gain experience in the art of compromise, soothing hurt feelings, and avoiding conflict as they adjudicate sibling quarrels and other family difficulties. They learn that conflict is disruptive in the family, where relationships are stable and must continue. Developing alternative ways of managing difficult situations suggests alternative strategies for managing differences in public encounters. "I think women can build bridges, because they can approach something acceptable to two confronting parties. After all, they have to do it with children."

Women also learn the art of coaxing in the stereotypical dependent role of daughter and wife. And they see no reason not to use such arts in volunteer work.

> I suppose it's the public relations coming out in me that I want to say the right thing to people and apple polish a bit to get what I want. I have asked for a lot of favors from people who said I'd never get it, but I did.

A stereotypic expression of women's wiles is to "chase someone until he catches you." And women who wheedle and insinuate their views sometimes do so in order to have others (as more powerful men) take up the cause, believing it their own. "If you do it right, you sort of—it turns out to be their idea, not yours."

These tactics may be learned at home, where these women not only mediate among family members, but adopt wheedling tactics toward husbands in order to win favors. Such tactics then acquire considerable practical value in the formation of a career; for the women civic leader's position rarely has any direct power attached to it. Tactics of persuasion thus become elevated to principles of organization and leadership in developing careers.

Of course, the work of civic leaders requires some hard decisions (staff are hired and fired, organizational policy has to be hammered out) and it is only to be expected that compromise and negotiation are not always easy . . . or even possible. Accordingly, these women were asked whether they ever had occasion to criticize co-workers and if they felt they could speak openly on such occasions. Three women specifically mentioned that old adage about catching more flies with honey than with vinegar; but the majority interviewed (39) indicated, one way or another, allegiance to the strategies of ingratiation. In this group, a hard core of eight women denied the validity of open criticism (whether or not they ever engaged in it). They said they didn't like it, that it was too difficult ("I find it easier to set up guidelines and develop manuals that can be followed"), that it didn't fit their style ("My style is to discuss alternatives rather than outright criticism"), or that it was "not useful" or "not the thing to do." One woman refused to consider the question relevant to her situation ("I just got my way by being gentle and soft-spoken"). But most women (19) in this group responded by modifying or qualifying the notion of direct criticism to place it within their understanding of conciliation or negotiation. The clearest theme was that of indirection. Indirection is important because confrontation is counterproductive; and so many community leaders say they work "in a roundabout way," that they can do more "with a low profile."

Clearly one reason to use indirection is to avoid confrontations whenever possible. One spares the feeling of others and leaves one's own feelings or judgments ambiguous.

> [The Junior League] wanted me to put in 150 hours of [low-level] service. They wouldn't count the work I was doing [in decision-making positions within community organizations]. So when they asked me to join, I just kept putting it off. And then when I was older, I told them how sorry I was that I let the time slip by when I might join.

Another way to mitigate the danger of criticism is to keep it from becoming public. These women favor taking someone aside for a private discussion of differences rather than voicing them before a gathering of board members or staff. And they deplore airing difficulties before the public (general membership of the organization or the media).

These strategies of indirection and conciliation include another theme already touched upon: the fear of antagonism and the association of criticism with it. Therefore, when these women speak of criticizing, they are careful to set boundaries "within the realm of politeness," "without yelling or screaming," or "sniping."

For some women, conflict over differing opinions is seen as a personal threat as well as an unnecessary unkindness to others. The traditional upbringing and life style of women civic leaders makes any kind of criticism look like confrontation; and confrontation is alien to their life-style. Eight women spoke of their inability to face conflict. One woman spoke of her difficulties at home as well as in community work. "I don't find head-on confrontations very easy. I have problems with confrontations just within my own family." Thus, situations set up for conflict have such women at a disadvantage.

Some women can sidestep the difficulties that conflicts present for them. As their reputation grows, they rise above the necessity for battle. Others come to realize that criticism need not be so damaging as they feared. "I will say I don't agree. And what happened? The world didn't fall apart."

But even conscious efforts at direct criticsm do not open up a context for confrontations; for it is not the style of one's colleagues.

> I felt very strongly about [an issue] and I wrote a letter to Sydney as head of the board of trustees. I wrote to say I thought the new membership proposals were too inward, that we must have community balance—representatives and expertise outside that board. And she gave me no answer yet; but I noticed three names were withdrawn. I always do it directly as long as I feel comfortable in my reasons. Criticizing Sydney took guts because I adore and admire her so.

The ideology against confrontation and conflict is so strong that most deplore these tactics, irrespective of whether or not they ever use them. A few women recognize their own ambivalence about direct action and open criticism; for the moderate, conciliatory style doesn't suit them. Sometimes they joke about it, in comments about their own working style. Or they deplore their tendencies toward outspokenness.

Whatever these women say about their style, they require forcefulness and determination to rise among the women of their class to the prominence of civic leadership. Some, accordingly, provide only lip service to the notions of how they should want to behave. It may be merely ideologically correct to show concern over the issue and to see aggressive impulses as a "problem." But for the most traditionally oriented women, the struggle between ambition and independent initiative on the one hand and the urge to be conciliatory and facilitative without wounding anyone's feelings on the other can set up an uneasy internal dialogue. One civic leader, considered among the gentlest, kindest, and best-liked, still struggled with her own impatience and interest in action to preserve the conciliatory stance considered so essential.

> [I try to speak out] in a noncritical way. But openness is important. In fact it is a liability of mine. I'm afraid that liability [leads me] to try to redirect a concept to match my vision and to almost smother other ideas. I have resolved to correct that. When I [build an organization] I usually have a vision and I am so enrapt that I steamroll to make a fit.

The woman just quoted is also noted for modesty and a willingness to help others in community work. She seems successful in reconciling both the urgency to accomplish things and the value placed on conciliatory behavior by helpfulness to others and modesty in sharing credit for success. The practices of conciliation and unobtrusiveness that many espouse suggest the usefulness of indirection in pursuing one's goals. Women in this study often stress this usefulness when they say they like to stay in the background. The strategies that emerge from their stereotypically gendered behavior are integrated into career activity.

Women can imagine the benefits of work behind the scenes in the community on the basis of their successes in gaining their wishes with family members through indirection, conciliation, or wheedling. Thus family experience suggests the usefulness of traditional gender behavior in strategies for accomplishing goals of community work.

One expression of preference for the second fiddle role connects the chance to work behind the scenes with greater effectiveness. Even women who are aggressive leaders, as is this president of an important women's group in the city, talk of it.

> I don't like to have my name out in front like [a prominent civic leader whose name appears in the papers frequently]. My greatest joy is acting as a catalyst, sitting on a board and explaining to the members how funding is available from a source if a grant can be written in time. It is far more rewarding than chairing.

The distance one can maintain from the seat of power is another advantage; for distance helps one see things more clearly and keeps one out of the line of fire. "I like the analytic part—seeing where the pieces fit. As the president you get sniped at. I think there is more power working through someone else."

An underlying theme for those working behind the scenes is that this work offers greater opportunity for understanding the larger picture and coordinating activity for the greatest benefit of an organization. In their concern with the benefit to the group, women in this study focus on the web of affiliation rather than the need for autonomy in leadership (Gilligan 1982).

A slightly different set of reasons for sidestepping the spotlight are related to feelings of timidity or reserve. Some gender and class socialization encourages the expression of personality traits such as shyness or timidity in women. Women raised in families with conventional expectations about gender behavior can develop such feelings and see them as reasons for remaining in the background or not persevering in the volunteer career to leadership positions. "I'm probably not pushing enough. And I'm probably not affable or outgoing enough [in] making contacts and getting around. I'm shy that way." If they don't like to push themselves, these women are pushed to be more aggressive by their husbands. (Three of the seven women who made a point of not wanting to step into the limelight said they were coaxed into it by their husbands.) "Last year when I was invited onto the Trustee Board, I was floored. My husband said, 'Do it, do it!' He has gotten me into more things because I am not that aggressive a person."

A few women (four) speak of their persistent distaste for leadership roles. These women have gradually divested themselves of the presidencies and board chairmanships they have held. They say things like "being a leader never meant that much to me," or "I'm a rather poor executive—a better Indian than chief." These women exemplify one career trajectory that develops after some years of experience and opportunity to express personality differences— growing dislike for leadership roles and retirement or curtailment of responsibility. Another alternative is to overcome early socialization and previous antipathies to take on, and even enjoy, leadership roles. However, the ability to grow into roles that are not stereotypically feminine requires explanation—of the difficulties in overcoming one's own resistance, for example, or of the modest beginnings from which one could grow.

When women speak of their gradual emergence as leaders they sometimes measure the distance from their early stance to the present in order to show how far they have come.

> I had a real block in dealing with exhibitionism. For example, after a big political banquet it was announced that I had done all this and would I stand up and take a bow. After, I had to go to the ladies room where I vomited. So I've come a long way since then [to act as state and national political party committee woman].

This visceral response to public acclaim reveals how engrained the ideas of reserve and modesty are. Women contribute to the creation of their own invisibility, in addition to pressures from husbands or family. Giving up the retiring stance and becoming visible can be personally costly, as the woman just quoted notes. She realized some of the costs in a memorable moment.

Other women find this change gradual and hard to pinpoint ("I guess I'm a leader; it took me a while to realize it") or it may be embraced with pleasure.

> I started at the bottom and became president. When I first came here I was very shy. I got over that fast. [Now] I like to be an officer; I like to direct projects—the planning and the excitement of it and the problems in seeing the whole thing come off and trying to get it public.

However they learned, six women emphasized that they had grown into the leadership role. But the notion of leadership is so fraught with dangerous or pejorative overtones that the very term requires some qualification. These women find it difficult to discuss their leadership characteristics without *some* modification: "I'm a leader, but not a Hitler" for example. They would show, by their shrugs, smiles and deprecating gestures, while discussing the topic, that they wished to avoid the appearance of being domineering or even bold.

The emphasis in the preceding sections has been on the way women reconcile traditional expectations for women with volunteer work outside the home. For some, however, the intensity of commitment to work and the desire for self-expression can lead into a direct interest in leadership. An easy reconciling of personal ambition or zeal for a cause with acceptance of the status quo, a low profile, a conciliatory manner, and a modest demeanor is not always possible.

Ambivalence and Resistance to Traditional Roles

Difficulties in expressing direct interest in or enthusiasm for leadership are related to expectations about how traditional women *should* behave or wish to behave. When women try to accommodate their own sense of growing ability and desire for leadership roles to their notions of appropriate motivation and behavior, they often find themselves in conflict.

Whatever they say about the joys of vicarious living through family and the necessity for or even pleasure in subordinate roles, most of these women have to be determined, assertive women who aspire to positions of leadership and work hard to get and keep them. The positions on important community boards, such as United Way or the local symphony association, the mayoral commissions and blue ribbon committees, the boards of philanthropic foundations and university trustees—these are prized as prestigious appointments conferring influence and even power on those who hold them. Although competition is indirect, women in the volunteer world compete for them with men and women from the business and professional worlds who can realize tangible benefits as well as altruistic rewards from community service (Ross 1953). Even without any benefit to a salaried career, however, volunteer women enjoy such appointments and accept them with pride when they are offered. For example, a recurring theme in the gossip exchanged among friends was which women had long awaited appointment as university trustees or foundation board members and then finally received or been denied the coveted appointments.

The desires for such recognition—and the hard work leading up to it—place these women in a dilemma between the ideology of the traditional woman in the leisure class, whose role is different from a man's, and that of a modern woman who competes in the public market for jobs and working opportunities. These women manage the contradictions, sometimes by obscuring or ignoring them, sometimes by addressing them, even if indirectly or with some circumspection. Whether they explain their aspirations as zeal for a cause, or admit to personal ambition, or whether they are inspired by some variable mix of the two, their work is hard and competitive since many others vie with them for leadership. Furthermore, bold and assertive women face negative sanctions from elders, and even peers, who do not countenance that style. And, like others without direct power, these women must be especially careful not to antagonize key figures in the larger community power structure. Women who are ambitious, or just eager to work, thus have to preserve a nice balance between a display of eagerness and a delicacy about considering or consulting others. And the effort this balance requires appears in the various ways women discuss leadership.

One expression of assertiveness that emerges as a dominant theme (40 women mention it) is a tendency to take command, even for women who stress the importance of negotiation. Whether a natural or acquired taste, these women have come to enjoy leadership, even if such a trait is not entirely ladylike. Ideas about the necessity for self-effacement and modesty seem to become less important as women progress through their careers. Most temper their statements so as not to seem too assertive, but not all do so.

A small group (5) seemed to know they were born leaders and do not flinch from command. ("I can be brutally frank." "I frankly enjoy a leadership role very much." "I like to get things started; then I lose interest.") One woman explained quite matter-of-factly why she did not like the vice-presidency of her organization. "I had no direct responsibility and let's face it, I like to be first. . . . Sometimes I cringe a bit from the responsibility when I first begin; but I really want it."

These women show a taste for leadership like that of any "take charge" person. They think they know how to do it and how to overcome any resistance or other obstacle. But the difficulties of directive and authoritative leaders are exacerbated in the context of the expectations they hold for themselves as well as those from others. The life of a born leader in the world of volunteers is made harder by her assertiveness. In this world, antagonism toward any forceful leadership—whether good or bad—can be expected. Assertive behavior is contradictory to the values that traditional women uphold. And frank expression of leadership traits shows an unwillingness to accept the traditional position for women as helpers and facilitators, not leaders. Nine women commented on the difficulties their leadership tendencies might cause. Some associated their leadership qualities with unfortunate personality characteristics (impatience, unwillingness to be criticized, a big or loud mouth). And they talked about the costs. For some, the costs were acceptable: a loss of popularity in order to do what one believes right.

> I am ambitious and aggressive, but I never had to go looking for jobs. I believe in strong leadership [though] I was chastized a couple of times. They would know I was right, but they didn't want to hear it.

Others talked about how resistance to them—and their style—made the leadership role they loved difficult for them.

> I like the president's job. One reason is that I get to guide a group and not waste time. The problems are those of my personality—and lack of tolerance. . . . And so I come across as arrogant.

Two women told me how they learned to curb their impatience and assertiveness in order to gain, or keep, their leadership roles. The *style* of leadership can be modified to give the appearance of deference to others. An obeisance to the system of values which stresses cooperation and conciliation over directiveness can permit a basically authoritative leader to continue. A woman who was afraid of losing the presidency she loved explained how she successfully managed to avoid the loss.

> I have two and one-half years left to run as chairman of the board, but each year you get elected again. I was warned by one of the older group on the board that I was too outspoken and must not run that organization by myself. I thought that was quite strong. It scared the living daylights out of me, for she was the chairman of the nominating committee. She's an energetic woman and likes to travel, but she wants to be able to be gone for three months and still keep her finger on everything. I am careful with her and do try to keep her informed and bring her up-to-date when she comes back.

Assertive women face the difficulties created by the paradox that even when they lead, ladylike women (i.e., genteel women in the upper classes) are not expected to put themselves forward, take charge, engage in contending factions. Some of these "natural born leaders" learn to curb their assertive tendencies in order to conform to the expectations of how women's organizational activity in community work must be managed. Others are less successful and are sidelined or isolated in special jobs. (We shall see later how a few aggressive women specialize in the role of citizen's advocate.)

It is not surprising, then, that the largest number (18) in any category of responses openly claiming leadership still show deference to the traditional role of modest, conciliatory facilitator-leader. Some in this category say chance projected them into leadership. Or they don't know why they are chosen or how their course of action led them to the top of an organization. ("When I began in the woman's board I had no idea I would become president of the council or be appointed to the Opera Board.") A few express difficulty in admitting that they are leaders, because it says something they don't like to face squarely. It may also say something about others ("I guess it's embarassing to say that I was more of a leader than those around me").

Those who wished to stress their flexibility as leaders pointed out that they were equally comfortable as followers. And a few wanted it clear that their leadership was not authoritarian ("I'm a helper and a leader too"). Others distanced themselves from interest in leadership by self-mocking remarks ("I have a certain kind of charm, I will say blushingly, and that is an advantage along with my militance") or by giving no personal opinion but referring to the opinions of those around them ("Others say I am a leader"). One woman gave an indirect example of her leadership capacity.

> I led a group of people to the Soviet Union and one travel-ing companion was an irascible labor leader with whom I have had differences. He gave me a real compliment when it was over. He said he was accustomed to being in charge, but it was a pleasure to be able to sit back and let another take charge.

These qualified responses to assertions of leadership show us the limits that women civic leaders work within. The stress on co-operativeness ("I'm a leader through friendly pursuasion") and willingness to consider opposing views ("I like to listen to those that don't as well as those that do agree with me") is a constant theme. Even some of the women with reputations as tartars (for fir-ing staff without prior negotiation and ousting board members with whom they had disagreements) expressed these views.

This theme has striking parallels to feminist and radical political notions that groups should be organized nonhierarchically and op-erate under a consensus model (Mansbridge 1980). It is paradoxical that these traditionally oriented women, with allegiances to the upper class, would espouse some of the same approaches as radical groups. However, for these women the emphasis is as much on ap-peasement and maintenance of appearances as it is on the develop-ment of consensus.

One theme implicit in their expression of qualifications sur-rounding leadership is the concern to avoid even the appearance of competition and bullying tactics in the desire to do good. Another theme implicit in the qualifications is that leaders should not grow away from (or rise above) the rank and file. And yet these women realize that ambitiousness requires hard, concentrated effort; lead-ers usually are different from rank-and-file members, not only in their level of effort but also in the ability they exhibit.

How to resolve this second dilemma presents a particularly deli-cate problem, for the stereotype of idle society women seems to fit many of the occasional helpers or contributors necessary to some kinds of community work. And the stereotype fits many in the family and friendship circles of these women. The problem, then, is for women to formulate a view of themselves as conforming to traditional values but *not* conforming to the pejorative stereotype of leisured women. In developing a rationale for distancing, women both resist association with the stereotype and also express sympathy for those who do seem to conform to it.

As noted earlier, these women of Pacific City belong to that group making some effort to become more than privileged, ornamental appendages to their husbands even while working within that guise. Of course, they are hampered by accepting the advantages—and costs—of their lives as appendages while striving for their own accomplishments and activities. Whatever the contradictions and consequences of wanting to have their cake and eat it too, these women do want to act independently. When we examine their career patterns and working styles, we shall see how they do it. Here I wish to suggest two elements spurring that effort. The first is desire to put distance between themselves and the dilettantes and idlers around them and the second is the desire to develop one's own identity and to overcome personal troubles. These elements suggest the less attractive aspects of the traditional role for upper-class women: the woman as a senseless, if ornamental, appendage and the woman as directionless, problem child.

Distancing strategies require some tact in expression; for community leaders can't forget their dependence on the people they don't want to be confused with. The foot soldiers who only require occupation and accept limited responsibility and the socialites and climbers who attend benefits to parade in their finery—and have their pictures in the papers—do not take on major tasks or work independently. However, they play their parts in the "big package" a civic leader puts together. Both of these social types are the objects of some invidious or condescending judgments from the women in this study—as well as from social critics who observe them in action. Yet most women interviewed showed consideration and sympathy for these people in society even if they patronize them. As one women put it:

> The Junior League is an attempt to discipline a spoiled, rich girl. Yet they do take young women who are really lost. And a lot resign after a year or two. These poor little people, lost souls. No real work. They are parasites, and yet everybody has to have someone to listen to them.

In this view, the women who put "lost souls" to work, no matter in how limited an area, are performing a social service. Community leaders, then, if only as a byproduct of their major focus, do their bit to integrate the work of even the dizziest socialite into some part of the social structure. In this effort they are helping to legitimize their social class by helping their own friends and families to maintain a world where all the participants have some reasonable occupation. Civic leaders, then, remember both their dependence on and their relationship to the people they distance themselves from.

The limitations of other women are noted—but their good qualities are presented as well.

> These ladies are very hard working even if they cannot get along with everyone. They will lick and stick [envelopes and stamps] at someone's house and do yeoman service hour after hour. And they will bulldoze the sale of tickets to their friends, practically holding them up. But they do not mix [with people from different social classes] because they cannot change worlds.

Another woman explained how she distanced herself by moving out of the superficial, "social climbing" category of volunteer through her discovery that superficial activities were boring and that even influential women in society were insecure about their social position. And another woman, herself involved in a salaried career in addition to her volunteering, viewed the old-fashioned "lady bountiful" with distaste.

> In those days the doctors' wives were well-intentioned ladies . . . interested in things like a social center to entertain visitors and other social events. Many even resented that we were taking on a couple of decent projects [like developing a volunteer staff for the children's clinics]. One of the things I like about the board I chair currently is that there is none of that.

In sum, these women talked about their feelings of reserve or even distaste with regard to other women in or around the volunteer world. Three (one from an old Pacific City family; one from the middle-class Catholic community; one from a prosperous middle-class Jewish family) wanted it clear that they were not interested in social climbing as so many others are; two said they had been earlier and then gave it up. (One of these women, however, did make it into society.) But all respondents wanted to dissociate themselves from those who were not serious, committed community workers and leaders.

A related theme to the desire for distance from the frivolous or limited women of the upper and upper-middle class is the desire, expressed sometimes almost as yearning, to be something, somebody on one's own and *not* just an appendage, no matter how privileged, to a husband and family. These respondents want to share actively in the American values of individual achievement and recognition, not just indirectly as the helper-facilitator to their families.

> In volunteering, I gained personal esteem. I found out I could do something. I could get some self-identity and some confidence. Hubert was very popular, handsome, and personable. He had a big smile. And people would be attracted to him. "Oh, your husband is so marvelous," people would say. "What does Hubert think?" they would ask. It was never, "What do you think?"

While a number of women imply it, one woman said she was pushed into finding a life of her own because of her husband's busyness.

> The fact that my husband works terribly long hours makes volunteer work a necessity for me. The symphony and museum are my own things. My husband is important in the medical world and I need something that's my little area.

Some women say they began to develop their own life in volunteer work early in marriage for their own reasons. The women fear alcoholism, weight problems, or some vaguely defined depression and mental illness if they cannot have some life of their own. The euphemism used is a necessity to "keep busy." These women came to realize they were not searching for scut work to fill the day but for the challenge of an independent career and the opportunity to exert influence. They want to escape some of the consequences of the traditional bargain implicit in clearly differentiated gender roles and priorities discussed earlier.

Six women spoke quite strongly about their need, at some point in their lives, to find a cause and espouse it. One of these women wanted to escape a difficult homelife.

> I was deeply unhappy in my first marriage. Jane . . . said ". . . you should consider The League of Women Voters." And I did. I just ate it up. I just liked everything about it, even sitting all day and listening to the city councilmen. Eventually I became president and got my start in politics.

And another wanted to escape the monotony of homelife.

> My children were four, five, six and seven; and the repetition of housework almost drove me crazy . . . I tried all sorts of philosophies, even Christian Science, to get over

> this feeling of repetition. I began to ask questions. People were starving in the midst of plenty. The radical movement gave answers and saved my sanity. Once I was busy on issues I didn't mind . . . about making beds.

The general theme, whatever the cause or the avenue for change, is a sense, almost of despair, at some limitation in their lives. These women then take themselves in hand and work out a career pattern that will bring some satisfactions and overcome the limitations of traditional lives for women in their class. But they use the traditional avenues available through volunteer work to do it.

The traditional avenues provide the best compromise between the desire for an individual identity and the desire to put family priorities (and class responsibilities) first. However, the style of work suggested by this compromise may not provide the kind of reassurance or gratification that some women need. The stress on modesty or indirection, vicarious achievement through family, general subordinate status to husbands and parents—all can sap assertiveness and diminish self-confidence. The costs of managing a subordinate, traditional role at home while aspiring to an independent status in the community can be seen in lapses of self-confidence that occasionally appear in interviews.

These lapses may reflect the difficulty of reconciling the conflicting messages that these women have received. Rubin (1979:45) summarizes these messages in a way that highlights the conflicts traditional roles create for women.

> Achieve, but not beyond what is appropriate for a girl! . . . Strive, but be careful never to damage your marriage chances! . . . Be smart, but not smarter than your brother! . . . Be knowledgeable enough to impress, but never so much as to overshadow a man . . .

Rubin (1979:44) argues that the repression required by the focus on indirection never works completely. Sometimes the demand for self-expression "sneaks out" in some unpredictable mood display. Perhaps that is the explanation for the indicators of self-doubt and the moments of sadness that sometimes appeared in these interviews.

Indicators of Self-Doubt, Timidity, or Self-Deprecation among Civic Leaders

It is sometimes difficult to sift out expressions of genuine uncertainty from conventional expressions of modesty. Yet the number of times such expression arose, and the contexts in which they occurred, led to a serious consideration of the problem of self-confidence. Why should these highly successful women exhibit so many signs of uncertainty to an interviewer? They are all women who have received acknowledgments of their community work that include national, regional, and local awards, special appointments and commendations from presidents, governors, and mayors. Perhaps it is because there is some ambiguity in the assessment of a volunteer career. In their own class, as well as in the larger society, success in the business world wins the greatest kudos. The respect offered community service is somewhat more ambiguous. Consequently, women are not always entirely sure themselves how their accomplishments are regarded by others. In addition to the appropriately modest disclaimers, then, women may express their own sense of uncertainty when they make self-deprecatory remarks. In all, thirty-five women in this study offered "put downs" of themselves: they cast doubt on their abilities, denied they were worth the time spent for an interview, despaired about their own achievements in some way, or were anxious about the future.

Some of these expressions do seem only conventional disclaimers, as when a notable leader would say "I'm not worth interviewing" or "I'm not a good person to talk to." Furthermore, self-deprecation and a modest demeanor are seen as "good form" in the upper classes (Cookson and Persell 1985:116). Yet since these women know they are seen as civic leaders, and since they have received many tangible indications of their leadership ability (in awards, appointments, presidencies, consultantships), their modest protests seemed strange. Other conventional disclaimers arose when mentioning accomplishments. Women would say "I hate to brag" or "It sounds like I'm tooting my own horn and I don't mean to" or "I hate to talk about it" when asked to review their honors and major responsibilities. Finally, conventional expressions of surprise were attached to statements about special notice. ("I don't know why they were so loyal, but they kept me. I was the youngest member of the board.") Here, as with women who claimed surprise at always being chosen president, the statements may represent conventional disclaimers rather than genuine uncertainty. Yet their frequency, and their association with serious efforts at self-evaluation, make them worth noting.

Stronger indications of wavering self-confidence emerged as women spoke of their doubts about their ability. These doubts are a common problem for women struggling to achieve positions in male-dominated professions as well (Ruddick and Daniels 1977). Some aspects of gender stereotypes are belittling (women are weak and frail) or derogatory (women are flighty and overemotional and therefore not always competent at work). They make it difficult for women when used against them by others in evaluating women's work performance. These difficulties are compounded when women themselves wonder about the grain of truth in these stereotypes and struggle to shake off self-doubts. The women of the volunteer world are particularly vulnerable to these worries because they do espouse so many aspects of the traditional role and live with their own and their family's expectations about the appropriate behavior for women. At the same time, their work—and the awards or other recognitions they win for it—does not offer the ongoing reassurance (provided by remuneration and prestigious occupational titles) given the men and women in paid careers they know and work with in the community.

> I consider myself a professional volunteer, but that's hard to explain to professional people. I find myself rather intimidated by this group. What can I say, by God, that can make them take notice when I'm not earning the almighty buck? And there is the lady bountiful image [to fight against]— the little rich girl who's never worked in her life.

Sometimes doubts can overwhelm women for a time.

> The first year [on a city commission] was scary; I don't know why. Males dominate the groups and I felt shaky. It takes a year to feel at home. During that time the labor people asked me, unofficially, if I was interested in running for City Council. I wondered for a while if I was competent and its funny how women will do that.

Women are sometimes very critical of and anxious about their own achievements. "I have done a fairly good job, now that I look back. But I think I am doing a terrible job when I am closely involved. I see the flaws and not the total picture."

A recurring theme, already touched upon within the context of family responsibility, is the necessity to put the family first. Women sometimes mention their guilt about family responsibilities in a self-denigrating way ("I'm probably a lousy mother"). Even while experiencing guilt at not doing their homemaking responsibilities better, women find themselves caught in conflicting expectations and wishes. And so they also express their sense of guilt about not doing more for themselves. "I have trouble recognizing my own talents and abilities. I still come at the tail end in the family situation and sometimes in a few others." Inability to resolve the conflict between duties to family and self are not seen as external social problems but internal signs of personal inadequacy. Women recognize that the fragmentation and consequent inability to concentrate on intellectual matters is produced by myriad calls on one's attention, although they do not see it as a problem produced by others—by family demands for example. Nor do women see it as produced by traditional social expectations that do not recognize their requirement for, or right to, uninterrupted time in order to develop some types of independent careers.

The most striking signs of an unassuaged problem in self-confidence were the occasional spontaneous comments made during interviews that seemed to go beyond conventional modest disclaimers. At least seven women made such comments (there may have been more; these unsolicited expressions were only recorded toward the end of the study when they began to appear as a recurring pattern). They apologized for signs of clutter in beautiful, tidy homes; they peppered their discussion with questions and disclaimers ("do I sound dictatorial?" "I have done nothing of any importance, really"); and asked for reassurance about the quality of their responses ("I'm afraid that was a rather rambling answer"; "I'm afraid I am giving you more than you asked"). Two women astonished me: one by saying, in the middle of an excellent explanation of fund-raising politics, "I am taking up your time?" and the other by stopping after a lengthy discussion of her career by remarking anxiously, "I am talking too much." My astonishment was mixed with exasperation; for both women were interesting informants and I was hanging on their words, taking notes as fast as I could. Their modesty seemed beyond the bounds of sense, for I had requested the interviews and I found them to be real repositories of information. Another woman, known for her aggressive, even domineering qualities as a leader, said at the end of the interview that she had been extremely nervous about facing it and did not sleep well the night before. After these encounters I began remonstrating with my informants about their disclaimers. Two women wept during their interviews as they spoke of fears or insecurities they had not yet overcome; three women had eyes filled with tears as I argued with them about the significance that might be attached to their work, the impressiveness of their resumes, and their potential for employability in the salaried world.

Expectations that women will find their gratifications in family responsibilities combine with other aspects of traditional upbringing to encourage modesty, reserve, and diffidence. This pattern may lead women to be thoughtful of and attentive to others, humble, cooperative and pleasant, but it also can sap self-confidence and drain the spirit of independence or assertiveness women may wish to possess. The women in this study deal with the problem of conflict between traditional expectations and the desire for self-assertion with considerable success; yet their reactions suggest that the dilemma is not always or easily resolved.

Perhaps the difficulty lies, in part, in ambivalence about the value and prestige of volunteer work. The difficulty of assigning cash or salary equivalents to their work leaves many uncertain about how to assess its worth. The experiences of women who have to find salaried work following a husband's death or a divorce exhibit the force of that difficulty. One divorced woman spoke bitterly about the lack of opportunity for executive-level paid jobs for women with many years of executive-level experience as volunteers. Another spoke resignedly about her lowered status after widowhood, even when she was appointed to a good position—one that many had applied for and the best job in the country for a woman with her experience. Or the change in status to widow or divorcee may simply raise questions about one's worth that one has never had to face before. It is not surprising, then, that some to whom I spoke were most tearful and tremulous over their potential for salaried employment after a change in their marital status. Doubts, anxieties, and sadness surrounded the issue of their worth on the job market. Some women who reported they had supportive families also expressed doubts. Talk of accomplishments and speculation about potential future careers to an interviewer sometimes elicited surprising amounts of uncertainty and need for reassurance. Some women were startled when I said I thought their resumes were very impressive. These women seemed anxious and upset when I said I thought their skills and accomplishments were transferable to the salaried world of work. But women with a substantial history of salaried work experience (either before marriage or after a volunteer career) were less likely to express feelings of anxiety about self-worth (see table 2.2). When I think of the self-assured, directive, and self-contained male professionals I have encountered in other studies (Daniels 1966) and the confidence of women in salaried careers (Daniels 1980), I see the importance to self-esteem of fi-

Table 2.2 Expression of Self-Doubts

	Yes	No
Divorced and Widowed	13 (1)*	18 (10)*
Married	19 (2)*	20 (3)*
Totals	32	38

*Numbers in parentheses indicate salaried worker experience of five years or more.
$N = 70$.

nancially remunerative work within a generally accepted status structure.[2]

Not all volunteer community leaders reveal this streak of doubt. For about half, the traditional resources provide enough support. Women married to successful men have a recognition equal to or better than any salary they could command. Nor are all high-status salaried professionals without their moments of anxiety and indecision in the course of an interview, but the context of their work provides paid careerists with a greater social validation (in addition to money) than is extended to volunteers. Paid workers have job titles, fringe benefits, and the social understandings about the value of paid work to support them. The social supports for volunteer workers are more amorphous, especially for those who are no longer married. Perhaps that is why they provide less reassurance.

The perspectives and values presented in this chapter show how these women view the advantages and limitations of their place in the world. The priority placed on family life makes the volunteer career a good alternative since putting the family first generally precludes a demanding professional career. When family and husband support the volunteer career choice, conflicts arising over priorities generally can be resolved. When family and husband are not supportive, the conflicts between a traditional woman's place and a career in the volunteer world stand out more sharply. Yet for

2. Steinem (1986:78) supports this view in her analysis of the undermining effects of dependence, even for rich women. She argues that rich women may be resented or ridiculed if they try to learn self-sufficiency by entering the world of paid work. Men may require the service and attention of their women that is symbolized by total involvement in the worlds of family and volunteer service. In addition, Steinem argues that women's self-doubts are deliberately nurtured to keep them docile. "The deepest reason for the self-deprecation and uncertainty of rich women may be the simplest: the closer we are to power, the more passive we must be kept. Intimacy and access make rebellion very dangerous."

most of these women, conflicts are successfully resolved and careers as community leaders are positively reinforced by family and friends.

Women use the conciliatory tactics learned in family life in their negotiations on community projects. And they wrestle with the problems of leadership and independence in their work just as they do in problems of management within traditional patriarchal homes. The conflicts these desires create for independent women appear in their fears and doubts about the basic importance of their contribution.

Despite these worries, the value placed on conciliation, indirection, and modesty in leadership does contribute to the success of ambitious women. And the strategies and tactics suggested by this value offer a sufficient range of alternatives to guide these community leaders along the stages of their career. The next chapters describe the experiences women encounter that guide them into the particular niches they occupy, the kinds of work these women do, and the particular skills they develop while doing them.

Finding the Career Content and Style

3

Patterns of Growth

The construction of a career, outside the ordinary understandings of how salaried careers develop, is a theme touched upon by admirers or eulogizers of these women. In his introduction to the autobiography of a notable woman civic leader, for example, Wallace Stegner (1978:x) writes:

> She discovered that she had more energy than could be consumed by the needs of even a close, affectionate, and growing family. Inevitably she was led outward into a career—for it must be called a career even though she probably never earned a dollar from it, and undertook it without reference to what it might do for herself . . . She could not help wanting to be somebody and do something. She could not help wanting to matter.

In this tribute to Josephine Whitney Duveneck, Stegner mentions some of the common notions of what a volunteer career entails—the placement of family responsibility first, a concern for the community, and an altruistic desire (including refusal of salary) to serve it. The tribute also suggests a less well understood aspect of the career: an outlet for untapped energies and a desire for self-actualization through some activity significant in the world beyond the family. Finally, the tribute touches obliquely upon the desire for power; "to be somebody" and "to matter" suggest the desire to have an impact on the world. This last idea is quite antithetical to the boundary on women's ambition set by tradition and so it is framed by the idea that this woman "could not help" it.

Most clearly, the tribute suggests the aspect of career presented in the concept of profession (or calling). Max Weber (1946) in his descriptions of careers in politics and science discussed the notion of commitment to a career that stresses intrinsic over extrinsic rewards: the love of the work is similar to that of artisans who take a pride in their craft independent of financial reward. In the ideal type, the professional following a calling into a career also has some concern for social betterment. In modern western societies like the United States, however, the concern with affluence and prestige of some professionals (particularly physicians and lawyers) raises questions about their motivation. The descriptive power of this ideal type is diluted by the exposés of professional behavior and the venality of many professionals (see Harris 1969; Gross 1966, for examples).

Nonetheless, the desire to serve humanity through the practice of a profession is still discussed by the recruits. Such motives are even more relevant for those workers who become committed to work without the possibility of financial rewards. The most notable civic leaders exhibit some of the characteristics of this idealism and become revered for it in the manner suggested by Stegner's remarks, but it is not always clear when they begin their volunteer work that they are headed in the direction of a professional calling. The path to take for training and special focus in an area is not institutionalized nor formalized as it is in the professions. There are no academic courses of study leading to diplomas, certification, or licensure; no required titles for practitioners, established consultants, or teachers.

As Heimer (1984) points out, we ordinarily think of career development in terms of a series of elements. They include access to information about jobs and their availability. Jobs are arranged in a clear sequence; tasks or training enhance the ability of recruits to climb the ladder implicit in that sequence. Those who judge a worker's progress collect information about it to pass along when fateful decisions about advancement are to be made. Such a process occurs within the framework of what Heimer calls either the organizational or the market model. In the first, individuals bank on the organization to reward them; in the second, people act as entrepreneurs to sell their accomplishments to the highest bidders. The first model rests on assumptions about the location of the workplace and the authorities who judge competence there—in an organization. The second offers more latitude, suggesting that individuals can organize their own training and experience, then shop around for customers—in various organizations. Neither model focuses on even more entrepreneurial alternatives where individuals use their own experience, seek out training, arrange the sequence of events as they go, and thus develop a notion of career without any clear picture of what advancement might mean.

This problem of how to make sense of a career is the one facing these women as they undertake their own development. They must, as they review their careers in retrospective accounts, piece together their experience to pinpoint and evaluate what natural talents they had, what they learned in the course of their activities, where, when, and from whom they learned it. Under these circumstances, when career development is amorphous, the other aspects of a professional career—the ideology of commitment, altruism, and service—are especially important. Women use the idea of a calling to explain why they keep trying: seeking self-knowledge; learning special skills; seeking advice about how to proceed; clinging to mentors who inspire them; facing up to responsibilities they must meet. The volunteer career has to be understood from a woman's own view of how this line of endeavor becomes possible.

Volunteer careers initially develop in the interstices of family life. Women put in time, as family responsibilities permit, during their years of child rearing. The development of a focused working life may have to wait until these responsibilities are substantially over. However, from their first tasks in the PTA, church, or political party, women begin acquiring experience and achievements. One successful performance leads to another; one indication of special interest or ability leads to more assignments calling upon the same skill or working in the same area.

Since no formal organization directs them, these women are especially sensitive to what they see as the pushes and pulls that lead them in one direction or another: the family concerns that guided their earliest interests; the experiences that touch their own lives or their consciences; the inclination toward work they have a talent for; the opportunities to develop a career line through experimentation. At the same time women can afford to be sensitive to their antipathies, allowing their selection of tasks to be explicitly guided by repulsion—as well as attraction—in a way people tied to salaried work generally cannot.

Developing Interests

While women find their way into the volunteer world by the variety of pathways discussed earlier, they choose the particular area and way of working within it out of an idiosyncratic mix of personal experience, chance, and special interest. This mix corresponds to what, as noted earlier, Hughes (1958: 122) called "the running adjustment" between a person and various facts of his or her life that form and shape the direction of a career. These patterns of developing interest are examined here to aid our understanding of the volunteer civic leader's record. She finds an area of work and a style of working in it that suits her. And then her organizational memberships and offices, her consultantships and advisory positions reflect those interests.

Through chance events, some problem or interest may be pressed firmly into consciousness . . . and conscience. One woman became active in mental health organizations in memory of a schizophrenic sister. Another did public relations and made movies for the heart association because she herself had had open heart surgery. Another organized a rehabilitation society after her recovery from a crippling disease. A reformed alcoholic created county and state services to combat alcoholism. One woman who had been raised in an orphanage became a leading light in improving the lot of orphans and dependent children more generally.

Not all these interests developed out of personal experience with adversity. Four women were active in societies for the preservation of various European cultures and languages because of their own affection for particular countries where they had lived or visited at an earlier time. One woman became interested in career counseling for teenage children through her desire to broaden her own children's awareness of alternatives. Three women became involved in the local crisis over school integration through efforts to keep their own children in decent public schools. These last concerns show one way traditional family concerns can provide the impetus for personal experiences. Some women find their own individual metier from their traditional understanding about their responsibility to help their children. Eventually, the experience, competence, and commitment a woman develops can transcend the original impetus: educational and political issues become the focus of attention.

These fifteen women used their earlier experience in various ways to build their careers (see table 3.1). The following specialist in education suggests how her career began to take shape, branching out from interests centered on personal experience to larger issues.

> It's interesting what kind of volunteer energy comes out of the co-op nursery movement. A couple of years of this is very fine management training. From there I went to the PTA. And after that the League of Women Voters began

Table 3.1 Developing Interests

Earlier experiences affecting career lines		15
Provide major focus	5	
Provide springboard to other related interests	7	
Create only one among several career interests	3	
Having a talent that encourages long-term interests		15
Always liked figures	3	
Artists	2	
Musicians	3	
Mixed business and artistic interests	7	
Took interests from family		4
Stayed with health interests	2	
Diversified in health, education, and welfare	2	
Trial and error		11
Interest in a cause		19
Art and culture	10	
Social reforms	5	
Social services, intellectual pursuits	4	
Discovered administrative ability		6
Total		70

hovering. But my real focus was PTA. My husband was president [during] the beginning of the integration. I was president of the PTA in another school seven or eight years later when my oldest child was in junior high. It was an active PTA with twenty on the board. Then when I was President of the PTA, I became a delegate to the citywide advisory council on school integration. During this time I also was a volunteer in the schools. I did individual tutoring in math for ghetto kids. When my kids went on I was president of that PTA and then secretary of the citywide PTA. At that point I left the PTA . . . [But] the PTA had gotten me into the political scene. Through the labor friends I had developed I was appointed to various commissions by the mayor. I'm just going on some state and national boards [concerned with integration, civil rights, and equal opportunity].

The career path of the woman just quoted is paralleled by two or three of her colleagues who became advocates, eventually running for office as she did. Although she was not, one of her colleagues was elected to a prominent position on the City Council. Many women follow this pattern of entering volunteer activity through concern for schools, then, when they see the place of education in the political structure of their city, developing larger political interests. This pattern is also found among working-class and lower-middle-class women (Gittell and Naples 1981:17). Both proponents and opponents of busing for integration (Rubin 1972; McCourt 1977) have developed larger community organization careers through these initial concerns.

Other developing interests focus on children, with particular concern for their protection and welfare. In addition to the woman noted earlier who was interested in protection of children because she had been an orphan herself, four women began working for children early in their volunteer careers (as a special interest beyond the very widespread pattern of work for their own children's schools and activities). This pattern of early—and continued—interest seems related to an understanding of what concerns are appropriate for women who intend to be mothers as a major part of their life career. They like children, have a knack—or sympathy—in dealing with them, and expect to have their own. This work, then, is most clearly an extension of a woman's traditionally appropriate role, even if it leads to an independent career.

> I did a survey for a day-care center in college. It was really an excuse to do observations of children in the community. When I transferred to the university I took a childcare course and worked in a day-care center. I assisted in children's art at the neighborhood center when I was in the League. I didn't work on organization parties but I did do the Christmas party on the children's ward. Then I did tutoring of a child. By then I had a child so it meant getting a baby-sitter and deciding to do it. When I moved down here, I worked for the junior museum and the crippled children. Later I helped organize the Family Service Advisory Agency. The area that really came to interest me is children's protective services. It has all been like building blocks. I have learned how to read budgets, legislation, I gave testimony before the board of supervisors, unsolicited. I knew about the possibility of cuts for the children's protective services. And so I have done lobbying. During this period I decided to move into the private sector and build an organization to deal with parental stress and prevent child abuse.

While this woman had other interests as well, the care and protection of children was her real focus and, ultimately, the impetus for learning the varied skills of the civic leader.

Other careers do not show this progression from activities rooted in personal concerns to more general political or social interests. One woman, for example, lived in Italy before her marriage. When she returned to America, she was active in the Italo-American society. But after she married she developed interests in a variety of religious and local charities. She continued working for Italian societies in several states, but added board memberships for volunteer services, a hospital auxiliary, a museum, a family service, a retirement home, Campfire Girls, the symphony, and a federal commission. "I'm all over the lot," she said.

Whether some personal experience creates a stepping stone to, or just another aspect of, a volunteer career, it provides a focus upon a substantive area for work. However, many women begin to organize their working pattern not around the substance of an activity but around a special capacity or set of skills they acquire or discover within themselves.

Women who possess business and artistic talents, but are too embedded in the family to consider serious professional development, turn them to some use in the volunteer world. A good head for business, then, is turned to promotion, budgetary, investment, and fund-raising problems in philanthropy. Artistic talents are used in decoration and design—or sublimated in organizational work for the arts. Some women in this category have both business acumen and artistic flair. Fifteen women (see table 3.1) developed careers that seemed initially to be influenced in these ways: three who had always "liked figures," two who were amateur artists, three amateur musicians, and five with an early mixture of business and artistic interests. The remaining two are women who worked all their adult lives in family businesses and organized their volunteer careers around that work. They used their talents both for profit *and* volunteer work.

The women who "like figures" were in great demand; for traditional women often succumb to the sex-role socialization that makes such topics as accounting, mathematics, and budgets particularly repugnant or fearsome. Early in their volunteer careers, women with mathematical skills could turn them to advantage; for many jobs involving numbers could be done in spare moments at home. Yet these jobs were not time-consuming, low-level, repetitive tasks. Throughout the women's careers, these skills proved useful in any of their organizations. "I teach [new board members] about the books and the financial status and reading the budget. Even those who can't really understand a financial statement can be taught to read the minimal four pages of the report each month." These skills are sometimes discovered within family situations:

there are investments to look after and no one else responsible or comfortable with the task. "I have a mother and some sisters not really capable of business. None of the ladies in the family can manage. So I have always managed their investments and properties in the East."

The women with artistic talent saw their talents primarily as avocational. The one practicing artist avoided total commitment to art and art causes and diversified her volunteer interests: some were in the art world and some in educational and social reform causes. The other artistically inclined woman divided her volunteer interests primarily between art and health care. She received a master's degree in art history and worked as a fashion designer for a short time, branching into window display and advertising copy. Once she married and had children, she left salaried work and concentrated her artistic interests in the volunteer world. She worked on museum art committees, chairing arts and crafts committees and building committees (to choose designs, work out plans with the architect). She taught mosaics, worked on Christmas Bazaar projects, served as a museum docent, prepared junior museum exhibits. These activities, as well as her interests in the health field, took the place of the practice of art. Her family pointed out how this career line has diverted an original impetus. "My children tend to say, 'Mother, why don't you do more things for yourself?' Boy number two is the most artistic of our children and shakes his head. He thinks I should be putting in my time on mosaics or paints, something personally creative." This woman, however, had responsibilities to her family, including special care for the very boy she mentions during his long and difficult childhood illness. Such responsibility encouraged a sublimation of interests in personally demanding artistic pursuits that require discipline and regular practice to more easily fragmented activities in volunteer work for artistic causes—and health interests developed while attending to her sick child.

The pattern of sublimating artistic interest in good works to benefit art is also common for those who are musical. All the musical women maintained some proficiency on the instruments of their choice—and all saved some regular time for practice. In this way they kept to their discipline and their allegiance to their early show of talent.

The women described thus far have used business or artistic interests as an organizing principle in career development. The remaining women in this section have expressed a strong interest in business *and* art (see table 3.1). Three of these five working women were in public relations, advertising, and purchasing until marriage. Thereafter they worked intermittently in firms connected with their husbands' interests while volunteering or else they retired and devoted their energies entirely to community work. A fourth woman continued her work for the family firm throughout her career as a volunteer, and a fifth is said to have increased her family's fortunes through shrewd investments. Their work often involves producing the society benefits which collect money to support artistic endeavors. But these women with combined artistic and business interests are very concerned to show a profit.

> I like buying and selling property and playing the stock market. I have been very successful at it. I feel that if I had gone into business I would have been at the top. But my specialty is decorating. I just had a natural bent. It was just learning scale and budgeting. We who have gone the gamut and raised from fifty dollars to sixty thousand, we know what it means to budget. In the museum guild, our accountant is from a national firm. And he never ceases to be amazed at the profit we show. I was at a meeting recently for the Music Conservatory. And they figure they took in two thousand and made seven hundred dollars. That is a failure because expenses were greater than profit. When I went on the [music and art boards] I used my business ability giving rummage sales and my artistic talent overseeing the students who would do the decorating for the Art Institute. More of my business acumen was used in fund-raisers to see that things were gotten wholesale or given free.

The profit, then, stands not only for the necessary product of fund-raising activity, but also as a sign of the skills and talents these women possess: the ability to bargain shrewdly, to budget and manage carefully, and to coordinate volunteer efforts in order to keep down costs. It is an important indicator; for it is a tangible expression of financial ability, a recognized value in the male world and in the business world generally. Unfortunately, a woman's record as a great charity money-maker, though known, is not formally attributable to her; all communal efforts require a wide sharing of credit. Some ambiguity in assigning major acknowledgments eliminates invidious comparisons and preserves the image of wholehearted participation from all.

Women often get their special interest for, as well as their entry into, volunteer work from family members. Women acquire their substantive interests from parents, and women learn how to take the appropriate role in an interest area from the models provided by parents. Fathers or mothers in medical fields inspired four women in this study to find health-related interests for work.

In this group, two women began and continued with health-related interests throughout their careers and two women diversified—though keeping within the areas of health, education, and welfare (see table 3.1). As often happens in developing career patterns, very strong interests in these areas seem to preclude an interest in cultural affairs. The social network required for cultural interests, the expenses, life-style, and working patterns required by the schedule of benefits and parties take up too much time, energy, and available funds for most women to be able to diversify so widely.

Other women found their major interests through trial and error, or they stumbled upon their talents. They entered volunteering with no special focus of interest or expectation of what they might eventually do, so they followed the path suggested by family or in-laws. They also put themselves in the hands of organizations that gave instruction and offered a preselected array of alternatives: the Volunteer Bureau, the League of Women Voters, the Junior League. During this phase, some learned what they didn't like, recoiled from it, and started off in another direction. From the opportunities to work for a variety of organizations and to learn the array of skills used in volunteering, many discovered something they wanted to pursue further. For others, the chance suggestion or persuasion of a friend started them in one or more of their major career interests. The following woman provides a good example of how the drift or trend of interests, combined with growing disinterests, begins to emerge after a period of trial and error.

> I started with the Community Chest when we first got here. After that, Mrs. VanDeusen called me out of the blue to ask if I would serve on the Community Board of a half-way house. It needed to switch from federal funding to community support. I helped raise the money and learned how to find a power base to support an organization. This was a great contrast to the Conservatory Board where you learn to cater a party. I decided I didn't want to relate to music that way. And my party wasn't that good, though that experience was useful later on. But the halfway house experience focused an interest I had in education and coun-

seling . . . I started an organization to do youth guidance and used my fund-raising experience from Halfway House. As a result of that experience, I have learned to write grants and now consult on education projects. Since the organization I started has become successful, I have branched out into mid-life counseling programs for women. I was elected to my college alumnae board and have developed a network of alumnae associations in the city.

In the course of working on various volunteer projects, some women came upon a cause they care about. Seven of these women discovered that working for the cause of art was their thing (see table 3.1). One of them happened on this field in the course of fund-raising for a neighborhood center. Her "gimmick" was an artist studio tour.

I did five of them and saw where my interests lay. I met artists and thought they were the most fascinating and complete people I had ever known . . . I also joined the membership activity board of the museum. I went on a neighborhood center board but it soon became clear I was really in love with the museum and from there could further the interests of artists which I really love to do. I stopped teaching Sunday School and resigned from the neighborhood center board. The museum is almost a full-time job.

Another group of three have organized their main work around musical interests. One of them began at the suggestion of a college friend and continued by developing her own connections to organizations devoted to the promotion of music.

In addition to aesthetic causes, women take on social reform issues (housing for the poor, civil rights, urban blight). These interests can become a meeting ground for traditional and more radical women. They also move volunteer women into political and advocacy roles within the city, distancing them from colleagues in the more traditional service and cultural activities.

Some women were captivated by a cause and then devoted themselves to it—through a variety of organizations or ad hoc benefits. Three women chose intellectual pursuits, furthering special education and scientific projects. One of these women worked for associations to please friends and family until she discovered her interest in foreign policy. She then helped a national peace organization with public relations and fund-raising. Another woman followed suggestions given to her until an organization "captured" her. She then abandoned everything else. She described her rise in the organization she served for twenty years.

> Before I found the [Helping Hands] Organization, I would jump from board to board. And then I got ill and resigned from everything. I was glad of the chance to get out of those things. My whole career started here in the city chapter. At first I got my greatest satisfaction from service. And then I went to desk work which I thought I would dislike, but there were satisfactions in bringing service. As I became more learned I was involved in decision making, resolving difficulties between volunteers and staff. Sort of up through the ranks.

As she became more strongly committed to the organization, its requirements dictated the direction her career would take.

> I had no thought of staying more than two years in the area office [for twelve western states] but thought I owed it to an organization I loved so much. You have to visit chapters to promote the philosophy of volunteer leadership. At first I worked mostly with volunteers and very few staff members. Later it was the reverse with mostly staff members and very few volunteers. I set up the organizational structure to separate program and personnel tasks.

Sometimes women discover that management problems interest them more than substantive issues. The opportunity to develop and use management skills is what keeps their interest focused.

> I have been working for the museum a good fifteen years. I was an officer during the merger. As an administrative job it was the most exciting thing I've done, building an organization. I don't know much about art but I enjoy the administrative side.

Managerial ability can also move a woman away from one interest to a series of leadership positions. The women who diversify are often difficult to place, but they are found primarily in the field of health-education-welfare and politics. One woman has managed political campaigns, served on boards, and acted as outside consultant to rescue foundering organizations devoted to children and more general health and welfare issues. This woman gradually developed her management skills through the pattern of incremental learning shown in more detail later. She saw herself as slowly acquiring her skills. Others feel the experience they have just "uncovers" a preexisting ability that was waiting to be found. These are "organization women," interested in a special range of problems, trained in a variety of organizations (co-op nurseries, League of Women Voters, PTA, Junior League, political parties). They are specialists at organization building and rescuing, but their allegiance is never captured by any one cause. This group (see table 3.1) contains a number of women who have sometimes used their skills to become paid consultants of various kinds—to management, philanthropic causes, political parties, and citizen action groups.

These women illustrate a principle for even those most tenaciously associated with one organization or cause: one has to move on to grow. In this regard, volunteer leaders are different from men and women in salaried careers—where bureaucrats or professionals can prosper by rising within an organization or by acquiring more prestige and clientele while continuing a practice. These women have to move like entrepreneurs in a changing market, capitalizing on a successful venture but learning to abandon it for another as market conditions change. Both the ideology and structure of the volunteer career discourages too single-minded an approach among community leaders. Foot soldiers can remain year after year at the same job if they wish, but leaders are required to move on, if only by periodic election and limited terms of office for incumbents. Most women say they wish to do this in any case. One woman sports a ring that says "I've done that already." And a recurring theme throughout interviews is the wish to avoid growing stale and the need for new blood and new approaches to the recurring problems faced by organizations and causes.

> I was vitally interested in the Library Board until two years ago. Then I found I didn't have anything challenging to do. I had been on all the committees. All those young people coming along should be the ones. I found it a dead approach going to meetings to say: we did that years ago. This library . . . needs younger blood and people with new ideas.

One characteristic pattern is to phase out stale interests, remaining to give advice or work on occasional special projects while developing new activities. Another pattern is to resign very formally, then decide what to do next. The woman who had worked twenty years for one organization did the latter, and a series of retirement parties were held for her as though she were retiring staff. But even she returned as a consultant for a year or two while developing new interests in volunteer projects to aid the retired. She, and at least two others in this study, became more involved in retirement projects and homes for the aged when they themselves became older. While interests may change drastically, the characteristic patterns of work are not likely to do so.

The tendency to adapt volunteer interests to one's own place in the life cycle is a common one and, as we shall see in the discussion of career contingencies, a necessary accommodation to the changing nature of family responsibilities over time. But substance—as well as amount of work activity—changes over time. Initial interests may be focused by the availability of volunteer tasks suggested by parents, friends, sorority sisters, and placement committees. As young marrieds, most women work on day-care, turning to other educational issues as their own children grow older. They remain focused or diversify, slow down or continue, in their later years as their interests, health, and general life circumstances dictate.

Antipathies

Women often found direction for their careers as much by discovering what they didn't like as what they did. (See table 3.2 for a review of antipathies mentioned in this sample.) Some women dislike boring and menial work, welcoming promotion with relief, despite the ideology that all should be willing to help on repetitive, subordinate tasks. And some women dislike fund-raising. A key element in this dislike is a repugnance for hustling: coaxing, bullying, scheming to extract money for good causes from resistant donors.

An associated antipathy is one for open conflict. Three women left organizations over disagreements they preferred to avoid rather than face confrontation in order to resolve them. Accordingly, it is not surprising that a substantial minority (8) of the women say they don't like politics. The adversarial nature of political contests strikes some of these women as too abrasive and the conflict too public for comfort. In addition, a few of these women find the substantive issues of politics boring. Most (6) of this minority are also older traditional women who do not see politics as a "proper," ladylike interest.

Other antipathies can draw women toward activity. Four women spoke of their fear of idleness and their dislike of the traditional stereotype of how time is spent by well-off women: bridge and the hairdressers. For some women, the traditional stereotype also included participation in "Mickey Mouse" activities of little value

Table 3.2   Antipathies

Hustling	4
Conflict and politics	8
Idleness, frivolity, stereotypes	4
"Mickey Mouse" activity	6
"Social" volunteering	5
Lady Bountiful image	4
Numbers and letters	7
Sad things	12
Other idiosyncratic distastes	5
No response	15
Total	70

("whether to serve fish or chicken to senior citizens"). Six women grumbled about it. A related antipathy appeared in response to the "social" aspects of some volunteer work. Five women abandoned organizational work in art and opera because they disliked the socialite overtones in the promotion of culture. Even those with a personal interest in culture would move into other areas of community work when they could see no significant connection between the work they could do and the content of the field.

Four women resented work associated with Lady Bountiful imagery or staffed by women who resembled this stereotype. Two of these were renegade doctor's wives who resisted joining the doctor's wife groups attached to hospitals. They resisted the narrowness and conservatism often associated with the image as well. ("I really couldn't stand it . . . Almost all of them were [know-nothing] Republicans.") Other women do not necessarily dislike elitism and "social" volunteering, but they cringe from the self-display involved in amateur theatricals, costume balls, and fashion shows. Some mask their diffidence (by making costumes, rather than modeling them or acting in them), but others resist invitations to join or resign quickly from even the most exclusive and important volunteer groups in the city if such activities are important components. Some women in this study enjoyed the limelight and appeared frequently in newspaper columns and photos. Other women said they didn't care for publicity yet seemed to be photographed and mentioned anyway. Still others shunned publicity in society columns but enjoyed recognition as notable community leaders in news stories and public commemorations. Others were tenacious about avoiding notice and substantially kept out of sight.

Women sometimes bear the stamp of conventional education for girls in their dislike of figures. Four women mentioned this dislike as an impetus steering them clear of organizations and tasks requiring any mathematical skills. Another problem mentioned by three women was their difficulty with writing and organizing reports.

If some women can't face certain tasks, sympathetic community leaders will help such fearful ones avoid their *betes noires*.

> We have a young member who has been president of various organizations already. The president of the board thought this new member was officer material and put her in as assistant treasurer. And this young woman was terrified. Next year the president wanted to make her the treasurer. I asked her quietly what she thought of such an idea. She said, "I will resign if I am asked to take that job." So I told the president and we were saved from losing a really good board member.

Or a seasoned volunteer can find her own way to sidestep a hated responsibility.

> I am not a scholar. For example, I think I come back each year to manage the big benefit because if I didn't I would have to write a report for the next chairman. Someone else is going to write the report this time. I work well that way; I'll talk about it and she'll write it down. And we now have someone who can take over without a hitch.

Sometimes, as in other activities considered vital (fund-raising, mailing chores), women will grit their teeth and get through them. "I stopped smoking but broke down when I had to write the annual report. The business of sitting down at the typewriter and getting the report ground out is the hardest thing for me." If the activity doesn't get any easier, or less painful, it stands a good chance of being jettisoned.

Twelve women said they disliked the health field, or some aspect of it, because it depressed them. Two wouldn't work for the Cancer Society: one because she hated the stress on symptoms and thought it created an unfortunate and unnecessary self-consciousness and fearfulness among the healthy; another because she found the medical approach incompatible with her belief in Christian Science. In general, these women found things like hospitals, the aged, the blind depressing, so they turned their interests elsewhere. Many of these women hope their preferred choices will be of some help to those they are really not interested in or don't like to work with. Like the women who want to make cultural events available to the poor and underprivileged, women who avoid the sadder side of good works nonetheless stress their abiding interest in the public weal.

A few women "took" against something in the course of their career for various personal reasons. Someone or something bothered them so much in the course of work they decided to leave it; but no clear pattern appears among the five women discussing this kind of antipathy. For example, one woman stopped fund-raising for a Jewish group as a policy decision; she disapproved of the group's focus on Zionism. Another woman discovered she couldn't stand providing a service after she trained for it; she liked the museum, but hated having to guide screaming and unruly children on tours.

Responding to Antipathies

As noted earlier, women believe that one of the great advantages in this work is the opportunity to experiment once one learns what one's likes and dislikes really are. Traditional women are sometimes tentative about this opportunity to pick and choose employment; their upbringing and current social expectations of them as daughters, wives, and mothers does not necessarily encourage the expression of much individuality. The volunteer world is a relatively safe arena for such exploration. Yet even here, traditional women often endure hated jobs they feel are expected of them for quite a while. Often they are given encouragement from mentors and older community leaders to resist pressures to take unwanted jobs. One woman, whose organizational talents were taking her up the stages of committee work and offices that would lead to the opera board told me how she appealed to an older woman for advice on how to escape gracefully. Now that the process was well under way, the younger woman realized that she didn't care for the opera and hated the society benefit aura within which much of the fundraising and policy-making of the board would take place. Yet she wanted to remain on good terms with the volunteers and staff, and she needed some support and guidance on how to accomplish this end while resigning from all further responsibility. For another woman, the problem of how to avoid a disliked assignment was serious enough to remember the woman who helped her avoid it long afterward. This civic leader encouraged the troubled woman in the idea that one shouldn't have to do tasks one hated.

For some women this process takes a while, but then they figure out for themselves that they hate something and so had better stop doing it.

> I was active in the Red Cross when my husband was in the service. I had a five-day week, and sometimes longer, as a volunteer. I gave the staff assistant courses and I got women in the area interested in volunteering for the soldiers. Then all of a sudden I knew I didn't want to do it anymore. I couldn't bring myself to get up in the morning. Or I would wake up in the middle of the night thinking: Oh how I don't want to give a talk in some little town or wherever. I realized that I had to stop.

Other women take their own resistance as a sign of something to be overcome. Sooner or later they may face up to it and learn the hated skills. Women learn about fund-raising despite their dislike of hustling ("I'm beginning to learn to fund-raise after twenty years of avoiding it"). Others conquer fears of hustling and public speaking as well. "I learned how you collect a crowd with a line of patter. The carney people taught me how to do it for a benefit circus. And I would do my pitch, even though my face was brick red."

The management of antipathies reveals some of the ambiguities in applying a concept like career to the work of women volunteers. These women maintain sustained work activity against pressures from the outside world that discredit or trivialize it. They also work against their feelings of boredom, dislike, anxiety, or fatigue with various aspects of their work. Some of their antipathies are related to intrinsic characteristics of the work, such as the hustling of fund-raising or the adversarial nature of politics. Other antipathies, however, are related to aspects of their life situation (for example, the imputation by others that these women are idle and frivolous, that they concentrate on silly rather than important matters, or that they are condescending to the less fortunate). The mix shows a combination of responses to pressures from others and specific dislikes of particular kinds of jobs that would be hard to parallel in paid careers. The main difficulty in the parallel is the absence of external structure in the volunteer career. There is no one or no institution to "blame" for difficulties at work. Women, consequently, address the issue as a personal problem to be overcome or circumvented by each individual. However, a successful resolution that permits a woman to continue working also suggests that she can become a leader and take charge of organizations as well as her own personal problems. The management of antipathies shows that work builds character or provides self-knowledge rather than supplying one with an excuse to stop working. In the absence of a formal structure with sanctions related to the presence of occupational titles and salaries, women circumvent or overcome antipathies while discovering what their real metier may be.

Learning Increments

Making sense of a career by considering learning increments is a reasonable strategy in both employed and nonsalaried careers. In the developmental perspective, for example, psychologists who study occupational careers assume that occupational choice represents an evolving sequence of individual decisions (Ginzberg et al. 1951). For women in this study, many of these decisions are recollected and then understood as part of a sequence.

These women have thought about how their interests took shape and how they made choices along the way. Most of them make sense of their career retrospectively. When receiving awards, accepting acclaim during benefits in their honor, giving interviews to the press (or to a social scientist), they would review their community work experiences. They may not have planned it or realized the array of career possibilities when they began, but they were ready to accept the concept of "career" and talk about how their careers developed. They were prepared for this task because women have had to explain or justify to themselves as well as to family and friends just why they work when they don't "have" to. Most of this discussion comes, accordingly, from the majority who have not held salaried positions for any substantial part of their lives. (Of the twenty women who focused on how their careers had gradually developed, only three have had any substantial salaried work experience. One has worked part-time and sporadically throughout her volunteer career; the other two are recent entrants to the salaried work world.)

The process of learning is easily divided into those aspects that are part of formal training programs and those that are somehow put together or initiated by the learner. In the first category are the various structured programs offered by organizations. The Junior League and League of Women Voters are known for their training programs in community service. Students learn how to chair meetings, plan agendas, use organizational procedures, and find their way around the community.

The training can be further divided into those parts that are relatively cut-and-dried, offering material to be ingested passively, and those parts that open doors and provide opportunity for independent initiative. Most early volunteer experiences have both these elements. The women studied here were most inclined to take the path of individual initiative, although they saw how special skills were developed through structured training.

Special Skills

When women point to the special skills they learn in training programs, the Junior League is often mentioned to show what volunteer groups can do for interested members.

> The purpose of the Junior League is to train you generally. It will give you skills to run a meeting, teach you how to set up an agenda in advance, be prompt in beginning and ending meetings. You can sit in the organization and learn nothing. But it does permit you to learn a variety of skills [if you serve on the board of this or another organization] by seeing and identifying with the women who have gone ahead. . . . It teaches you to leave things shipshape when you leave them. It teaches you to train workers to follow you and take over.

The impermanence of office and the issues that arise while serving on boards are both subjects considered in more detail later; it is also important to note here another topic to be considered in detail later—that boards of organizations are often the training ground and the source of varied experience for community leaders.

In general, the more structured learning contexts are not only places to learn skills; they also provide opportunities to build self-esteem. The knowledge that one has skills commensurate with those of salaried workers can bolster one's confidence.

> I found I was disagreeing more and more with the professionals in social work. I didn't want a Master's but I wanted to find out if I was on the beam. So I took a certificate. That was four semesters at extension and a summer session intensive course. I . . . got all A's. There were forty-nine professionals and I was the only lay person. When I was through I said, "All right, if I can survive with professionals and get good grades—I can go with them." And I needed that to reassure myself.

Volunteer training programs are often organized to provide this confidence. "The Junior League is truly invaluable as a training organization. You can work your way in and find your own place—it's a sheltered workshop in a way. You find out how to use what you have to make things happen." The key to this confidence building is the opportunity to watch oneself develop skills and then to see them validated through management of some leadership position. The importance of successful performance in creating self-confidence and self-esteem cannot be overestimated. Women who dread performing in public are like any women with little experience in the public arena who are often afraid at first. But success is a very positive reinforcement. McCourt (1977:226–27) speaks of this experience as creating dramatic changes in the self-esteem of working-class women in Chicago. She offers an example of the process from the life of one such woman.

> The first time I made a public statement . . . I always had this kind of feeling that a man is better informed, a better speaker. And it was that public hearing, and I got a public ovation and I thought, by God, I did that just as well as any man could have.

Validation possible from *publicly* acclaimed behavior encourages self-confidence. Despite the ideology surrounding the importance of home life and women's activities in creating or protecting it, the importance one has in one's private world is nonnegotiable beyond it. Accordingly, women have little opportunity to develop a general sense of self-confidence there; the territory is too restricted. Entry into public worlds reveals both the limitations on confidence building that family life offers women and the opportunity available to them outside it.

The foregoing provides examples of learning discrete skills which lead to positive reevaluation of the self. More generally, in this stage of their experience women learn about the community and how to operate within it. Hence, women often mention their interest in the Junior League or the League of Women Voters when they are newcomers to the city because these organizations will provide ready access to that information.

Mentors

While the opportunity to learn about the community may be provided by a relatively well-structured organization, individuals have to want to use it to learn. Women are sometimes taught the usefulness of these skills when they become the apprentices of mentors who provide inspiration as well as practical training. Mentors also provide confidence when juniors accompany these more experienced elders making their volunteer rounds. This pattern is almost an institutionalized practice for learning—and teaching—the finer points of fund-raising, for example.

Mentors offer inspiration and access to new and desired opportunity. The literature of the feminist movement—as well as popular and social science articles on career advancement for either men or women—has made it fashionable to speak of the importance of mentors in various kinds of career mobility. Even the neologism, mentoring, is now fairly well accepted as a way to describe the process of developing protégées.

Kanter (1977) shows the importance of patrons or sponsors for new talent in the business world. The importance of the "right" sponsors for professionals—as in the introduction of physicians into the medical community—has long been recognized (Hall 1948). The importance of sponsors for women in academic careers is currently a topic given much discussion (Hall and Sandler 1983; Daniels 1979). The search for such sponsors, the discussions of appropriate expectations for the sponsors and their apprentices, the advantages and limitations of this informal system of patrons and neophytes, these are all included within the concept of mentoring.

The importance of mentoring for women in this study lies in the learning they can do with a teacher, advisor, or sponsor in a role outside the formal and institutional channels for learning. The relationship can be more fragmentary or fleeting than in a formal relation with institutionalized duration and set responsibilities assigned to teachers and students. Experienced and knowledgeable people may intervene to give counsel on one particular occasion, then move away.

Since women who become civic leaders carve out their careers relatively independently of any formal process and outside well-understood patterns of career development, the informal and even evanescent relations that can be encompassed within the mentoring concept do offer many of the tips and guideposts to help them build careers. Not all these leaders have a reputation as mentors, but those who do are seen as leaders in part because of their influence on their juniors.

Some of the mentoring reported in this study comes from accounts of the mentored. Women reminiscing about their early experience spoke about those who had helped them. The earliest influence upon many, as noted in chapter one, comes from family members who through example and precept show informants the importance of philanthropic activity. The example of family members may serve as inspiration as well as model. The following informant saw her mother-in-law that way.

> My mother-in-law was a remarkable woman. She was probably my greatest mentor and I admired her most in her interest in others, her creativity and accomplishments. She had the ability to recognize others' talents and help them develop.

When newcomers arrived in the community, spouses and in-laws would also offer example and precept, adding introductions and suggestions for specific tasks to women finding themselves at loose ends. As noted earlier, a sister-in-law could provide entry to an interesting organization, another in-law foot the bill for the household help, enabling a wife to become active in volunteering. Such help suggests mentoring activity in that it is tailored to the particular problems of the junior, at that time. The younger person has shown some indecision, or even distress; the mentor has hit upon a plan to resolve it. Or the two have negotiated a plan—as when one woman reported that her mother volunteered to baby-sit a few hours each day so that the daughter could get out of the house to volunteer. These examples suggest the combination of assistance and precept that mentoring can involve. An older, more experienced colleague goes out of her way to solve a problem for a younger person. At the same time, the senior shows the importance of the volunteering activity she is encouraging by the lengths she will go to promote it.

While family members can be mentors, the general use of the term suggests a search outside the usual institutional contexts, either familial or educational, for guidance or instruction. The concept of mentor has some overtones of a disinterested but kindly disposed observer to the junior's progress. And these kindly actions are reported, both by those who offer them and those who have been recipients. Helpful advice is particularly remembered when it is offered and received at crucial stages in the career. The woman who reported that she was referred by an older friend to just the right organization after a divorce is one such case. And the woman who said she intervened to save a promising young woman from the treasurer's job she would have hated enough to resign is another.

Within organizational contexts, the mentor can step in, and as in the last example, intercede both for the good of the organization and the person. The mentor may, as in the case of a leader in a national self-help patient group, persuade her junior to start a local chapter and find her the right assistants to do the job. Or the mentor may be remembered for support and encouragement in the teeth of systematic opposition from others. When women wish to work for political candidates and face indifference or hostility to their plans from the male party workers, the juniors particularly remember the sympathetic support of older, more experienced women political volunteers. Sometimes the mentor is remembered just as a prop or "magic feather," giving confidence that one can, like Dumbo the elephant, fly if one wants to.

From the perspective of the mentor, the personal interest taken in juniors *should* include a sensitive attention to the details of their lives. After all, that kind of attention is required to tailor a proposed line of action to an individual's requirements. Further, the mixture of personal attention and thoughtful advice also carries an implicit message of the essential worthiness of the junior. If the mentor takes so much trouble for her, the junior can feel enough self-esteem to have the courage to take on the plan of action suggested. Women remember a mentor for showing the patience and willingness to make special efforts, and for giving sympathetic interest in monitoring their progress when they were younger—along with the inspiration offered by splendid example. Special relations often develop between the mentors and their students. These relations are not limited to women volunteers; sometimes, as we shall see, special bonds develop between volunteers and staff women. In addition, men are sometimes seen as mentors. A husband or father may be mentioned as specially influential in career development. Or male community-service associates from staffs or boards may be singled out as significant teachers or sponsors. (In all, fourteen women noted the importance of some man—or men—in guiding their career.)

Despite the references to male mentors, the emphasis is certainly on the importance of women teaching women. In these interviews, some see themselves as self-taught or else have no special recollections of mentors; but twenty-eight women focused exclusively on women in describing their mentors. In these descriptions, informants mention the high ideals and standards of older women who would push their juniors to greater accomplishments. Challenging or difficult tasks, more sustained and disciplined effort in community service, more intellectually demanding problems were some of the expectations mentors would hold for their protégées. In addition to sympathetic helpfulness or understanding, their mentors provided models and goals for achievement.

The Gift of Charisma

Some of the women who serve as role models and who set standards for aspiration are not personally known to those they have influenced. Women in this sample sometimes mention such influences on them. Or community leaders will learn, in passing, how much they have unwittingly influenced others. A few women in this sample are sufficiently admired to be mentioned in many interviews. They have influenced, or trained, many of the current community leaders. They are also known for their speaking ability, intuition and good judgment, patience with information-seekers, knowledge of the community, and all-around acumen in any aspect of community service. In addition, they have, to an even higher degree than do these generally high-powered women, the gift of charisma. These are women with that extra quality that makes them stand out when they chair a meeting, manage a complicated merger, outface an opposition group, charm or neutralize an antagonist in a public confrontation. These great leaders have special leadership qualities above the rest. Such women attract a great following. If they wish, they have considerable opportunity to select the potential leaders of the next cohort of women community leaders and train them. One such leader reminisced about a great community leader who had trained *her*.

> She befriended a great many women [among] my contemporaries. People adored Mrs. Grant. She was always interested in . . . your problems. I think all the young women around her were anxious to be the primary one that she was really interested in. I had no idea I was the primary one. I think I was because later people said to me . . . I wish Mrs. G. felt about me the way she feels about you.

These women, then, not only capture the attention of their juniors, but they also focus a lot of affect in the process. Sometimes this focus can be a potential source of competition in the protégée cohort, as the foregoing suggests. Or the affect may be expressed in a determined, even willful, clinging to the great leader against her wishes. When one of these leaders fell ill and went into seclusion for a time, her many friends and protégées vied for the few visiting hours she permitted. One of these protégées, unusually anxious to reestablish contact, insisted on an interview. The mentor refused, on the ground that her needs for rest and privacy should now take precedence. The protégée, quite beside herself, came to the house anyway and stationed herself at the door for some hours in hope that her mentor would relent and permit at least a few words. In speaking of the incident at a later date, this civic leader said she had left the suppliant on the doorstep until she tired of waiting and departed. Always the mentor, this woman explained that she did not wish to seem hard-hearted, but that it was important for this importuning woman to learn that her own sense of anxiety, no matter how frantic, could not be assuaged at the expense of the very person she cared about.

Such a strong response to another suggests the depth of feelings followers generate for their great leaders. Whether or not the expression of affect is always appropriate to the occasion, it also indicates the power of the teacher and the attention her message will receive. The messages or precepts delivered from such sources have oracular overtones for willing acolytes. The great leaders, then, are revered and heeded. Their power lies in this capacity to capture the imagination and thus influence their protégées. Some of the flavor of this context in which precepts are learned is caught in the following reminiscence:

> [The organization was] having a hard time and Mrs. Jansen and I were worried. . . . A woman who wanted badly to be president . . . was elected. . . . She was a pathetic figure in a way . . . but she was such a bad organizer that I didn't have patience with her. Mrs. Jansen did, being an older woman looking at the situation. This woman wouldn't permit anybody to help her. . . . And I finally realized that I was so frustrated that I would have to get out of [the organization].
>
> Mrs. Jansen called me up and said, "Now, you go out to the beach, and you talk to the waves . . ." She wanted me not to shout at anybody else because, of course, she had the long view, which was that it wouldn't do anybody any good for me to try to destroy my . . . as it turned out . . . predecessor. [If] I did resign, I was losing all opportunity to be president; that was one thing . . . I really wanted. . . . And I thought, if I were just president, I would know how [to bring the organization back from the hard times befalling it] . . . so I was terribly frustrated that year. . . . But when my predecessor's year was over [I was asked to be president].

It is through the intervention of well-respected mentors, then, that even headstrong women, such as the preceding speaker, learn to bide their time, avoid confrontation, and trust in their capacities. Once these women have made their reputations, of course, this procedure entails fewer risks. But in the early stages of a career, it is that extra push from great mentors, who combine surveillance and sponsorship of protégées, that can make the difference in many women's lives. The charismatic mentor, then, has the special abilities that attract other women into volunteer work and persuade them to remain in it even under adversity. Three women in this study possess enough of this gift of charisma to be mentioned admiringly by most other informants. They are seen as "mentor of the entire community," or as "our mentor." And informants offer the highest accolades they can think of to describe their work ("A marvelous woman," "great wisdom and understanding of people," and "standards . . . of the highest"). When referring to new or rising community leaders, women will sometimes say these juniors are in the tradition set by a past, great community leader or that they are a second Mrs. Reynard or the most promising protégée of Mrs. Jansen. These comments show that community leaders expect a succession of women with great leadership gifts to appear in community service. The leaders also recognize the informal system for their selection and training.

On-the-Job Training

These dramatic figures and inspirational moments in the growth of women community leaders are reinforced and supplemented by working experience. Women may receive training from the professional staff of the organizations they serve as volunteer board members. The staff may also open doors to advancement—and new learning opportunities—in the volunteer world.

Women speak of this type of training as on-the-job, trial by fire, and training one's self. They learn, for example, that new tactics and strategies have to be adopted when transferring their skills from the more genteel world of private philanthropic organizations to the rough-and-tumble of public commissions.

> I learned a lot when I was appointed to the Mayor's Commission. It was a political thing. There's no orientation. You go in like a lamb [to the slaughter]. We wanted to change the general manager and didn't know about the Public In-

formation Act. So we had a meeting of about three or four of us in private. A reporter found out and there was a big story in the newspapers. I was really stupid, but they never explained it to us. The biggest thing I learned from this public work is that a community-oriented person privately started really needs more information. I found it crushing to deal on the public scale. But I was motivated to do something for the city. I was on for twelve years and some things took ten years from their original undertaking to fruition.

As they need information or skills, then, women acquire them in the course of their work. When new challenges arise, they may learn skills uncharacteristic of or even antithetical to their station in life.

I went as a PTA president to the Congress of African Parents—a group of black and community leaders working for a community school board. I was a straight white middle-class stereotype and that was something I had to work through. I ran into this group of men who would block anything creative that would happen at these meetings. And I couldn't figure out what motivation they had. So I would ask after meetings, "Why did you want to kill this motion? It looks pretty good to me." It turned out they were Maoist and interested in Maoist theatre tactics. The philosophy was that you had to destroy society in order to change it. And they would sit in after meetings and explain things and teach me. Turns out they were really quite nice people. And I learned all the tactics and manipulation of the language and all that.

Such experiences can crystallize the direction developing in one's career. As we shall see, they did just that for the woman quoted above. She became a formidable advocate with a combination of ladylike and Maoist tactics in the services of her projects. For her, as for most women, experience is incremental. Women may realize what they have learned only when they put together some "big package" and see how various bits and pieces they have learned helped them do it.

Some women see a linear progression to their learning after they came up through the ranks. But most women, as they reminisce about how they came to learn what they now know, present an interesting mixture of learning, at all stages and levels of work, about the city, the development of useful contacts and referral sources, and the development of specific skills. Some of their training in skills underscores the special problems of privileged women trying to get something done within the city. The woman, quoted earlier, who complains of the difficulties facing a "community-oriented person privately started" without the information about how the city is run refers obliquely to the limitations of the training received through volunteer activities in such organizations as the Junior League. The woman who learned Maoist tactics from working-class and minority group leaders expresses something of the same perspective: ladylike approaches reflect class interests that assume more acceptance of the status quo than is shared by other participants in the civic—and political—arena. The following woman, who rose through PTA and the League of Women Voters, explains the limitations of that perspective.

> My most intensive training came in the advisory committee to set up the PTA busing for integration program—a highly political setup by members of the board of education. There were seven members that each could appoint and we were sixty people from varying backgrounds. It was a training ground in style. People threw chairs at you and screamed in six different languages. You can't undergo that without learning confrontation and mediation techniques. And it is important training for women not used to it to learn [that] confrontation as a tactic is at least as useful as mediation— and have it as a resource. Upper-class women see it as their responsibility to put out fires and not to light them.

Some women stress the fortuitous aspect of developing contacts over time rather than the incremental nature of learning. From this perspective it is the accretion of friends and contacts over the years that provides useful increments.

> Recently I was in some desperation about how to get hold of labor support for this campaign. When I ran into this old political ally from the depression and discovered he was a prominent labor leader, I asked him for some help. And he volunteered to send out notices about this proposition to the various labor unions; and he showed me how to get endorsements for the proposition from labor leaders in the city. It's funny how these friendships come back to help you at another time of life.

Whatever their special skills, it is clearly a matter of overriding importance that these women know their territory. While a few women are tied into national networks through special interests, their base of power and influence is the city. It is the gradual or ac-

cidental accretion of this knowledge that they talk about in reviewing their careers. They make friends and allies, learn suppliers and
resources, develop access to information and influence networks.

Turning Points

While some women speak of their gradual career development over
time, with slowly dawning realization of the direction taken, others
come to crossroads and crises that force recognition of a change in
plans. Some women find their careers a previously unexamined
mixture and suddenly realize what the developing pattern means
and resolve to continue or change it. As we have seen, recognition
of a positive interest or a strong antipathy can help solidify this realization, as can some deeply felt personal experience or some
friendly intervention by friends and family. But such changes may
seem, at most, temporary and ad hoc adjustments. The seventeen
women who speak of sudden realization cover a greater scope than
that suggested in earlier discussions. These women see the "grand
design" in their careers and make a major decision to solidify or
change course, or "start over." Life changes sometimes force turning points upon women. Two women saw remarriage as the chance
to start a new life, change careers, take up new interests. Another
woman changed both salaried and volunteer career interests after
recovery from a disabling illness.

One woman presents the theme of renunciation. She gave up her
graduate study short of the doctorate, and her hope for eventual
professional employment, when she realized that she was needed
to build an organization that would benefit the community.

> The organization does work. And it has confirmed as right
> a decision I made with regard to how I ought to use my
> education. I remember commuting to the university and
> worrying how I could fit everything in. A voice inside said,
> "You have to give up more education for this." I thought it
> should be done and I was following the right voice for
> once. But in the beginning, continuing a volunteer career
> was a sacrifice.

This woman who experienced a sense of having been called is the
most dramatic example of turning points in careers. But many
women come to the realization of what they will now embark upon
in their careers after some soul-searching. Six women ruminated for
a long time over the direction they would take before it was clear to

them. For two of these women, the direction was determined by realizing the significance of their special skills in management.

> I was surprised by my ability at organization because I would have scorned it as not a worthy thing earlier in life. Someone said, "Why not be proud of what you do well?" Little remarks like that from thoughtful persons made a strong impression.

A few women also view certain positions as decisive. After election as president of a prestigious organization, some women saw nothing left to do. Accordingly, they marked time, diversified interests, and essentially retired from the role of civic leader at an early age. Two women saw the presidency of the Junior League in this light. They were content after their term of office to step into the background, taking less responsible jobs. Other women decided, for various reasons, to stop short of a retirement age. As one saw it, she was taken care of by her family for the first twenty-five years of her life, she gave the next twenty-five years to her children and the community, and she wanted the following twenty-five years for herself. Her hobby had always been painting and now she would devote herself to it seriously. Three women renounced their leadership careers after coming to the realization that the work no longer suited them.

Retirement, then, can be the turning point that marks the end of the career or the passage to a new stage of life. Women can find themselves in mid-life crises just as men do. And women may desire a new life-style, after many years in the old one, just as men do.

In the differentialist view of occupational choice (Lancashire 1971), any career can be studied in terms of the diversity of talents, abilities, and personal characteristics existing among people. Reviewing the patterns of growth and change discussed by women who are civic leaders suggests that their expectations, discoveries, false starts, management of interests and antipathies on the path of career development bear some resemblances to the experiences of anyone in the paid world, male or female, searching for a direction in work. While their language is restrained and their horizons restricted by traditional expectations for women of their class, these civic leaders show real concern for how they *should* work and how they may develop their talents and serve the community.

Yet these women differ from most dedicated professionals in their emphasis on the subordinate nature of the work to family. One consequence of this emphasis is that the work occurs in the interstices of their public and private lives. The ambiguous nature of this conjunction can be seen in women's varied responses to publicity as well as in their insistence on a personal or individualized effort to create a career. The way work is constructed to produce the configuration of each woman's career shows her concern with weaving personal concerns and public service together. This insistence, of course, is both created and made possible by the necessity for an unpaid career.

4
Interest Patterns and Work Styles

Once a woman becomes active, a pattern develops according to substantive interests and preferred style of work. The first category can be divided into cultural interests on the one hand and health, education, and welfare interests—with a small group interested in politics—on the other. The second category can be broadly separated into "bang and bust" versus steady incremental effort.

These categories are developed from the women's own perspectives as they reflect upon both the substance and the shape of their careers. This pattern of organization reveals some of their differences from women volunteers in other classes. Women who have the privileges and resources that these women do have the opportunity to get a broad view of their city early in their careers. In that sense, they are cosmopolitans with entry to a wide range of networks rather than locals who work only within a small community or on a narrow focus of interests.[1] Most of the women in this study become involved in a number of varied projects throughout their volunteer careers, but even those women with a distinctive concern or a special institution to which they are devoted are connected by family and friends to other current philanthropic issues in the city. They understand where the interests fit into the "big picture" of various competing concerns for volunteer services and charitable donations. This understanding comes as part of their class and family position, their experience in volunteer training agencies that try to lay out the varied picture of community services to new re-

---

1. The pro-life activists that Luker (1984) studied are examples of this second type of volunteer. They do not participate in such community-oriented organizations as the PTA and local church societies but concentrate on a single issue. Consequently, they do not see—or are not concerned with—how their issue affects or fits into the ongoing life of the community around them.

cruits, and the contacts they make in their efforts to use the accessible networks for their own special concerns. While these connections may not show them all the communities within a city, these women are still in an excellent position to survey both the needs and the opportunities for serving them within even a fairly large metropolitan region.

The major distinction that women make in organizing their sense of the range of areas in which to work is between culture and everything else. Culture is the area which most conforms to the "society" line of intersection referred to earlier in placing these women at the intersection of society and philanthropy. Everything else includes those with special interests in health, education, and welfare—and politics—as well as those who resist the connotations of society and "social" interests in organizing a career. The resistance reveals both an appreciation of the privileged position these women have by virtue of their class connections and a reluctance to be too closely associated with the stereotype of how women in that position may pass their time on the gala events associated with benefits for culture.

The second category of preferred style of work reflects a common opportunity for volunteer women throughout the class structure: the opportunity to organize a work schedule according to individual, temperamental predilections as well as around one's schedule of family activities. Women may work as hard and as systematically as they wish. However, the exigencies of volunteer work suggest there are two major divisions in the organization of work. These are sporadic but furious work under a deadline and steady incremental application.

Let us consider each category and its variations in turn and then examine the important overlapping areas (table 4.1 provides an overview of interest patterns in work).

Culture

I use the term here in the common usage as "high" art. The core of these interests is some focus on symphony, opera, art, ballet, and theatre. As Bernard (1981:413) remarks, "According to 'Veblen's Law,' culture is high in terms of the expense required for either its production or its appreciative consumption." The women in this study fall into the second category, consumers. But they are also patrons. Those who take cultural interests seriously conform to the stereotype that women in the upper classes preserve the finer things

Table 4.1   Primary Interest Patterns in Work

Culture		14
Art	3	
Symphony	2	
Opera	2	
Mix of the above plus ballet, chamber music, theatre	7	
Health, Education, and Welfare		28
Education and public schools	4	
Health	9	
Welfare, mainly child protection	4	
Education and world affairs	4	
Health, education, and welfare	3	
Child welfare and conservation	1	
Health and community welfare	2	
Ecology and conservation	1	
Politics		5
Mixed Culture and Health, Education, and Welfare		10
Education-Music	1	
Youth, aging, art	1	
Art-World Affairs	2	
Art-Welfare	2	
Culture-Health	1	
Culture-Health-Education	3	
Sporadic Interests		13
Total Number in Sample		70

in life while men make money.[2] When women become patrons of the arts, they also fit the American stereotype of the rich society ladies who engage in such patronage. They are suspect as to whether their primary concerns are related to art or related to supporting and participating in "social" interests.

Whatever their motives, the women I met had clearly worked in the service of community fine arts. Some had spent their lifetimes in regular service on auxiliaries, boards, fund-raisers, and outreach programs for the art museums, the symphonies, the repertory theatres and local opera, and the development of a ballet company. These women are an integral part of the cultural institutions of the city. In all, I could identify about fourteen women who focused their main volunteer activity on cultural interests: three focused on

2. Bernard (1981:415) cites a subheading in a book by Cohn (1943:72) entitled "My Culture Is in My Wife's Name" as an indication of the way appreciation of culture falls to women. See also Tuchman (1975:186–89) for a discussion of women as patrons of the arts.

art, two on symphony, and two on opera. The rest had mixed interests, including the above as well as ballet, chamber music, and
theatre.

Successful women in this area receive communitywide recognition. They are written about in newspapers and city officials invite
them to important civic events. The women who helped found the
symphony, the opera, and the ballet sit on the major policy-making
boards (where men of the business community predominate) that
oversee continued support and growth of these institutions.

The visibility that this recognition assures for these women is
mixed with (or tainted by) the public stereotypes of society ladies
and their cultural interests. The recognition is also affected by
some public ambivalence surrounding the news of women who
have chaired an important cultural benefit one month and were
then off to St. Moritz for the season in the following month. One
reason the overtones of frivolity adhere to cultural activity is that
the highly public aspects of the work are seasonal or intermittent.

In fact, although the cultural interests of most of these fourteen
women are steady, three of these women are really "bang and bust"
types. That is, their main talents lie in "doing" events and organizing fund-raisers rather than in steady service to maintain an organization. These activities require considerable effort over a short
period of time. They culminate in a big event after which the exhausted organizers and workers may congratulate themselves and
take a vacation. Their skills and connections in the community are
indispensable for the production and success of the ad hoc programs, exhibits, conferences, parties, and other managed events to
raise money, create good publicity, and heighten community awareness of the significance of ongoing cultural activities. Of course,
there is some truth in the stereotype of socialite philanthropists; for
some, organizing benefits is a way of filling time or a way of maintaining or building their social position. Yet an emphasis on this
aspect of their work ignores its significance in maintaining class
structure. In constructing benefits, women provide the arena where
their peers can meet socially. Women also provide the opportunity
for the socially mobile to become known and to be socialized to
philanthropic responsibility. Both newcomers and old-timers in
this social set are enticed into good works through the promise of
the glitter and gaiety surrounding the events. The work that is accomplished assures that the desired arenas (the opera, the symphony, the ballet) will continue, not only as valued additions to the

cultural life of the city, but also as the favored background for the mingling and public display of a smart or social set.

The stereotype also neglects an analysis of the personal effort involved in constructing benefits. This work requires a fertile imagination and a vision of how various elements in the community work together to provide an even bigger and more profitable benefit each year. It also involves concerted planning; and women pride themselves on raising great sums of money through their campaigns. The money they raise is important in keeping local cultural activity going. Here is how one accomplished organizer and public relations specialist helped keep the opera solvent in Pacific City.

> After the Opera Follies (when I was chairman) I talked to the producer who was also a volunteer. And we came up with the idea that there should be some way of opening doors so that the gross could be our net. We thought of a program to sell a program. At the start the Follies magazine grossed about $2,500. The last time I was chairman was for the twentieth anniversary and we netted $19,000 and then it was $33,000 last year . . . I was the one to say "get the Follies out of the Grand Hotel and into the Armory" [thus tremendously increasing participation, publicity, and revenues].

Such examples of success that an informant can be proud of show more than skill at raising increasingly large sums of money. They show what a woman knows about her community: how to find the right location to maximize the impact and the profit of an event; how to conceive of gimmicks (like a program) to extract additional donations from participants; how to estimate the potential interest in a community that is still to be tapped. Finally, the examples show the element of daring in such innovations. Like other entrepreneurs, these women take chances when they hire a larger hall or invest in salable gimmicks for an event. When they are successful, these efforts to break new ground raise more money; they also attract a wider range of participants. Consequently, new elements of the community become interested in the cultural institution that benefits from the event (see Zolberg 1984 for a discussion of the development of new audiences in the art museum world). The money raised to keep the cultural activity going thus serves more purposes than just keeping it solvent.

In addition to these entrepreneurial skills, the women who take a steady interest in culture often combine organizational skills—in the regular management, fund-raising, and policy setting of boards and auxiliaries—with specific substantive interests. Those with art interests develop special art history and criticism specialties in the development of docent programs (where women serve as volunteer guides and lecturers for visitors to special collections or exhibits). Or they become knowledgeable intermediaries between artists and potential buyers. Such women also serve on museum boards, presiding over or organizing the ad hoc activities that provide necessary funds. They show the mix of substantive interests and abilities to manage the one big event necessary for many volunteer activities. In this way, even the steadiest workers need some of the talents of the "bang and bust" specialists. Their efforts to construct big events show how women organize to raise more money than individual board members can donate themselves. These women turn to the production of events that will attract a public willing to contribute (and to make purchases) on a larger scale than can be managed within their own immediate circle.

> In 1971 my board lent $3,000 to the museum; eventually it became a gift. This year I gave the curator a check for $35,000 as a result of two fund-raisers. One was a giant sale. The project started as a way of clearing the basement to deaccession materials we didn't need. And it was padded out with stuff from our membership and museum boards: painting and bric-a-brac. . . . Antique dealers and decorators came in droves.

The group of women who focus on culture includes those who only manage events to promote art and those with artistic interests themselves. Some of these women begrudge the time to do ad hoc benefits and fund-raising. But they understand the importance of these activities and, at the least, help their organization or find others to do it.

The relation of community supporters to artistic endeavor constrains them to focus on fund-raising rather than on programming and performing issues. Since they do not perform professionally, the women who work for cultural institutions are limited to being members of the audience. The "higher" the culture, the greater the tradition, training, and general mystique associated with the art form—and these aspects separate the judgment of the performers and producers-managers from that of the audience. The community boards of directors and sponsors are limited in the sphere of their authority accordingly. The women with cultural interests have to work within these understandings, focusing on the problems of organizing the community to care about and contribute to the up-keep of the city's cultural institutions. This work is *always* pressing, for these institutions do not receive much tax support nor wide general concern in the public view. Women active in this area need to be well-off financially; contributions are always needed, and they are expected from highly placed participants on boards and fund raising committees. At the very least, women need connections to money. Finally, there is little opportunity for women to use volunteer experience as the main avenue into salaried work. Should they wish to become paid development workers and fund-raisers, their knowledge of the needs of their organizations would only permit them to accept small salaries. The well-off women contribute their work with this understanding of the situation.

Health, Education, and Welfare

The highest proportion of "steadies" with serious, substantive interests as well as organizational and fund-raising responsibilities are found among those who are concentrated in the area of health, education, and welfare. Of the twenty-eight women interviewed from this category, none could really be called a "bang and bust" worker. For, while most have worked at many different volunteer interests during their careers, each woman has developed a specialist's familiarity with at least one discipline, social problem, or community concern, and each continues beyond seasonal or short-term activity. These careers include education and public school improvement, hospital management, childcare and child protection, ecology and conservation.

Here, women of the privileged classes become more integrated into the operation and management of the agencies they work for than is the case for culture. First, the interests are more vulnerable to intervention at all levels of management than are cultural interests; for everyone has an opinion, and, as a citizen, feels qualified to speak. Further, agencies in this area are often subject to the demands of changing community networks. After elections and public pressures following media exposés, new appointments and re-organizations can alter the direction of policy in such areas as education or conservation. Women, as citizens and as members of various networks of influence, can participate in these changes. Second, women initiate some of the developments themselves. In the areas of child protection and environmental conservation, for example, women in this study have created their own organizations to serve as watchdogs over juvenile detention practices, or to protect a forest preserve, and used them to develop or change city policies. Third, interests in these areas require participants to form alliances across class lines and with a variety of people in professions, city administration, business, and local neighborhoods. These requirements force women community leaders out of a limited concern with fund-raising among the wealthy.

Like those with careers in culture, volunteers in this area may find an alliance with the society network a valuable asset. However, these alliances are not absolutely necessary: eight women in this group have no connection, either by birth or marriage, to that network—the largest number in either of the two areas. Instead, the women without society network ties develop political connections (as three have done). They also can develop important ties to the business and philanthropic worlds they come to know through a salaried career (as did another three). But all of these women have developed skills through their work in health, education, or welfare that give them the entry to and working experience with many other leaders from both volunteer and salaried sectors of Pacific City. The experience gained and the contacts made provide these women with their own place in the city leadership even without the advantages of family connections.

Six women (of the 28) have become community leaders on the basis of their combined interests in health, education, and welfare and are among the most widely known leaders in Pacific City from this sample. They have the greatest number of awards, honors, and prestigious appointments; they are also the women most clearly recognized as outstanding by the community at large. All have been named in the local newspapers' annual awards for Pacific City's most important contributors to the general welfare. All have received testimonial banquets and special awards for their service from presidents, governors, and mayors. These women are also most often pointed out by other women in this study as truly outstanding volunteers. In addition, they are also noted by male leaders (in the symphony and opera associations, the two political parties, and on the area's major university boards) who were asked about the most important of their women colleagues. Finally, in contrast to their colleagues with cultural interests whose activities are reported primarily in society, arts, or people's sections of the paper, news of these women also appears in the main news section and in the sections devoted to business and political commentary.

It is difficult to give a sense of these extremely active, diverse, yet systematic careers in overview. However, a close analysis of one career can show how a career line reflects the substantive interests and the skills a woman develops through community service. It also shows how the conservative political outlook of an upper-middle-class woman can lead to ready acceptance and approval by powerful business interests in the community. In this case, the combination of substantive interests, sympathies, and opportunity have led this woman to for-profit corporate directorships in addition to her lifelong volunteer activities. Sydney Harrison is one of the most distinguished women in this study. A former Junior League president, she has also been active in League of Women Voters, held a policy-making position on the board of the Volunteer Bureau, served in various posts within the Community Chest and its later organizational transformations. The earlier positions signaled her successful completion of training in community service and her serious interest in community welfare. The later positions enabled her to specialize in budget, grant allocation, surveys of community services and to advise on where support for these services might be found.

Early in her career Mrs. Harrison helped an older, very powerful volunteer leader develop hospital auxiliaries. Afterward, Mrs. Harrison served as a hospital trustee. These positions showed that she could help create a new service and then use her experience to guide policy for the organization. Her ad hoc or short-term activities include chairing programs for national professional conventions, when her husband or his friends asked her to do so; developing community interest groups for several local colleges and universities; consulting on merger and fund-raising problems for boards of local private schools, where her own or her friends' children had been educated; and serving on library and public broadcast service committees. All of these activities indicated how successfully she could solve problems, organize events, and manage ongoing services in the community. They also showed where her interests and abilities lay and suggested further appointments to city officials and business people in her community. Her long-term interests and track record in welfare and city planning issues led to her appointment on foundation boards (that award research and community service grants), as well as blue-ribbon educational and city commissions (that review federal, state, and local allocation of funds for important public services). At the same time, Mrs. Harrison has shown some shrewdness on matters related to finance and corporate responsibility. The connections she made while serving on boards of philanthropic or government welfare agencies provided the right entry to promote her appointment on several for-profit boards. On these boards, Mrs. Harrison is expected to represent community relations interests; she also serves as liaison between corporate spokesmen and community organizers and leaders in various advocacy groups. She is not questioned in these circles about which part of the community she best represents, but the implicit assumption underlying her appointments to corporate boards is that an undifferentiated or general public will be served by someone with her background and experience. This widely respected woman is also regarded as a "safe" representative by business interests. I was told by other informants that corporate representatives see her philosophy and style as sympathetic to their own. While this view of Mrs. Harrison is what made her a likely candidate for positions where few (or no) women have served previously, it also suggests that she may actually represent a limited rather than a wide spectrum of the public. Yet, even if she serves as a "token" and is regarded suspiciously by some more reformist or radical colleagues, she does have wide experience in the city that is useful to business interests and knows how, when, and why to tap representatives of special interests for advice or assistance on projects in both her business and nonprofit corporation activities.

In this way, highly respected leaders from the volunteer world make bridges between public and private welfare services, special areas or issues requiring service, public and private finance. Their value to the corporate and business worlds is that these women can use their judgment to sift through applicants to find the "worthy" candidates for philanthropic investment. Causes that provide for the welfare of some community but are not too strikingly in opposition to the establishment are desired; women volunteers know how to make judgments about this desired category. They can introduce potential donors to worthy applicants, build a consortium of donors or develop grant applications to systematize philanthropic contributions in a particular area. In a sense, then, the most highly respected community leaders are brokers. They do not deal in for-profit investments or make commissions. But they can assemble philanthropic investment packages by introducing different elements of the community to one another. For example, one distinguished volunteer met with adolescent gang leaders, seeking to improve their local neighborhood. She coordinated meetings with members of the banking establishment who could secure the necessary financing for the project. In managing such connections, women acquire reputation and respect for their brokering ability even without commercial returns. Only a few find some financial return for the broker herself. Mrs. Harrison has bridged the gap between volunteer and paid work; but she is one of only two women in this study to receive large salaries from service on for-profit corporate boards. The anomaly she presents in this respect highlights the nature of the career pattern as separate from salaried opportunities.

The remaining twenty-two women are divided among specific interests. The four women in education have developed careers and skills around the struggle to upgrade public school education and the effort to promote effective integration in their city. In that struggle, these women moved away from the conciliatory patterns characteristic of community leaders such as Mrs. Harrison to become political advocates and critics of the educational establishment. As part of that move, they began to work actively in political campaigns and three eventually ran for office themselves. They resemble, in their determination to change society—even if they have to work against their own class interests—some of the women who work in welfare.

The four women whose main interests lie in welfare worked a great deal with child-related problems: recreation for children, placement of homeless children, protection of runaway and juvenile wards of the court. The women in this category have created special niches for themselves in the city. They have founded organizations (for example to counsel parents or provide new types of services for abandoned children) as well as leading already existing ones. They have developed a service where they saw unmet needs, built an organization around these needs, and then moved on to something else. For example, one woman helped close down outmoded orphanages, built up alternative systems of childcare such as small group homes, and then established new institutions to maintain the system—a city commission to monitor the activities of the new system, for example. She then turned to work on changing systems of child management in the juvenile courts, instituting civil service rather than politically appointed directors.

These women span the spectrum from reformists to strong advocates. In this group, the most (upper-class) woman with the best connections to the social families and political networks in the city is also one of the kindest and best liked by a wide circle of colleagues. She has persuaded powerful interests in the city to support educational reforms in the public schools. The most intransigent advocate in this group has a somewhat less prestigious standing (upper-middle class) and a much narrower following, but she has organized political action groups that force changes (such as firing agency directors and hiring new ones) upon reluctant city officials. While the working tactics of these two women are strikingly different, both are successful. The first promoted educational services that the "social" community as well as the general public supported; the second developed citizen groups to protest scandals in the local management of juveniles and then promoted legislation to safeguard against further mismanagement.

These women in education and welfare share in their determination to change some aspect of society with a specialist in ecology and conservation. This woman had started with larger social concerns in race relations, housing, and general social welfare; she then focused on conservation. Like the citizen advocate in child welfare, she had organized friends and supporters for political action—to defeat a freeway construction, save a forest, and protect wilderness areas. Like the educational reformist she is well connected socially and is admired and respected for her work by a wide array of citizens.

The women described thus far from education, welfare, and ecology present a mixture of interests. Some of these interests can make a few of them seem renegades from their class in their insistence on advocacy and troublemaking for the city fathers. The middle-class women are a bit more intransigent and less concerned with maintaining pleasant relations with more conventional colleagues who support the status quo. Perhaps they feel they have less to support and less to lose in alliance with upper-class interests. The more well connected members of this group have a "softer" approach; they are more conciliatory and less demanding. Their concern with compromise and mediation rather than confrontation and attack—even when they believe very strongly in a cause—may not just be the ladylike resistance to aggressive tactics that their traditional upbringing teaches. It may also stem from a sense that it is in their best interests to gently urge others from their class rather than alienate them.

Four of the women I met were very involved in disseminating information about social and current issues. They worked for the education of their own social circle (through reading clubs and discussion groups) and for more general education as well (the development of school programs and curriculum models explaining current events, principles of international cooperation and law, the language and cultures of other lands). One such effort to mix public and private interests involves a yearly weekend symposium on some serious educational topic. Admission is open to the public (although the cost is steep; in 1979 tickets were priced at about $175 per person) but the social occasions that commemorate the opening and close of the event are private parties. These are the "social" events that receive attention in the newspapers and reinforce the notion that a small group continues to promote its own amusements under the guise of broadening the interests of the community.

Those who work the hardest and gain the most are often the serious amateur scholars who plan the events. These scholars provide a real education for the other women and gain an opportunity to use the experience they already possess as well. As spokespersons and translators of difficult-to-understand social and economic issues, they educate people in their own world. The women also provide these educational opportunities to the city at large. Their public programs and the forums reported in newspapers and on television allow them to be mediators between city provincialism and larger world affairs.

These women resemble the women who focus on cultural activity more than many involved with health, education, and welfare in that a primary focus is on benefits to their class. They also confront some of the same problems facing amateurs among professionals in the worlds of culture. Women interested in information about the larger world do not see themselves as dilettantes. They are supported by the admiration of those in their circle, and they are validated by a larger public when they are asked to appear in public forums or are interviewed by the media, but amateur status makes their position somewhat ambiguous. A major avenue for validation would be the transition to paid work, but only one of these women has made this transition as a writer and a journalist.

The largest cluster (9) in the category of special interests forms around health issues. The health of a community is a traditional concern for volunteers and an elaborate, institutionalized pattern of volunteering has developed around hospitals, clinics, Red Cross services, blood banks, and community programs of education and fund-raising for these and for special health areas (alcoholism, mental health, planned parenthood, muscular dystrophy, cerebral palsy, and a host of special diseases or health-related problems, afflicting some members of the citizenry).

Women from families of wealth and social position were most

likely to rise quickly through the ranks of hospital service, as pink ladies and members of auxiliaries. They are sponsored by family and friends and need remain only a token period in minor or drudgery positions before they are promoted to more interesting and prestigious tasks. Soon they become chairs of important committees and attain membership on the more prestigious boards. Some hospital boards, as Joan Moore (1961) has noted, were formerly composed exclusively of such women. Many women in this study were like those Moore described: they were members of prestigious hospital boards and known for their society connections as well as their community spirit and the industry required in serious enterprises.

Separation of the serious workers from those participating because their friends or their families did is not easy. Many volunteer leaders come to their work, as their career paths indicate, through a mixture of interests and obedience to duty. Acquiescence to the requirements of class and family expectations can dictate volunteer as well as family responsibilities. The element of obedience in performance of duties notwithstanding, some of the most committed workers focus on health interests, rising to executive positions on boards and minimizing "social" projects in cultural areas.

For some, hospital service is the main activity in their volunteer lives (two in this category have been president of their board). Two other hospital board presidents have additional health interests—one in health care planning and another in outreach programs for the disabled. The former combined hospital board activity with regional health care planning. The latter combined a family tradition of board service with a continuing interest in the problems of mentally retarded children.

Three more health-centered volunteers have each made lifetime commitments to one community health agency (and two of these combined volunteer interests with long and prosperous full-time salaried careers). In each case, they have worked on one specific health problem, taking every position necessary (administrative, public relations, fund-raising) in the process.

The one woman in this category who never held a salaried job spent a lifetime working for one agency. She rose through the local chapters to a prominent position regionally and nationally. After about thirty years, she retired—but only when her husband asked her to on the event of his own retirement. Then she turned to less strenuous and more varied volunteer work outside the health field.

The careers of the women with health interests presented thus far all show a disinterested concern for what was discussed earlier as noblesse oblige. This motivation also includes concern for maintaining the class and family interests that were involved in the founding of many of the institutions these women support (hospitals, old folks' homes, clinics). These careers generally involve no plan for an eventual move into salaried work in the health care field, although a few women have had professional training in that area earlier in their lives. However, the careers involve the satisfactions associated with having recognized power in the community. The knowledge that one is in the thick of a field recognized as important by the general public—and where one has both influence and some explicit power—contributes to the motivation for a high standard in work performance. In contrast to those working in cultural areas, women in health, education, and welfare can feel they escape the pejorative overtones of socialite frivolity and point to their volunteer contribution as "serious" work. Women in the health care area often have the added legitimation of large operating budgets, technical and professional personnel, and building projects for which they take responsibility. The last two women in the health field have had distinguished careers in both hospital and community health center service. Both are now interested in some form of part-time salaried career in addition to volunteer work. Their volunteer experience and recently acquired educational credentials already open the doors to paid short-term consulting. They reflect a growing change: even among women who once accepted the idea that women should not take salaried employment unless they need it, many now want to be paid for this work.

This desire is seen in the interest many women of her class focus on Mrs. Harrison, the corporate board director. She receives many calls from friends, acquaintances, and even strangers who are active in the volunteer world but interested in the transition from nonprofit to business corporation directorships. However, most volunteer work in health, education, and welfare areas does not lead to work commensurate in pay and status to the positions these women hold as board members. Four or five women from this study have moved into well-paying positions as consultants, city agency directors, or directors of philanthropic organizations; but, like Mrs. Harrison, they are unusual. The high-level positions of volunteer leaders are not easily exchanged for executive salaried positions.

Whether or not they wish to make that transition, these women work in a professional manner. Their careers require responsible and regular attendance at meetings, regular contacts with others in the community—volunteers, establishment members in business and corporate structures, political leaders, community agency executives, consumer group representatives, specialists in financial and social problems research (such as alcoholism, mental health, childcare, transportation, open space preservation). In this work, women acquire expertise and specialized knowledge, even without formal credentials. This knowledge develops incrementally through long experience. Women with a "bang and bust" style cannot work here. There is too much persistent, steady effort required and too much regular patrolling, too much need of a reputation for ready accessibility for any who prefer to do a stupendously big job and then lie dormant.

Mixed Careers in Culture, Health-Education-Welfare, and Politics

Causes, like conservation or child welfare, do require women to participate in political campaigns involving both steady and crisis work. They are joined by women active in political parties in their ability to meet a steady stream of obligations and also to work night and day on a short-term effort. And they are joined by those with a mixture of interests that includes both culture and health, education, and welfare.

Some women are so skilled at organizing programs, benefits, and membership drives that they are called upon for these services in promoting a wide spectrum of causes. They may offer no service to their health-education-welfare or cultural organizations except organizing the big party or other one-time event. Others with careers that span a variety of causes become known as organizational generalists: they advise others on how to promote *their* causes.

Alternatively, one might regard some of these women as specialists; for they are known throughout the community for their skills at public relations, party throwing, and event organizing. Consequently, many careers resist classification by areas of interest. Of the twenty-eight women in this category, serious interests (in several areas) dominate the concerns of fifteen women and the other thirteen are a mix of so many interests they are hard to assign within any one area. They have sufficient family, position, influence, or wealth to suggest that their privileged position in the community enhances their volunteer status. Their connections to wealthy and powerful families in Pacific City provide the entry to support for charities and assistance in producing benefits. Further, their connections provide the opportunities to serve on a variety of prestigious boards and to become known to celebrities, business people, and political figures important in the network of philanthropy. Their wide range of leadership activities may not develop primarily from their own commitments, then, but from their family connections.

Politics

If we look at the fifteen women whose careers are some mixture of stable, incremental interests (see table 4.1), we find a group of five who have developed political skills and a reputation in the Democratic party. This group is somewhat anomalous in a community of mainly Republican women where many express a strong distaste for politics, and at least five others often cross party lines to work for family or friends. The five who have important political careers have risen to local, regional, and national appointments—one sits on an important city commission and three have run for office. Others in this study hold such commissions and even elective office from time to time, but these five engage in party politics in an organized and consistent manner just as other politicians do. They differ from male politicians in their manner of entry and in their length of service prior to recognition. They are women from volunteer organizations like the PTA and the League of Women Voters and, with a much longer apprenticeship than men, they serve as precinct workers and fund-raisers. They have more experience as campaign managers before their leadership capacities are recognized as equal to that of men in the party. These women also differ from many serious politicians in that they continue a large commitment to other philanthropic interests at least as important as their political careers. Three of these five women are Jewish, and they are active in Jewish welfare organizations. (All the Jewish women in this study state that whatever their major interests, some appreciable time is allotted to fund-raising, organizing, or developing educational programs in Jewish welfare.)

The final category of women with long-term volunteer interests contains those who systematically and regularly bridge the gap between culture and health, education, and welfare with one or two specialties for each (see table 4.1). They learn enough in each area to work as liaisons for their interest in the community, moving through community reform groups, state and federal agencies, and high society. They are widely consulted for organization development, fund-raising, and program planning.

The Mixture of Talents Found in "Bang and Bust" Specialists

The remaining thirteen women in the group of seventy are the most comfortable with the traditional priorities assigned to women of the upper classes. These women also most closely fit the stereotypes of the Lady Bountiful and the society lady with dilettantish and narcissistic concerns. But even though they come closest to fitting such descriptions, they cannot be dismissed as no more than social butterflies. At the very least, they are iron butterflies; for the work of party giving can be demanding, and creativity and imagination are required to plan new themes, novel decorations, and fresh gimmicks that combine fund-raising with fun.

These women stress their good fortune in coming from wealthy or well-established families (9) or in having married wealthy or powerful men who provided entry to philanthropic and social circles (4) more so than the wealthy women with long-term interests. They do not see themselves as deprived of an independent, salaried career. All of these women explain how they have used these resources to work cheerfully, if sporadically, at good works in the city by underwriting charities and lending their names to good causes. Generally, they accepted their place in a philanthropic network rather than developing their own interest areas as many in the health, education, and welfare arenas have done. Five stepped into the tasks assigned by their parents or followed in their mother's footsteps. This pattern required some serious service on prestigious hospital boards and attending to management, but it also included planning the parties and benefits that are part of that board membership responsibility. Several of these women have also been active in children's dance theatre (a "social" group organized to perform dance programs for school children, offer lessons, and encourage the talented through scholarships for the needy) and in the opera-symphony-ballet- museum fund-raising parties and balls. It is not, however, the serious or substantive side of these activities they remember best. Their liveliest reminiscences were of events such as the following.

One woman took charge of decorating the Armory (in a hectic two-month period) for a carnival. In the process, she faced some of the problems that professional curators and exhibitors face. Another remembered the marvelous parties for the opera and animatedly recalled dragging two horses into one of the poshest hotels as part of a masquerade-benefit for a hospital. Still another recalled her own starring roles as a performer at charity balls.

But the real problems of logistics and training—the ability to maintain a dedicated cadre of co-workers and to sustain the sense of camaraderie and gaiety which spur everyone on to work day and night for weeks on end—should not be ignored. As one women put it:

> You've got to use all of your ingenuity. And you use every contact you have. I am known around town as one who never pays for anything. I enjoy [the challenge]. I call on all my friends with experience in certain areas—for example catering. I put a committee together and they are all super human beings [and work very hard]. . . . When I gave a luncheon for all my workers afterwards, there was much of the good feeling we had, working so furiously to get it done—everyone talking and laughing. Remember, it was an enormous amount of work to do in a very short time.

Here is how another woman described the complexity of producing a "fun" society affair.

> The Annual Muscular Dystrophy Extravaganza . . . was eight hours a day for seven-day weeks for a year. First you have to spend a month wheedling money out of Maison Suisse. Fortunately Maison thinks our organization is so classy they are willing to pay for the privilege of having the extravaganza use its costumes . . . and then you have to wheedle money from [the jewelers] who do the jewel sequences. Then you have to sell $30,000 worth of ads for the program. Then there are tryouts to select the cast . . . and then you have . . . to have a script theme.
>
> [Mine] was The Sheik of Araby. And the program was held in a tent. . . . We had to wheedle money out of the hotel which was new at the time. I went in my horn-rimmed glasses and very severely dressed, carrying a briefcase. And I'd take Marcy Grant with me—a tall gorgeous blonde—to look pretty. And the . . . publicity persons would come with the past extravaganza scrapbook to show the hotel manager how much publicity he would get if he would do this.
>
> Then . . . there were decorations for the table . . . an international outfit was wheedled to give us more money. For the Israeli sequences you would want some vaguely

Middle-Eastern music. The dancers and singers and actors all have to take special training.

The show is sold out months in advance and there are hundreds on the waiting list. . . . For fifty extra bucks you can have a table close to the stage . . . there are program committees for music and costume, prompters and starters. We used walkie-talkies to keep in touch with backstage. Then there was the problem of music and sound effects.

These reminiscences show how women construct ambience and understand the importance of its creation in developing group purpose. First, working together and coming together to achieve a goal engages the attention and allegiance of participants, making them feel part of a common enterprise. These feelings are reinforced in a sociable context. Through the parties, the luncheons, and the teas that workers share, organizers show their appreciation for such building blocks as food and drink in the construction of sociability. As Douglas and Isherwood (1978:72) remark, "Food or drink . . . are no less carriers of meaning than ballet or poetry." The sociability created when sharing food or drink is part of the desired atmosphere that develops and ensures a willing and even dedicated staff. This outcome is an especially important consideration for volunteer workers. Further, the atmosphere of entertainment that can create a general party spirit has to be constructed by the women who perform as hostesses in producing charitable events.

In philanthropic work, a sociable context has to be created in order to kindle commitment to projects in others. Yet successfully manipulating hospitality to further some end, even an altruistic cause, creates problems where such gestures should focus on the conviviality produced. As Simmel points out (1950:44), the pure process of sociation is a cherished value. Sociation to some serious end (obtaining the necessities of life through cooperative activity, for example) is a serious business; incompetence and mistakes can have serious consequences. But the forms of sociation, freed of this significance, can be enjoyed in playful activity. This activity, playful flirtation instead of courtship in earnest, for example, creates a sense of freedom and gaiety that is possible because the activity is not expected to have serious consequences. The exhilaration created by this freedom and the sense of shared intimacy that conviviality creates can be enjoyed by themselves alone. Any conscious design for utilitarian ends might destroy the ambience that has been created. Where play becomes part of serious activity, it is no longer an opportunity for creativity and disinterested sociable interaction (Huizinga 1950:199).

For play to remain interesting, however, it has to have some connections to the serious parts of life. The socialites who attend benefits find the cause a rationale for attending and partying. The significance of the cause as well as their own importance are asserted by the flocks of lesser lights who also come. An implicit understanding in the production of events is that a wider audience comes to view the social figures as well as to support the cause.

For the workers, the convivial aspects of their work are justified by the sense of mission. They remember the excitement and even the near hysteria of working together to meet a deadline as important and meaningful events in their lives. In those moments, women find a heightened sense of being needed and of belonging and participating in an important activity that their ordinary private life, no matter how luxurious, may not provide.

Women who create the ambience of sociability in the service of a cause thus require a special skill: the ability to create the sense of freedom that sociability provides while exploiting the situation to ensnare the workers and the donors required. The stereotypes about women's aptitudes and traditional skills obscure and mystify the process by which women develop and use these skills. Nowhere is this mystification more evident than in the manufacture of hospitality to promote sociability and commitment. The work is valued but yet it is regarded as basically silly work. If it is important, why do we regard the work as so vulnerable to ridicule? Even the women committed to the work reflect this ambivalence when they speak apologetically or defensively of their own efforts to promote sociability to produce services needed by the community.

It is important to underscore the significance of the work that goes into this combination of celebration and philanthropy. These celebrations require the hard work that creates the context in which a sense of communal solidarity can flourish. The workers who become successful producers have skills and techniques developed through practice and experience. But often these skills are hidden from public view by stereotypic notions of work and leisure. They are also hidden by the notion of the product as communal. Individual effort cannot then be spotlighted and credited. Ironically, the skills that produce success are also hidden from the view of the practitioners themselves. They see their activities as idiosyncratic, "natural" responses to the diffuse requirements of sociability. Or they convince themselves that the most important aspect of the effort was that they, as well as other participants, had a good time. The work of creating good works through good times, then, is most often invisible work that is invisible to the workers as well (Daniels 1985).

While the real contributions of these efforts in building economic support for various charities by raising sums up to hundreds of thousands of dollars should not be minimized, the work does not lead to the same respect and position in the community as does long-term work in health, education and welfare. Only one woman in this group of thirteen with sporadic interests has risen to the same rank and holds the same stature in the larger community as the others.

Distance and Alliance between Interests

In consequence of the ambivalence toward the promotion of big events as a serious, legitimate endeavor, many who possess the skills to give benefits—and see the necessity for them—nonetheless shy away from too close an identification with these specialists in the one-time event. The women in health, education, and welfare areas are most likely to keep their distance from these specialists and their preferred activities. For example, none of the women in culture, compared to eleven of the women in some area of health, education, and welfare, made distancing remarks in the course of the interview. One of the most distinguished women in this sample, for example, was asked to join the exclusive Children's Dance Theatre Group because of her earlier interest in and talent for dancing. She declined, though many of her friends were members. When speaking of this event, some years later, she explained that her more serious interests took her in a different direction. Perhaps it is difficult for the women who come from this social group, despite their commitment to accomplishment, to escape an uncomfortable awareness of the stereotype of the socialite and its undertones of frivolity and greater interest in the event than the cause for which it is given. Another of the acknowledged community leaders in the community made it clear that she wished to disassociate herself from this world. "Society life bores me to extinction. I can't stand [the parties]. I would rather be working out organizational problems."

The desire to disassociate themselves from those activities associated with traditional female behavior often leads women to overlook the significance of what is accomplished through sociability. Stall (1982:14) reports that the small-town women she studied downplayed the consequences of their community contributions. Although the woman's club had succeeded in electing one of their members to the school board (the only woman elected in the last few decades), the current president saw the club program as primarily social. "As far as being a vital part of the community, I really don't think [the club] has to do with it. With many of the women . . . though in many of the programs they'll learn something, they go for the sociability of it."

Despite the mixed feelings about the commitment of their colleagues, the women civic leaders in this study know the aims of volunteer work are advanced through the efforts of women who must be motivated. And these leaders also see the importance of the women who can motivate the rank-and-file workers, as well as the organizers.

Some of the most serious volunteer leaders recognize the importance of parties, sociability, and opportunity for acceptance or recognition in the lives of women less directed and ambitious than the leaders themselves.

> I generally attend every [social event] they give. A little lady said it better than anything I could say. I said [this organization] was more than tea and cookies. And she called me on the phone afterward to say, "Don't forget that tea and cookies are also very necessary." I have come to realize that social functions are just as important [as other aspects of volunteer work].

The significance of tea and cookies is reaffirmed in estimations of their importance in fund-raising. The formation of the esprit that makes a volunteer organization work is also vital in the development of fund drives. But the negative feelings about the women who drink the tea is reflected in the following observation (Toffler 1965:81). "A staff member of the Louisville Symphony Orchestra complained about the affairs of the symphony after the tea party-DAR set had let things deteriorate there." The trivialization of women's activity is also seen in the praise of what they now accomplish, compared to what they used to do. The California State Superintendent of Education, for example, is quoted as praising the PTA for how far it has advanced. "The day is long past when the PTA can be considered an organization of cookie pushers" (cited in Cohen 1979:402).

Yet, in reviewing ingenious methods of raising money, Colonel Samuel Rosenbaum, a member of the Board of the Philadelphia Orchestra is quoted as saying: "Give me six women, a bag of cookies and a box of tea, and you will have a symphony orchestra" (Toffler, 1965:163). A hospital administrator quoted in Stall (1982:17) shows a cautious respect for both the money-raising abilities and the power of women engaged in characteristically feminine activities to promote community welfare.

> We have a Guild at the hospital. You know, a bunch of little old ladies who started out selling jams and jellies for the hospital. But they're a very important, very influential way to deal with the community. . . . They can do anything. . . . [They raised public support to keep the hospital open.]

The comments quoted above imply a mixture of respect for a product and amazement at the trivial means which can produce it. The notion of what is trivial, of course, comes from a system of priorities developed in the cash-nexus economy. Those priorities reflect the experience of men and of public life, primarily. Yet both men and women find the value system persuasive. It thus becomes difficult for anyone to accept women's worlds as equally serious or important in comparison. The women who want to stress their "serious" interests are aware of the ambivalence in the male world toward women volunteers and toward such manifestations of the female world as tea and cookies, jams and jellies. They are also sensitive to the implicit condescension—even in the praise for their strategies to create esprit. At the same time, they do have sympathies with, and alliances in, the female world that keep them sensitive to the importance of activities in promoting sociability and parties that feature female interests (like tea drinking) or crafts (like jam and jelly making) to aid social and cultural projects. Consequently, these women present various strategies for reconciling a wish to be taken seriously and an enjoyment of their own skills in managing social events combined with an enjoyment of the events themselves. Some of the women discussed thus far are more ambivalent than others and try to separate themselves as much as possible from idle sociability. But the women who specialize in the creation of benefits and charitable events—the women of the museum shows and extravaganzas, for example—are clearly more willing to enjoy, and work hard at, these affairs without reservation. For traditional women, who accept their privileged position and seek useful occupation within its terms, careers are built upon the special interests, talents, and time requirements formed around conventional family expectations.

Some women with conventional life-styles focus their volunteer interests so intensely that they transcend the usual expectations that their work will be an avocation or a part-time occupation. Much of this all-absorbing work revolves around the problems of fund-raising, a topic to which we will turn in the next chapter.

Becoming a Specialist

5

The Specialist in Fund-raising

Women develop specialties as they recognize some of the functions that must be performed and that apply to any pattern of work. As in other forms of complex work, there are parts that one prefers and becomes more skilled at than others. Even with work such as domestic labor—commonly considered as unskilled and offering few choices to the worker—employers find that workers like to specialize. Consequently, housekeepers or other domestic workers may be excellent seamstresses, or launderers, or cooks, or caretakers of children or shut-ins, but may hurry quickly over the other aspects of their job. Lopata (1971) points out that housewives organize their occupation around three major axes: housework; child-care; husband's companion. Women can expand any one of these areas to the relative neglect of the other two.

Areas for specialization can develop wherever initiative and judgment are required in performing a variety of tasks. In areas where workers earn little and their efforts do not garner much social respect (such as domestic work), these specialties go unnoticed. Similarly, with unsalaried work (housework, volunteer work) the development of special skills is not validated by systematic, formal recognition.

Yet, women who work as volunteers—and others in the community who use their skills—recognize that certain special talents are valuable. One of the most valuable is fund-raising, and in volunteer work it is an important area for specialization. Women who know their city learn how to collect from it so they can redistribute some of the wealth. They know how to skim the cream from affluent citizens (collect big contributions) and how to glean or scavenge (find small donors; develop new pools of potential donors). They know how to find special publics—those who will donate to some causes but not others. Their successes indicate that they have found a great array of possible donors. But success has another meaning; it is an important indicator of skill at knitting communities within the city together. These women can identify the potentially interested, draw them in, and then act as liaisons for individuals or groups that could work together on an issue. Through this process these women may create new publics or interest groups.

Fund-raising is now an acknowledged specialty in the salaried world and sometimes draws high salaries for its practitioners. National charity drives, the departments of development in private universities and colleges, private nonprofit hospitals all employ such specialists.[1] This work requires both experience and natural aptitude, although many women in the volunteer world have to overcome their distaste to become skillful in what is after all, and even at its most genteel, a form of hustling. The volunteer enterprise, however, requires fund-raising, so there is no way to avoid it completely. Since it is for a worthwhile cause, those who find the work uncomfortable grit their teeth, smile bravely, and learn to do it. Among the women I studied, all but two said they were experienced in some form of fund-raising.

Fortunately the field is extremely varied, so one can pick and choose among types of fund-raising. A woman can make door-to-door solicitations or personal requests to friends. She can give some part-time assistance in a gift shop or she can stage an enormous affair that takes weeks or even months to produce. Since these women are the leaders among fund-raisers, they spend more time organizing big events, dreaming up new fund-raising schemes, and consulting on how to raise money than they do on minor tasks. But many start with menial, repetitive, or tiresome jobs (phoning, writing, or walking door-to-door for solicitations) and rise to leadership positions. They first show their ability, energy, and responsibility in what one woman called the "grubbies" of volunteering.

1. See Galaskiewicz (1985:42–44) for the importance of the federated drive. For the history of fund-raising in America and the place of women in it see Blair 1980:13; Brumberg 1980:5–8; Stall 1982:11; Rosen 1977; Lubove 1965:53; Steinfels 1980:334; Sills 1957:157–59; Warner et al. 1963:141; Glanz 1976:125–30. For a discussion of fund-raising efforts abroad, see Smith (1981) on France; Stott (1978) on England.

The following analysis of fund-raising patterns, satisfactions, and problems comes both from interviews and participant observation. Building upon what I learned to learn more, I have worked in a few fund-raisers myself. I have attended expensive functions, have helped organize symposia and luncheon panels on the subject of volunteering, and have advised on fund-raiser "themes." I have helped construct lists of potential donors and useful contacts in the private foundation world, and I have also acted as a board member.

The major categories of work in this area, whatever the specific cause, are one-time events, regular or annual events, revenue-producing businesses, personal solicitations, and research grants or service awards from private or governmental agencies. Any or all of these fund-raising efforts can be supplemented by mailings (appeals for contributions through letters) and other forms of public relations (a separate specialty discussed later). Any of these can be accompanied by some combination of others, and any of them can be undertaken for the receipt of large sums (several million) or small (several hundred dollars).

Fund-raising Patterns

The One-Time Event or Production Number

Most single or one-shot affairs are based on principles that are also workable in regular events. In fact, extremely successful events are often institutionalized as annual affairs. Other events are spin-offs of the already successful: a regular fashion show for one charity may in time spawn several special shows for a variety of other charities. Or it may be that the type of event, over time, comes to be expected as appropriate for certain fund drives: the political campaign dinner, picnic, lunch, coffee, cocktail party, or breakfast are examples. Throughout the country, understandings have developed about the kinds of events that members of specific communities will want to attend, how glamorous society implications may be attached to an event so more people will be willing to spend money to attend, what events will draw small or large crowds, and what strategies can be employed to sell tickets. The success of the event is gauged by the amount it makes. Evaluations of successful events in each of these categories show that interests and sentiments of community members have been tapped—that segments of the community will turn out (or fork out) for a specific kind of activity. These one-time events often become regular or annual affairs as well: the big productions entailed by dinners and luncheons; fashion shows; "theme" balls and parties; house tours; raffles-bazaars; auctions and cake sales occur in this city as they do elsewhere. All of these events are, by now, institutionalized "gimmicks" with an established reputation for popularity and attractiveness. They are products of the activities characteristic of women's worlds. It is women—of any class—who generally take responsibility for gender-related products: entertainments and cakes; clothes; homes and their furnishings.

In the previous chapter, the complexity of assembling a production number is suggested in the description of the rigors of successful partygiving. The woman arranging the Sheik of Araby extravaganza learned skills of theatrical production. The illustration suggests how many skills, how much discipline, planning, training, and coordination are required to produce an apparently frivolous event. Any fund-raising involving a theatrical or staged event, especially one coordinating volunteer and professional performers, will have similar requirements. The elaborate fashion show, "theme" ball, or party are in this category. Like the production of sociability, these events require the submersion of the effort in an apparently effortless happening. The producers are successful when they arrange things so that participants and the audience come together in what appears to be a recreational rather than a serious event.

A basic requirement to create this effect is community contacts. Ties to small and large businesses (willing to supply decor, refreshment, service, space at little or no cost) are essential and are discussed under the topic of solicitation. But even without soliciting favors or donations, it is important to know what suppliers are best, most conveniently located, and most reliable.

The constant need for innovation also demands a flair for originality or a knowledge of where to get it. Within the boundaries of what a party, show, dance, or carnival can contain, new ideas for things to eat and how to serve them, exotic arrangements in decor, the latest new successful entertainer or social lion must be involved. The woman who can ring another change on limited variations and still make money is undoubtedly creative and certainly a skillful manager. She is also a woman who knows her community: the range of businesses and suppliers who can help her; the array of talent, themes, and interests that will draw the appropriate public to her cause. One woman describes another who had these talents: "Carmen is talented at organizing events—arranging the right service. Basically, she can jew [sic] everybody down so that they could kill her at the end of it, but she gets the best prices. And she has bright ideas. She managed the best flower ball ever and the best talent show." An entrepreneur-administrator with ties to many networks can do much, yet women in this category acknowledge the stereotypic (and somewhat pejorative or condescending) perceptions of such efforts others may have. "You might think that's just a fluff," as one woman said, captures the spirit in which women resignedly or defiantly construct great production numbers. They know quite well how others may view them, but they also know these efforts will tap otherwise inaccessible segments of the community and persuade them to serve or to give. The treasure hunt, raffle, bazaar and auction are all similar to the big dinner, theme ball, or fashion show in that these events require preplanning, coordination of persons and skills, as well as ties to socialites who will lend "cachet" to the affair.

Several women in this study (10) spoke of their elation at meeting this challenge, as in this description of an important charity raffle.

> The group works six weeks . . . to distribute and sell tickets. . . . We'd be on the streets . . . sometimes till 10:00 P.M. in groups of people. And we had booths downtown and sellers . . . they would get commissions on the books . . . and we would gather up the money in paper bags and walk down the street with it. . . . I remember once when Harry called me up and said he was at the Greyhound bus station at five o'clock in the morning and . . . would I come down and get the money. I got right up and went down there and took an enormous amount of money off to put in the bank. . . .

> I went to [an outlying fishing town] and contacted people [I had known from my husband's army days] and asked a man who drove a beer truck to distribute tickets. He said he didn't know how many he could get to the other drivers but he would get them to the bartenders. And then he won first prize [$10,000]. When I called him, he fainted. The telephone operator was still on the line and she said she would take care of it and get back to me. He really needed the money . . . and after he paid off his bills he bought a fishbar on the waterfront. Next year he sold an unbelievable amount of tickets. Those were the things that were . . . exciting.

The raffle was exciting not just because of the crisis involved in having to raise large sums, but also for the success in reaching people across the barriers of class and life style to tap new sources of donations. This success might also be seen as an example of the ability to find and use resources in the community for philanthropic purposes. Getting the big donations is both an opportunity and a challenge. "I raised more money than ever in a one-shot deal [for the museum]. I ran the first treasure hunt. Things were given to us. Mr. Giddings gave us the entire contents of an apartment and that was to support a Giddings room event."

Local charities become the vehicle for members of a social set to shop for quality items. The possibility of a return for good works is one way to inspire the workers as well as the public. The following suggests some of the ethics of this mix of fund-raising and personal acquisition.

> Many weeks the work is more than forty hours . . . as in times of buildup for the treasure market. . . . We have a thing about we do not buy ahead of time. And there have been things I was dying to have. So I would take the job of opening night so I could honestly say I could buy at . . . the sale.

The events in the preceding quotations were each part of larger fund-raising packages for museums, combining these and other activities as well. This is a common pattern in the art world where a museum auxiliary will plan annual affairs and previews of exhibits. The auxiliary will also organize house tours, ongoing businesses, and "gimmick" benefits (as when architectural displays of complex and original design made of pastry and candy, feathers or fabric, are presented to the public for an admission fee and then auctioned off at the end of the show).

Women can take pride in their success at organizing diverse talents, people, and resources in these efforts. But no matter how huge the effort, most events are tied either to support of culture or to medical charities with "social" auxiliaries or boards. Boards and auxiliaries for culture carry a heavy overlay of society interests. They attract those who will use the arts as an arena for recreation, consumption, and interactions that maintain and reinforce class position. The culture arena is a suitable one for this activity for many reasons: the historical association of aristocratic patronage and culture suggests that this activity is an appropriate one for an elite; the noncontroversial or nonpolitical nature of many cultural events suggests that they are a "safe" concern for those who wish to be public benefactors; the general belief that cultural activities are enriching for any who participate suggests that this undertaking is a useful public service.[2]

Society page editors often comment ironically on the consequences of the linkage between cultural and upper-class activities.

> The rituals of society continued, but they seemed empty . . . each year there was less glitter at the opera opening than the year before. Even more devastating was the fact that more and more people were going to the opera . . . to hear [it]. If you couldn't talk with friends during *Aida*, what was the point of going to the opera in the first place?
> (Moffat 1977 : 253)

These comments take account of the use of culture for an arena of interaction among the upper classes, but they ignore the fact that opening night festivities help produce the funds to support the rest of the season for everyone else as well. The comments also ignore the great efforts involved in producing such charitable events as the pre- and postopening night parties that support culture. Further, they ignore the skills displayed in the big events described so far to serve opera, symphony, ballet, museums—or the causes supported by social auxiliaries in hospitals and other health-related activities, childcare, old-age homes, and historical preservation societies.

The ironic commentaries, however, do touch upon the self-aggrandizing aspects of the great or glamorous benefit. Fund-raisers capitalize on these self-interested motives to be charitable in this area just as they do in their art and museum shops. In addition to the opportunity to buy and donate merchandise that shops or bazaars provide, participants may rub shoulders with the wealthy and well connected at some benefits.

A fund-raiser may package a ball or banquet to suggest that subscribers might extend their own social life by attendance. They might, for example, meet—or at least glimpse—socialites and local or national celebrities. Serious fund-raisers, as in the foregoing, learn to capitalize upon the foibles (or interests) of those who will only be philanthropic if they can see the homes of—or rub shoulders with—an elite group.[3]

2. In the United States and Great Britain, corporate philanthropy is heavily weighted toward donations to the arts (Useem 1984:118–25; see also Galaskiewicz 1985:39–40). Corporate directors see giving to culture (particularly in the prestigious arts) as being good for the company image.

3. An interest in this strategy comes naturally to liberal-minded civic leaders who may see it as a painless way to redistribute money, with a benefit to everyone con-

Not all social occasions are "social," however. Like any generalization, there are some exceptions to the categorization of the big bash, the auction, or other fund-raising "event" as a vehicle for social partying and camaraderie as well as good works. Many political dinners and parties, activities for the public schools, and church-related events succeed—and may even be attended or sponsored by a few social luminaries—without much social "cachet" attached to them. These events tap the political and business communities of a city where members may have commercial or political interests to further or protect through these social contacts. The political events may tap business, corporate, and labor leaders for heavy contributions (dinners for $100 to $1,000 a plate) or raise small sums locally for a local candidate or a national fund drive (as the Dollars for Democrats in the 1952 Stevenson campaign).

All of these fund-raising activities, whether single or recurring events, require the engineering, mobilization, and plan of attack necessary for a small-scale war—or a major theatrical opening. In addition to preliminary negotiations with businesses, service people, publicity people, sponsors and helpers, these events mobilize energies, call forth entrepreneurial and creative skills, test the mettle of women under pressure to meet deadlines, solve last minute crises, and make large sums of money. Sills identifies some of the community fervor these activities can generate in his descriptions of raising funds to fight polio (1957:156–65). He shows the "gleeful pride" of both men and women in their efforts to give the war on polio a Mardi Gras character. They thought up new gimmicks for catching donations, such as wheelbarrow collections, a Robin Hood Campaign where the sheriff "held up" passing motorists for donations, and mothers' marches at night and noonday. Not all fund-raising, however, requires this warlike or "show must go on" spirit.

The Business

The worlds of women provide the staff to operate a variety of business establishments where all profits benefit a charity. The most common enterprises are the hospital gift shop, coffee shop, and baby photo service; the museum gift shop and rental gallery; and

cerned. Redistribution via fun rather than through imposed taxes can also be a mechanism for providing resources to those who need them without questioning the existing distribution of wealth. I am indebted to Rachel Kahn-Hut for this observation.

the thrift shop for the resale of used clothing. Initiated to provide a steady additional revenue for ongoing institutions or charities, these businesses require abilities found in the salaried world: managerial acumen, buyers' abilities, reliable staffing for sales and service, annual inventories, and budget analysis. When the goods to be sold include contributions, the organizing, collecting, and wheedling abilities of the women finding merchandise or services for their businesses are also required. Some community leaders who organize hospital auxiliary gift shops, for example, run cottage industries on the side where women take piece work sewing and other handicrafts on consignment for the shop. And thrift shops (or turnabout, next-to-new, and second-act shops as they are often called) require collectors, sorters, repairers and pricers of apparel in addition to sales clerks and general managers.

The value of these enterprises as revenue producers is well-known and some national organizations suggest them routinely, wherever a local chapter develops. In 1981, for example, the association of Junior Leagues raised 18.1 million dollars for their projects; almost half that sum (7.1 million) came from thrift shops and the sale of cookbooks. The remainder came from short-term events such as holiday bazaars (where cottage industry finds an outlet) as well as fund-raisers like cultural events and fashion shows (AJL Newsline 1984). The Association of Junior Leagues also spends time on public affairs activities, but the streams of money pour in from the merchandising and celebratory activities. Making this money requires faithful attendance, some sacrifices, and administrative ability.

Women in this study show the executive and entrepreneurial ability to assemble a string of projects like the women cited above. About eighteen have a strong interest in business management activities, and some of these women are also found in the ranks of the larger group (46) who have successful records staging fund-raising events. But there are others who prefer putting together the activities or people to create the funds required for some philanthropic cause. These people are negotiators, planners, liaisons who can assemble a big package.

The Big Package

Master planners and organizers for fund-raising are found among the oldest, most experienced, and most knowledgeable of the civic leaders. About twelve women in this study work in this area. They know how to collect a variety of resources to get things done. Some of their activities resemble those of women coordinating, bargaining, coaxing, begging, and recruiting to collect the paraphernalia for the big event.

> I [received a prestigious appointment] to a women's prison board. . . . I got up a sponsor group which [an important male community leader interested in prisoner rehabilitation] had tried [to do] for years and we got some money so we could do something. I went to [the director] of [an important local] foundation. I told him those girls come out with $30 and a prison wardrobe. I got the Salvation Army to give them a month's free room and board while they were looking for a job and I [asked the director] if we could get the money to loan them. He took it up with his board. They'd give one or two thousand and more. The Soroptimists [a women's service organization] . . . they took over this program. A wonderful woman invited people on parole for a weekend at her ranch.

The organizing involved in getting such a package together not only requires coaxing and wheedling, it requires a vision of what the community can do, how a service can be constructed, and the ability to communicate such ideas to others. The appeal or the strength of this vision then inspires the potential donor to donate. The good fund-raiser thus develops a new possibility. She extracts funds from the uncommitted by developing interests donors didn't have previously. In this process, a visionary fund-raiser also creates a service that did not exist previously and that makes a difference for the community it serves. As Ryan (1981) points out, these services are constructed out of energies and activities that create something new without using already developed resources. Thus they add to the array of services and funds available in a community.

One woman developed skills at coordinating efforts of grant seekers with funding sources to develop a service in a new way. She combined research and grant-getting abilities with substantive assistance and liaison work for those she assisted. At the same time she helped younger volunteers find their niche in community service. In this combination of coordination and assistance she brought granting agencies, services providers, volunteers, and clients together on an innovative project. But she also structured sororal ties, both for the young women in the group and also between herself and them. This woman repeated her successes for and with another group of women whose activities she focused and directed.

These activities show a community leader who can formulate a project and get the best out of otherwise inexperienced women. In her efforts she not only helped to create a service that did not exist previously, she also strengthened and focused existing women's networks.

While success in these activities does not require family social position—or other connections with the local establishment from earlier work—such ties help. One woman attests to their importance in putting together a big package.

> I know I need to win over some friends [to] thinking the same way. . . . I wrote to some of our senators [for help] because I know them personally. Now I feel the organization is more solid and we see our role as directors as much more political. One of my friends helped. And I called another who was the president of [a major bank].

Still another woman has developed her abilities at liaison work through her influence with individual philanthropists as well as foundations. She can lead those working on good causes through the maze of establishment connections and guide these applicants to success. The "daring" nature of the pimp metaphor that she uses in the following remark is neutralized by its patent incongruity; for she is a wealthy, respected member of the upper class. The question of what serious evaluation should be placed on a woman of such formidable talents is sidestepped.

> Someone once said to me, what I am is this city's biggest pimp. And I think that's a good way to put it. It's getting people together. For example, I took Laura around to the [major local] foundation for a grant. And that's how I got to the X Family Fund and got them to grant an overseas project—because of my pimping . . . .
>
> Jim Lyons is going to run for governor. And so I have done a concert for him and gotten some of the people who did the concert interested in organizing his campaign. That is what I call Byzantine pimping . . . a lot of what makes volunteer [fund-raising] work.

What is not stated in this anecdote is any reference to the place of personal or family wealth in providing initial entry into establishment networks. However, the observations in this section come from women of wealth or position. While wealth and family connections are great advantages, not all of these "big package" assemblers are so fortunate—four of them come from middle-class backgrounds and have acquired the experience, connections, and skills for assembling a program to fund a worthwhile project through their years of volunteer experience.

Personal Solicitation

Most people think of the door-to-door or telephone solicitation as the major effort for volunteers. And so it is for the many who act as block captains in drives for the United Fund or in the national campaigns for the heart and cancer associations and for those who volunteer in telephone campaigns for public radio, public television, and political party causes. In the past, these volunteers were virtually all housewives. Today, views of the telephone banks staffed by volunteers during major auctions or other appeals to support public television suggest a greater mixture of men and women, old and young, salaried and unemployed. Whatever the mix, this is not where the training and skill for the personal solicitation of big funds occurs. Most women in this sample have done some door-to-door solicitation when they were young housewives with small children at home. Cheerful and responsible performance at tasks that many others find tiresome or distasteful enough to shirk can be the first step in establishing the reputation that leads to a leadership position. Yet skill in one kind of solicitation cannot guarantee skill in the other; asking for big money requires having it as well. Sometimes one's own wealth and connections are useful in assembling the big package, as indicated previously. Other times the process is simpler, involving genteel extortion from members of one's own set. The trade-offs occur when others want you to contribute to their pet charities. Generally, the ties of friendship help one fund-raise and save face when one's own plans go awry.

The woman who hustles her own set is well known; often friends tease her about it. One woman mentioned, somewhat ruefully, a note she had recently received from a friend who said she would like to talk sometime when it didn't cost her money. Others look to their families for help with big contributions. Two mentioned their fathers—either as contributors or as having provided introductions to big contributors. Another mentioned the value of her husband's corporate connections.

Some women focus their big fund-raising efforts around their own substantial fortunes. They can squeeze philanthropy out of others through matching grants. Here is how one woman reminisced over the skills of another who was famous for them. "Mrs. Smythe Morgan was a marvelous dame. She had the dough and the guts to get into people. . . . She would say she would give $25,000 and then [play off] Mrs. Garnick [who] would say *she* would give $30,000." Another woman described showing the "guts"—or risking the antagonism so antipathetic to women in this group—required to ask for large gifts. "I went to see a man and asked him for $250,000. He turned pale and I thought he would faint. 'I admire your nerve,' he said. But he didn't give that much." The large expenses connected with big time philanthropy are sufficient to give even the very wealthy some pause. One woman described the family problems caused by these donations. "It cost me plenty [to head a major fund drive]. We always discuss . . . any major gift. . . . We have stayed up plenty of nights over that. If the campaign chairman doesn't give an expensive gift, no one else will."

Further, if people find it difficult or impossible to turn down someone from their own set, it may also be because reciprocal understandings govern expectations about how requests from members of one's own set should be honored. Warner et al. (1963: 141–42), in their discussion of Yankee City, point to the symbolic significance of the giving and taking of money in fund-raising as a way of defining a set of relations (Mauss 1967). Women who fund-raise in this class understand these relations and how they strengthen them by successfully tapping them for money.

Some women of relatively limited wealth—but with excellent connections to the business world through some combination of having served on corporate boards, membership on very prestigious philanthropic boards where many corporate executives also serve, and family connections with corporate boards—are asked to participate on major gifts committees for universities, hospitals, and the arts, even though they cannot make a major donation themselves.

Some women may enjoy the advantages of community connections and relish the "savvy" that permits them to shine in this area. One woman who is not Jewish knew how to extract money from Jewish philanthropists and was proud of her skill. Many women also enjoy the puzzle of putting together connections and prior experiences to help manage a giant fund raiser. The ability to tap the business community for in-kind donations as well as money, the knowledge of how to put together a big package, all contribute to a sense of mastery. All together, the ability to do any or all of these things produces the accomplishment—the big donations, the financial success of the big event, the formation of the hardworking fund-raising board.

Once women have reputations as successful fund-raisers, opportunities for further successes arise because other sponsors—and business interests wishing to show their wares—feel they can profit from the arrangement. Fashion designers, for example, will offer to show their line at an event benefiting any charity a fund-raiser may designate. Or a theatre may volunteer a percentage of the box office receipts at a benefit performance sponsored by the fund-raiser for any cause she wishes. Some of the most successful fund-raisers in Pacific City are besieged by such requests.

Fund-raising takes many forms, with various projects requiring somewhat different skills. Some require a greater array of skills than others; but all fund-raising requires initiative, determination, knowledge of the donating community, and some amount of crust. Big events require business connections, many friendships, administrative skills, the ability to be direct and pushing as well as indirect and placating. They require collaborative efforts and the ability to generate worker esprit. Major fund-raising may be solo or collaborative, but it need not require a great assortment of skills if one's own wealth or prominence is great enough. The lustre of one's name on the board or the appeal letterhead is expected to do the work without further personal effort. Again, however, additional skills and determination make one more successful.

Some fund-raising can be done without the network of necessary connections. If one has business management and other technical and artistic skills, one can be a steady and reliable contributor. But like door-to-door solicitation and hard work within a larger campaign of selling ads or telephone appeals, these skills do not show leadership abilities. Often, they are the token efforts of women who seek leadership in other ways but show allegiance to community causes by helping out.

Goals of Fund-raising

The causes that spur the volunteer into fund-raising are well known in every community where churches, schools, libraries, museums, parks, hospitals, and other civic interests require private contributions to operate. The structure of fund-raising activity, however, depends upon the nature of the sums to be collected. Whatever the cause, common patterns of fund-raising develop around such questions as imminent collapse of a good-cause organization, whether small or large sums must be collected, whether the collection is a one-time affair, an annual affair, or an ongoing enterprise to collect regular income. Volunteers learn to adapt their skills and to use their ingenuity to meet these goals of fund-raising. Style in fund-raising helps meet goals: it also encourages both community and worker esprit in the general service of philanthropy.

Solving the Crisis

Many women say they dislike fund-raising yet learn to do it under threat of some peril to a worthwhile cause. The peril effectively prods some women into the desperate appeal . . . and then a sense of competence.

> I was very shy and did research. I didn't know about my capacities. But when the rehabilitation center was folding, I just had to go out and see these people. And I found . . . interviewing [a rich philanthropist] was not so terrible, that [an important city official] wasn't so bad. So you start a little slowly, but you know you have to do this. You know no one else will. And if not you, the center will close tomorrow. And you are forced to do it.

In the course of meeting a crisis in funding, such women learn enough about the community to make them competent at putting together "the big package."

> I helped form the board [of a halfway house] and served as the first chairman. And then I found out just when we were leaving the office that . . . we were $10,000 short. This peril thrust me into the nuts and bolts of how to get funding to an organization. . . . If I had not faced such peril I wouldn't have the moxie to step out.

The crisis forces women to take stock of their resources (connections from family and friends) and to overcome squeamishness about using them. As they search for money, they make new connections and acquaintances, reassessing and pyramiding these resources. This kind of skill has much in common with the search for major contributions, where connections are terribly important.

The Major Contribution

Large sums are generally, though not always, collected for a one-time project: the university endowment goal; the new building for

a school, museum, or social service; the big development or purchase of park land. While some who construct "the big package"
know how to organize one of these fund drives, only the most
wealthy and well-connected can actually make the requests for
contributions.

> Certain things I can do because I am [a well-known mem-
> ber of a rich family]. It's the first time the board members
> went to foundations. And I called on [the president of an
> important bank to support the building fund].

The actual sums involved in the gifts these women have to be
able to contribute themselves were never specified; these women
were quite reticent on the subject of money and this reticence created some of their fund-raising problems. However, reticence about
naming sums of money donated may also indicate the wish to
downplay class differences with others (like the interviewer) who
could never afford such charity. Ambiguity on the extensiveness of
spending guards the privileged against envy and possible appeals
from the less fortunate as well. Despite these difficulties in assessing just how much women give to their charities, some estimates
are possible. Major gifts can be designated as those over ten thousand dollars. Relatively small major gifts (one to ten thousand dollars) are most likely to be regularly incurred, as donors or "friends"
of an organization contribute to its maintenance or meet the deficit
between income and operating expenses.

Some projects require a mix of large and medium contributions.
For this mix, fund-raisers go to individuals and corporations in
their search for donors. For example, lists of the bright, young
(35–45) leadership in the city are compiled. The names on the list
include rising professionals and corporate executives the fund-
raiser hopes to interest in the cause. These people can then be
tapped for a mixture of personal and corporate gifts. In a series of
individual lunches, site visits to the cause, and special entertainments, the prospects are lured into a greater commitment. They
then are expected to help recruit other prospects. Perhaps, if they
show the leadership qualities, these young business people will be
tapped for board membership themselves.

Fund-raising often means extracting sums from philanthropic
foundations. Here, as when soliciting business in the community,
genteel extortion methods prevail. They include the prod to awaken
the conscience of community responsibility with an amorphous
threat of unfortunate consequences if there is no awakening.

There was a need for a Boys Club at a time when the local charities were not supportive. One of the ways a volunteer can bring pressure is shown by my activity at that time. I was chairman of one group [and member of various other organizations] that wanted this club. Young Morris Gruenwald wanted it too. The gal that headed local charities said, "We can't do it yet." But she would go to Gruenwald Senior and he would always give this gal hunks of money. So there were political negotiations about this. I said to her, "How will it look if you keep taking money from Gruenwald Sr. and the pet project of his own son can never get approval through the Local Charities?" So we got the Boys' Club. I am trying to show you what a volunteer can do, show the angles.

The Small Contribution

Raising small sums of money does not require as much wealth and position, but it does require a similar amount of persistence and ingenuity in understanding the community and knowing how to extract funds from its various components. Some small sums are raised for contingencies. A woman who raised money by selling Democratic jewelry used the proceeds to pay the rent and phone bills at party headquarters. She could depend upon the good nature of strangers and well-wishers, for the sums requested were quite small. "Stevenson buttons . . . would be sold for a dollar, but in the bars people would give far more money. I set up a booth and sold at the labor convention."

At other times, they capitalize upon the single event to offer special entertainment at a moderate price. Such events will cost far less than the big ball or social event, yet they will have some of the same cachet. The profits become significant if all the materials and labor are donated. Often the community that will benefit is tapped for the small contribution. "You can do more if people eat together. The amount of shashlik I had to eat to get the park down there in Greektown. We raised money for benches and every bench has a plaque with the name of some ancestor." The importance of the small volunteer-run business collecting small sums regularly (that mount up to sizable yearly contributions) has already been noted. Activities, such as those selling admissions or raffle tickets, mitigate the request for funds by giving something desirable to the purchaser—albeit a sale in a good cause. A similarly mixed form of fund-raising is involved in the membership drive. Generally, the

group is formed around a common interest, such as art. In return
for their memberships, contributors receive special favors (invitations to previews, rehearsals, and cocktail parties). This type of return can be substantial (as in free or discounted admissions) or it can
be token (as in the publication of members' names in a program).

Volunteer groups are often divided on the issue of whether to
provide service or to raise funds. The idea that fund-raising (in
seeking donations through memberships or participation in some
combination of frivolous, social, or cultural events) is not an appropriate activity for "serious" persons interested in service to the
community is quite pervasive. But practical women with experience in service organizations see that some combination of serious
and frivolous interests may be required to keep an organization solvent. (This combination is institutionalized in the separate functions of hospital volunteer services: working with patients, running
gift and coffee shops on the one hand and auxiliaries on the other,
fund-raising through events such as the ball, fashion show, bazaar.
Both functions can overlap and some members of each service will
participate in the other.) In overcoming the reluctance of volunteers
"from all walks of life" to be associated with any activity carrying
both social class and frivolous implications, one community leader
showed them how to keep their organization solvent by producing
a dinner to honor outstanding women in the community. At the
same time, she provided a new organizational structure, the auxiliary, for them to use to produce events like the dinner and to tap
new resources (the honorees) in the community.

Building Worker Esprit

These activities raise money for good causes. But they also develop
the solidarity and purposiveness of the organization itself—both in
its fund-raising capacity and in its ability to keep members interested in the cause that inspires fund-raising. The effort to keep
fund-raisers working at their jobs—and volunteers at their functions in the organization in general—is an important part of the
overall fund-raising activity. Fund-raisers realize that this goal is inextricably entwined with the direct task of raising money. Skill in
this aspect of the work is thus much highly prized.

> Carmen and I did a marvelous party on the stage of the au-
> ditorium. A picnic on the stage. There were all these ladies
> making hero sandwiches on huge loaves and then tying

them with yarn so we could slice them later. And there were hanging loaves and sausage and garlic for decoration . . . I never ask anyone to do something I wouldn't do myself. And that's why I get along so well [with everybody and why they want to work with me].

On occasion, work and play are so inextricably entwined that the stereotype of the socialite interested mainly in partying for philanthropy is used, almost defensively, by the very person who is caricatured.

I worked for organizations that were more social and we did volunteer work . . . with a fun group of girls. We would raise money for a nursery school—scholarships. And we made money by giving parties that we all went to to have a good time.

The comment reflects the views of others as much as this woman's own perspective. She downplays the significance of what the "fun group of girls" accomplished, and she ignores the importance of creating esprit and commitment among workers for a cause. Yet, here, as elsewhere in the reminiscences of women who produce events, women describe how they encourage the affections and personal loyalties of other workers and participants through parties and shared effort.

Fellowship is not just the "by-product" of charitable work, it is the product of a particular kind of work that contributes to a sense of community responsibility. It provides an avenue for collective representations, in Durkheim's (1954:376–88) terms, to be reaffirmed. The party is a collective representation that asserts membership. The esprit that develops in these fund-raising efforts may bind a working group together so that a cadre remains when the activity is over. Such a cadre is an extremely valuable resource to call upon for future efforts. Thus even when great sums are not raised, creating esprit is a worthwhile investment. Friendships can provide some of the extra impetus to persist in a long, drawn-out fund-raising effort.

About four of us became very good friends [working to raise money for public television]. If we had not worked . . . quite so seriously, it might have been that the station would not be able to continue. There is a good feeling in . . . helping establish something like that. In addition, we made strong friendships.

From this perspective, collegial relations have to be associated with the work and the development of fellowship presented as incidental. The excitement generated by hard work in a cooperative venture, particularly under time and other pressures, is a favorable medium in which commitment to the cause at hand—as well as friendship—grows. The capture of commitment is sought as a means of building community interest in the cause as well.

Building Community Esprit

The fund-raiser, whether seeking large or small sums, regular or one-time donations, has to gain the attention of some part of the city in a zero-sum game. A working assumption is that only so much money will be donated and many good causes must compete for this finite sum. However, a competing assumption is that new markets or communities of donors remain to be tapped. The market in philanthropy is thus still expanding.

> You come down to raising money [for musical events] and it involves you in different ways to increase the audience and get new groups. . . . We do all kinds of [cultural] things and that gets the ethnics. And we do in-school programs [to get the young] . . .

The greater the enthusiasm for one's own cause, and the greater the number of enthusiasts, the more likely that both large and small donations can be attracted.

> Take something as frivolous as the Opera Masquerade . . . it's brought out . . . people and embraces everything you can imagine. . . . Young people would come . . . the whole city was involved. We kept the price of the tickets low. . . . When I persuaded the Board to do it, I told them it must be a city thing. It should be elegant and in that spirit—this is a dancing city.

The important ability, then, is to tap civic spirit and harness it in the service of one's own cause. This ability is also seen in organizing special publics within the larger community. It is closely related to the development of an attractive personal style.

An important aspect of this ability is skill in creating the background where contributors and potential fund-raisers can develop the appropriate commitment. Women often speak of their facilitative ability in this area, quite independent of any ability to raise the large funds themselves.[4] Such women see themselves, to use Parson's (1955) terms, as agents of expressiveness who pave the way for more instrumental activity by the big fund-raisers.

> I put on a dinner recently for big givers. We have a director of development. I was his chairman and he organized it. I followed through to make sure everything was right and to see that everyone was sitting at the right places. I am happy to fill the need [mediating between the "right" social connections to make the dinner a success] where he couldn't.

The contribution such women make may be mainly in providing the background, but they also emphasize the importance of their own efforts in creating the particular scene. "I like to have the best hors d'oeuvres and make them myself; and give [the guests] the most expensive bourbon. And flowers all through the house because I want it that way." When women speak of their accomplishments in this way, they stress their desire to achieve a certain quality for an event, the setting of a tone and style which becomes a goal in itself. This notion of the importance of ambience permeates the work of the fund-raiser—and the world of volunteer work more generally. Ambience, then, corresponds roughly to what, in another ideological system, is called the "quality of life," and to ideas of craftsmanship as well. Volunteer women need to pride themselves on the strength of their commitment, their successful accomplishment, and their special style in fund-raising to overcome the problems fund-raising presents to them.

Problems in Fund-raising

The paradox of fund-raising is that it requires women to "work" for money although their own careers as nonsalaried volunteers proclaim they don't need monetary reward themselves. Fund-raising also forces women to engage in directive, "pushy," and entrepreneurial activities in opposition to the ideal traditional feminine role. As we have seen, the range of these activities involves genteel extortion, business management, and entrepreneurial skills. Some women enjoy using these skills; others do not. In addition, the "so-

4. Sometimes men become known for skill in this creation of background. When they do, they too stress their facilitative role in constructing community spirit. In the case of Joe Gorman (Bellah et al. 1985:8–13), however, his work in creating a big package of events was abetted and supported by his occupational role as director of public relations for a large manufacturing company located in his community.

cial" aspects of fund-raising, that is the dependence of fund-raisers on society, entertainments, and the social cachet of an event, bothers some.

In this study, twenty women complained that fund-raising was the least desirable, even the "dirtiest," part of their work. ("I hate it. It makes me shrivel up.") Some expressed their reluctance to solicit by putting it off. Others decide to give it up. Thus, another paradox for these women that fund-raising reveals concerns the problem of saying "no." Women often get involved in volunteer projects because they have a hard time saying "no." Yet they have to learn to say "no," turning down jobs they detest, to remain committed and successful volunteer workers. They also have to learn to accept "no" in reply to solicitations.

Those women who don't like raising money, but do it anyway, stress the importance of the task in various ways. Some stress the impossibility of avoiding it. Or they stress the disinterested nature of solicitation. As noted earlier, women start, and then persist, at fund-raising when they become convinced that they must or a worthwhile project will disappear. They also mention how burdensome they find this sense of responsibility. Some women "try harder" because they do not have the ability to give large gifts. Some women, however, feel that their inability to give big gifts excuses them from fund-raising. Others excuse themselves from fund-raising responsibilities by pointing to the connections between fund-raising and frivolous "social" activities. ("Money raising is not my bag and it's all social.") These women prefer to give a major amount of time and effort (equivalent to a half-time job), as well as their own contributions. ("I feel I contributed my time and, of course, I gave to causes I believe in.")

Despite these negative feelings about fund-raising, the woman who said "everybody does it" was quite right. No one in this study (including informants who try to avoid it and downplay their participation) has escaped fund-raising duties. It would be difficult to set a clear figure on the monetary achievements of any woman; for each often works as a part of a team, a facilitator, an advisor, as well as a direct solicitor. But as a group, they have, in their careers, helped to raise millions of dollars for citywide projects.

Perhaps it is just as important that they have, in learning how to fund-raise successfully, learned how to bring segments of the city together in philanthropic efforts. They know how to find special interest groups and develop committed publics by putting together the big package, or how to catch the attention of the idle and curious through production numbers and other glamorous events. They know how to scrape together accumulated small sums in small businesses that depend on volunteer staff and craftswomen. Finally, they know how to make these various segments of the city work together.

In the process of using all these skills, women help create community purposes and concerns. The significance of these activities has also been noted by other observers of community life, such as Warner et al. (1963:141). The act of working together, coming together for a purpose, engages the attention of individuals and makes them feel as though they are part of a common enterprise. They "save" the cause they work for when they attach the interest of major or minor contributors to it, and they develop a cadre of committed workers as well as a larger peripheral group of donors in the interested public. The contacts made and the fellowships enjoyed in the process help develop commitment to the cause and the idea of community responsibility.

The opportunities for developing a community esprit may suffer when women are not readily available for this task, as Stall (1982: 11) reports.

> You know one time in the history of the church . . . you served church dinners [on a regular basis]. . . . They don't do that anymore. And one of the reasons is that a large percentage of the women are working away from home. Dinners are lots of work, and they just don't have the time for that . . . you know there was more to that dinner than making money. . . . [T]he by-product was the fellowship. Well, we don't have those anymore, so we don't have the fellowship.

Part of the ideology of volunteering, as noted earlier, is that this effort must be fueled—or inspired—through volunteer efforts. While fund-raisers are now often paid professionals, it is unclear how much of this activity can be effectively delegated to salaried workers. Many givers, for example, object to the high administrative costs of charities that use large numbers of paid professionals. In addition, the tireless gleaning of small donations and the legwork involved in developing new groups of givers may require many local, decentralized efforts that are expensive to duplicate or replace through computerized mailings or other appeals to a general audience. The question of whether these contributions can be developed and then collected without the grass-roots efforts of countless volunteer women is now being seriously considered. Even if money can be efficiently collected through mass mailing appeals to special publics, can new donor publics be developed or wavering interests sustained without volunteer community workers who make personal contacts? As more and more women enter salaried work, the question is likely to become more pressing. There may be no fully satisfactory replacement for the scouting and gleaning activities—the invisible work volunteers perform as a service to their communities.

6

The Specialties of Public Relations, Organization Building, Advocacy, and General Consulting

The central importance of fund-raising in volunteer work focuses our attention on the necessity both for money and social organization in the construction of philanthropy. The development of other specialties tells us more about the construction of work in philanthropy, as well as about the organization of work more generally.

In the study of occupations, we learn something about the nature of work from the requirements which benefit from special performance. Service workers are expected to be quick, sensitive to the needs of their patrons, cheerful and unflappable; physicians prize diagnostic skills; artisans develop standards for craftsmanship in their field. The heroes and villains of the workplace (Klapp 1962) tell us about the values and expectations of the participants there. (Was John Henry stubborn or noble to contest the steam drill? Should a captain go down with his ship?) Some standards are very idiosyncratic, keyed to a special setting. Families expect housewives, for example, to meet general standards of performance for meal preparation, cleaning, grocery shopping. In addition, women negotiate and tailor their performance to the expectations of individual family members (DeVault 1984). How do women know when they are successful? The issue of judging one's performance as a practitioner at something is complicated when the work is unpaid.

Volunteers always face this problem. They receive no increments in salary or changes in job title to indicate their growing experience and accomplishments. Their work does not have visibility as a serious career and the specialties within it are not articulated or given

151

shape and rationale through the formation of ideologies, as in medical specialties and subspecialties, for example (Daniels 1972). Nonetheless, there is clearly specialization as well as career. How does this pattern emerge without a firm institutional base, a strong occupational ideology, and a system of payment? To answer this question we must consider their work in terms of what these women have done in community service and how they went about it. This approach requires a focus upon the skills acquired as well as the product created. The civic leaders assess their work from these two directions: what they accomplished and how they did it. From that perspective, one can see that volunteers do other things besides fund-raising. This chapter shows how specialties in volunteer work are used and how women become skillful in using them.

Each specialty, such as public relations or advocacy, has some important relation to fund-raising while offering an opportunity for different talents to appear and skills to develop. Each specialty has some overlapping relationship to the others. Women turn to these specialties, just as they develop interests, through a combination of aptitude, prior experience, and opportunity. In addition, women see the need for someone to practice these skills if a cause or an organization is to flourish. As with fund-raising, public relations, organizational building, and advocacy are required in some situations. General consulting seems to be more of a cachet for the elder stateswomen, just as opportunities for consulting are often the sign that professionals, academics, and business specialists have attained eminence.

Public relations skills are useful in capturing the attention of the public for a cause. Most generally, a volunteer leader uses public relations techniques to attract a wide public audience by disseminating information through the mass media about how to contribute for a cause or participate in events celebrating it. When very successful, a publicist can create public concern for a philanthropic cause in the same way that successful public relations agents can create new media stars in entertainment or politics, new products or services in industry. Her causes are also like those of successful public relations agents in that they are apt to be noncontroversial and will appeal to a wide public. Such causes do not require social change or even very much reform. Instead, they help maintain the status quo by supporting cultural activities or hospitals and medical research.

The organization builder works closely with grass-roots groups. In addition, she combs her own community in search of likely assistants to help develop the kind of new group she envisions. In this way she helps to develop new talent in volunteer work. The women in this category have to be patient; some organizations take shape very slowly. These women are known for their ability to proceed step by step, deliberating as they put each each piece together. They may develop new groups or revitalize old ones. When they create new ones, they can be like the public relations specialist in developing a public awareness for something that did not exist before and uniting both serious and frivolous audiences. They are like the advocate if they build organizations that are reform- or change-oriented and so promote the development of partisan or even warring publics. Organization builders—especially those interested in advocacy—may work with a narrow constituency or a very specific cause. When they do so, their skills—and the reputation they develop—overlap with advocacy.

The advocate-lobbyist is the specialist least likely to develop in this group of women at the intersection of philanthropy and society. Although some women have been angry (or determined) enough about one particular cause to pursue this career for a time, very few embrace it for long. The conflicts which can emerge between fighting for social issues and maintaining class interests are especially difficult for traditional women to face. Pressures from family and friends to work within the understandings of how women of the leisure class should behave constrain those who feel loyalty to their social circle. Nonetheless, some women do become involved in a cause. Those who do make advocacy their specialty use the volunteer skills of all the other specialists, but with a special and persistent focus on an issue (such as integrated schooling, low-cost housing, childcare). Fund-raising, public relations, and organization building skills are all directed to that one cause. In this concentration, of course, particularly if sharp controversy requires an adversarial stance, the advocate may narrow the circle of potential subscribers or large donors who will be sponsors. She may, however, pick up enough grass-roots support to find, eventually, that she has developed a new constituency. This new group may draw her away from her customary social circles and into a new career line. The new constituency expects a somewhat different performance from its leaders than will other, more traditional, volunteer groups. Political careers, for example, may be an obvious alternative for leaders of social action groups interested in changing the existing system. Accordingly, this role is likely to lead women away from their traditional roles and into careers in elective politics. As these interests develop out of desires for some reform, the advocate-lobbyist often fights for something new in society (a new social service, or ways to integrate schools and improve education) as well as for the preservation of the old (a historical landmark or an environmental resource).

All these specialties require a mixture of skills and interests that reaches its fullest expression in the oldest and most experienced volunteer community leaders who become general consultants. They show nonprofit agencies where to find funds and other needed resources, introduce potential working partners to one another, suggest board members for organizations in need of new talent, and offer advice on how to manage mergers or major fundraisers. They are like successful financial brokers in that they understand their market and know how to develop a program of purchases tailored to individual clients. The investments are in programs for the city's welfare, and their rewards as a successful broker provide no financial gain. These women rise through the ranks of volunteer work and succeed in many or all the other specialties. Their experience and reputation for judgment and wisdom make them brokers and advisors to other civic leaders—both male and female. In addition, the great teachers and mentors for junior volunteers come from their ranks.

The Public Relations Specialty

Fund-raising and public relations require many overlapping skills; in each case, the development of a unique style or "flair" is especially helpful. The style of the public relations person enables her to draw attention to the event she is publicizing or selling. She not only stimulates the enthusiasm and public interest for fund-raising events, but she also provides the occasions—and the audience—to build communities within the city. For example, she may bring local women professionals together with liberal upper-class women to support a service for poor and ethnic women. The event will be staged at an elegant hotel with champagne, a fancy buffet, important speakers from the national and local feminist circuit to espouse the cause, and members of the benefited community to explain it. Many women and some men will find it politic and even interesting to attend and to offer contributions. In the course of this participation, they can also enter into substantive discussions, presenting various points of view and responding to questions. The occasion provides both organized and informal interactions for professionals, prosperous liberals, and women working to support or develop a service to learn about one another's perspectives, capacities, and problems. Such events help create and maintain a women's community and a concern for the particular cause around which participants have gathered.

Commemorative events, such as a dinner for a visiting foreign dignitary, are also used to strengthen community esprit. The media publicity surrounding these events tells a wider audience than those attending how much the citizenry can be proud of their city. And these events provide opportunities to repair as well as consolidate community esprit.

> For the Friends of the Aquarium I did a luncheon for businessmen on a tennis court in Greektown. At this luncheon, someone was saying we should do something at the Armory for the Bicentennial, because our city has its anniversary then too. . . . I decided we ought to have this great cake baked at [the nearby military post] because they have these great big ovens and surely that would be something to cement relationships [after a conflict between the military installation and the city]. . . . So I called up the general and asked to make an appointment . . . We didn't get to the point at first but talked about the weather and made pleasant conversation. Finally I asked for the cake. And you could see the general's sigh of relief. On the day the cake was to be erected in the City Hall Plaza I was downtown early. And you should have seen all those green trucks converging. It was like an invasion. First they erected a scaffolding and then they constructed a cake. And they slathered on the icing with those great cement smoothers. It was a big success and the cake was delicious.

This event brought Pacific City recognition in the national media and it united previously warring elements from the city fathers and the military in mutual congratulations over the good publicity. The organization of the event also provided experience and incentive for future cooperative efforts between business interests and the military installation. The crowds downtown were good for business and the importance of the military in making the event a success was clear to all. The woman who successfully initiated the plan illustrates the ability of the public relations specialist to mediate between agencies in conflict and to unite the city around a publicity gimmick.

The women who can dream up and orchestrate these big events

are in sufficient demand to get a taste for power. In the following case, a woman gained her power by showing political figures how to bring together various elements of the city to build community esprit as well as to extend a political base of operations throughout the city.

> I did some fabulous things, like running the mayor's inaugural. I said I would do it for him on condition that he had five inaugurals, spotted all over the city. One of them was [in the black ghetto]. It was a big success and written up in [national magazines]. All his honchos had to report to me. I loved it.

These examples suggest some of the exciting aspects of public relations work, including the publicity and deference accorded the successful public relations experts. The less pleasant aspects of the work involve courting publicity.

> I . . . resent the way society page editors have to be coaxed and wheedled. They are treated like little tin gods and behave badly—accepting invitations to dinners and then not showing up. On one occasion I was asked to be nice to Lana Gato [an important columnist] but I didn't understand or else I wasn't nice enough. Anyway, she left in a huff and all sorts of society people were relegated to rush out in relays to find her and coax her back.

Public relations experts realize the importance of columnists who can publicize benefits. Part of their skill as publicists, then, involves maintaining the level of friendship and intimacy that some columnists require.

In addition to the "flair" for promotion and the friendship of columnists, public relations specialists need to know about media production requirements in their own community. Organizations like the Junior League and the League of Women Voters teach their recruits some of the basic skills for promotion: how to write a publicity release, how to call a press conference to publicize a coming event or dramatize the plight of an agency, and how to prepare copy when it must be ready for morning and evening paper deadlines. Other women learn these skills in their salaried careers as buyers or department store publicists. One woman developed public relations skills as a recruiter in the Navy during World War II, but many learn through a combination of training courses and on-the-job experiences as a volunteer.

However they are trained, women learn how to promote ideas,

causes, and organizations by using the mass media to publicize the issue. The best publicists produce a news item or material for a special feature that reporters want to use, irrespective of its promotional value. These women, then, understand the requirements of the news media—what kinds of stories they can reasonably expect reporters to write and editors to print. The public relations experts develop symbiotic relations with journalists and editors who need copy just as the women need publicity.

In the course of their work, specialists in this area have developed a wide variety of personal connections in business and government agencies as well as in the media worlds. Like the great fund-raisers, the public relations specialists know how to package an event inexpensively and effectively. They can show business people and bureaucrats how helping to make an event big publicity will benefit them. In this capacity, these women are just like professional public relations workers in the salaried world.

In this study, fifty women have had considerable public relations experience. This work is in great demand. Like fund-raising, publicity for a cause helps to make it successful. And women learn to do it to help or save their causes. The work is also closely tied to marketable skills. Seven have worked as salaried professionals in public relations before and, sometimes, during their volunteer careers. And four women have developed salaried careers using their public relations experience from the volunteer world. The remaining women (39) have used public relations skills in conjunction with the other specialties.

Some women show their skills in this area through management of the wives' program for large professional meetings at which their husbands are officers. They will arrange events and publicity for the convention banquets, special teas, outings, or activities for the wives. This work includes union negotiations, space arrangements, invitations to and correspondence with special guests and speakers for the major public events of the conference. Many of these activities are part of the work of producing benefits as well; but here they focus on the task of producing an event which promotes the image of the association and the city that welcomes it. In this study, all the doctors' wives (10) have had such public relations experience—as did a few wives of lawyers and brokers.

A consistent flair for public relations appears in certain interests and work styles, especially in workers of the "bang and bust" sort and in those interested in culture, whatever their style. All of the fourteen who are explicitly culture-oriented and all of the thirteen bang-and-bust style workers have expertise at public relations. They are joined by the women with careers in politics developed from community organizing or advocacy. Thus, women from the most and least conventional volunteer interests develop similar specialties. They share the common concern of broadcasting a message to as wide an audience as possible. They are also the civic leaders who will find it least practical to remain invisible for part of the work of publicizing an event or a cause will bring them into public notice through press interviews and announcements. Women who really shun the limelight, then, will avoid this specialty.

The Organization Builder

As in the fund-raising and public relations specialties discussed thus far, organization building often overlaps other functions. The growth of an organization can augment fund-raising schemes (when membership fees are used to maintain the budget of some service or cause). And the growing membership can promote public relations through its own reports about the organization. Twenty women in this study could be identified as having built organizations. They have started hospital and cultural institution auxiliaries, developed private schools, taken faltering organizations and rebuilt them, and built new membership groups for political and other community issues. Often these women have built organizations by following the experience of similar organizations. They have visited other programs or learned about them through reading reports and manuals on how to establish a particular kind of service in a community. The organization builders have also responded to already formulated desires for support groups within established institutions. For example, they have established programs for hospital volunteers or museum docents at the request of the directors.

A few women (3) have developed their organizations entirely from their own vision of community need. They have formed organizations to fight for some cause—childcare services, an endangered neighborhood landmark or an endangered species, for example—where the organization, following early successes, became a permanent interest group with a growing membership. One woman developed a job counseling and placement service for teenagers from middle-class homes. Although this volunteer leader was recognized as the major force behind this organization's development, as well as the initiator of at least two other community services, she always spoke of it as a team effort—"we" rather than "I" made it work successfully. Consequently, her successes were somewhat less visible and not associated with her identity as much as they might otherwise have been. Nonetheless, in her own circle she is known for her special skills. For this particular organization she developed a public relations program in the business community to find jobs, wrote grants, recruited a finance committee to do fund-raising, and started an auxiliary for both the public relations and fund-raising arms. These last activities became extensive enough to merit a spin-off organization. Ultimately, the organization became successful enough and sufficiently institutionalized to require a paid executive director and a staff. To develop and expand such an organization requires much the same skill as assembling "the big package" in fund-raising. Here, as in the complex fund-raising scheme, wide connections and knowledge of civic resources are essential, as are the negotiating, bargaining, and persuasive talents so helpful in public relations.

Advocacy-Lobbying

All of the skills described so far show active women at work within the framework provided by the status quo. Whether fund-raising, doing public relations, or building organizations in any areas of interest across culture, health, education, and welfare, or politics, these women are clearly seen—and see themselves—as working within the system. They do not seem to see drastic changes in our sociopolitical system as possible or even necessary.

The women in this advocate group who try to change the system, while not exactly renegades, are still set apart. The assertive qualities required for insistent criticism of such social institutions as the public schools, the welfare agencies, and city government generally seem abrasive to many of their class and conflict with the widespread expectation that the appropriate tactics for women community leaders will involve negotiation and coaxing; women's efforts to coerce should, according to tradition, be indirect, and tactics of bluster or threat are unthinkable. Insistent public criticism of the establishment may seem disloyal and against the interest of their own class. Some of the advocates are so regarded by other civic leaders who express their disapproval, even if only indirectly or tacitly. As most of the women in this group are well connected within the establishment and socialized to traditional women's roles, it is not surprising that only a few (5) fall into the advocacy

role, and even these few do not directly challenge business interests. Instead, they concentrate on fighting for such causes as conservation, protection of juveniles' civil rights, integration, and
school improvements. They have followed the same evolution as
the early friendly visitors in the nineteenth and early twentieth
century who tried to help poor women and children in the growing
industrial cities of Europe and America. Blair (1980:170–71) points
out that middle- and upper-class women were close enough to the
abject poverty of cities to be perpetual witnesses. Once they came
to know something about the life conditions of those they tried to
help, the women gained an awareness of the social injustices that
kept so many in poverty. Some of the women then became advocates for the poor and fought what they saw as the vested interests,
speaking against them in public forums (Blair 1980:171).

The pattern set down by such women[1] is followed by the women
in this study who become advocates, even if they do not directly
challenge the capitalist foundation of the economy and the state.
They see the social system as needing repair, yet as still basically
serviceable. From this perspective, corporate executives, elected
and appointed officials are not in fundamental opposition to social
change, only ill-informed on what needs to be done. Concerned
women feel confident they can educate and convince members of
the local elite through persistent effort. Four women in this study
who developed advocacy skills began through their concern for integration in the public schools when their own children were in
them. Here is how one of these women described the shock they all
experienced upon seeing how a public hearing on the issue was
managed. This experience focused their work commitment for a
long time thereafter.

> [The public meeting at Jefferson Auditorium] had a pro-
> found effect on me, probably because [I saw] the rioting
> that took place, where three people, including a photogra-
> pher from one of the local newspapers, were beaten up . . .

1. The life of Margaret Dreir Robbins (Dye 1980:36) provides a historical example.
Her first social service was as a volunteer for the Brooklyn Hospital's Auxiliary. As a
member of the State Charities Aid Association, she also volunteered for the visiting
committee for State insane asylums. Genteel philanthropy gave Robbins the opportunity to see the effects of poverty in hospital wards and led her to question conventional charity. In 1903 she joined the Women's Municipal League and helped investi-
gate employment agencies as a source of organized prostitution. As chairwoman of
the legislative committee, she often testified in Albany and lobbied for regulatory
legislation to control employment agencies.

[and the] less than enthusiastic performance of their duty by the police . . . stationed there that night. I felt strongly enough about the whole situation to testify at [the Mayor's] commission . . . several days after the riot. And I really concentrated my [volunteer] efforts in the whole field of education [after that].

One woman who specializes in educational advocacy explained how she came to realize the wider significance of her own special cause and her affinity with other advocates who drew her attention to their feelings about racism and the strategies or techniques of advocacy.

There was a good mix of black and white and men and women in the Congress of Black African Parents. It was good for me because they would treat me as an equal. Finally they accepted me, but it took a long time. Now here I had this one area of absolute fury with regard to the school system. I knew it had to be changed. And this man said to me, "Suppose you felt this way about everything in your life? Your money, your job, your housing, your future?" Because I had reached the point of almost thinking you had to destroy the school system in order to change it. And then I understood how they felt. [And] I became confident with loaded language. And in later projects I used every tactic I learned from the radicals. The education bureaucracy is not happy with me. . . . But I have the freedom to use any tactic I want to.

Some advocates, like this woman, have an adversarial relationship with many established interests in the city. They stress their autonomy as unpaid workers and see volunteer status as the opportunity for independent action. The other side of that autonomy, of course, is that they have no institutionalized base of power or structural supports. They may choose to be noisy advocates but they run the risk of being ignored or discredited. An alternative strategy is to employ conciliatory rather than threatening behavior, seeking to collect a wide constituency. This strategy also includes a tendency to soften demands so as to make them more acceptable (see Thorne 1975 for the importance of this strategy among extreme protest groups). These advocates maintain sufficiently cordial—or neutral—relations in the city so that they can call on large numbers of helpers in mounting campaigns.

Whether intransigent or cautious, those proficient at advocacy have developed the ability to communicate and then mobilize some segments of the community to express outrage. An important component of this mobilization is often the letter-writing campaign. Stall (1982:18) reports how women saved their community hospital when new state guidelines would have resulted in a closing. The women involved in the campaign placed letters in the newspaper and drummed up enough support so that six hundred letters were written to the relevant officials.

The women in this study also report on the follow-through (including almost monomaniacal round-the-clock commitment to work) required to channel and maintain sustained public pressure for their causes. As one elderly, widowed conservation worker reported, "I just do [advocacy work] all the time. And late into the night, usually."

Another component of mobilization is tenacity in doing the research to support one's cause, even as professionals charge unwarranted interference.

> [I went to see one of the doctors] and she was very cold to me. "Mrs. Kline," she said, "just what are your academic credentials?" And I said I didn't think this was a matter for academic credentials but a matter any person would be alarmed about. She said that she thought everything was proper [in the management of children in custody], that she was a medical doctor and understood these things and it would be a waste of my time and hers if we continued the meeting. So I left. I remembered I had served several years before on the budget committee of Family Charities. At that time, they were questioning the infant shelter budget and program. And there were articles on the damage done to infants in institutionalization [written by social scientists, to show the damage that occurred]. . . . I went to the Charities office and saw [the executive]. . . . She dug out the dead files so I could learn how babies get to Juvenile Hall and get out [. . . to demonstrate how much unnecessary time they spent institutionalized because of the current system].

All the activities to mobilize civic concern are put to the service of the cause; so advocacy shares some characteristics in common with activities in the specialties discussed thus far. The knack of catching public sentiments and playing upon them involves public relations skills. This elderly conservationist is much in demand for advice on how to mount campaigns as spectacularly successful as hers have been.

I just see loads of jobs ahead. You never lack. For instance at this water conference someone came up to me and said, "In our district we're losing all our streams. The Corps of Engineers is diverting them all into ditches." I explained, "You have to have a burning issue. Is there some beloved stream?"

Advocacy patterns also develop when pinpointing the dramatic —and the unpleasant—so as to suggest that action *must* be taken; some reform is unavoidable. One activist personally marshaled support to shut down juvenile cottages over the opposition of the professionals in charge. She established an independent panel to evaluate what agency professionals were doing.

The judge, the chief probation officer and the two doctors [to represent the agency], and a psychiatrist and a psychologist [were among those on] the independent panel . . . and I. They started discussing procedures—the 48-hour isolation practice, the cage [in which children were left] and . . . other screening and medical procedures. . . . So I asked for the floor. And you could see that they thought I had no right to do it. . . . I told them about the horror stories I had heard—rats running around the garbage cans—two brothers who were in for six months and then discovered to have active TB but never [diagnosed] at the cottage—a child with a broken arm not properly set—how children almost invariably had head lice and impetigo. [One] doctor got up and, shaking with rage, read a long report [that] justified all of their actions.

By that time the committee was incensed. So I got them to put together a resolution to the board of supervisors and the [relevant agencies and commissions] for the care and custody of dependent children, that this [responsibility] be removed from the court and placed in the hands of a social service agency.

In the foregoing case, agency provisions were eventually changed and more humane procedures instituted. But any of these activities clearly require the ability to attack and resist attack from others. In this case, the advocate had to overcome the resistance of professionals to any lay interference and learn how to circumvent obstacles to change from entrenched authorities.

But once a cause catches on, the advocate may have to change direction and spend a lot of time encouraging, promoting, and cooperating. A cause requires much groundwork to sustain it. One of the advocates shows that varied talents are required.

> There are thank you notes and letters to write and phoning. There's lots going on [to develop, staff, promote] that conference and there's this bond thing [we are fighting for] and then an unusual dinner [for the interested citizen's group] and then a study [requested by the mayor]. And I have to write all of the regional newsletter. We get it out four times a year.

When manipulations behind the scenes will not avail, one alternative is to turn to the concerned citizenry in hopes that public pressure will force the decisions or actions that agency chiefs or elected officials will not take. An important cluster of skills within this general category involves organizing campaigns to place initiatives on the ballot. All of the women with advocacy skills have this experience.

The work required to develop a successful initiative involves many of the same skills involved in assembling "the big package" in fund-raising. Again, it is important to understand that a really outstanding specialist in any area has considerable experience in other areas as well. These advocates, then, know how to build organizations, raise funds, and accomplish a variety of research and publicity functions to make their projects succeed. For example, one highly successful campaign to protect children in custody got the bar involved, demanded that judges establish criteria for performance (for supervisors) in this field, got a charter amendment on the ballot, and a measure put forward by the city council. The publicity created by the local bar association resulted in citywide interest in the organization and added to its members. The pressure from the growing membership and the local bar created enough concern to warrant a charter amendment and a council resolution. In this process, the volunteer advocate helped stabilize the office of the Chief Probation Officer (CPO) in the judicial system through her efforts to assure protection for children under city care. The charter amendment changed the system. "In the past, the CPO was fired each time there was a scandal. . . . It was a very handy way of taking care of a problem without solving it. And you couldn't get any really reputable person to work under these conditions."

Throughout this process, fund-raising was essential; and so was the development of coalitions of existing organizations.

> We . . . raised enough money to publicize the charter. And
> we put together a separate committee to do it . . . I went to
> every organization with social concerns and I got them to
> use their own mailing lists. . . . Our measure passed by a
> larger vote than anything else on the local ballot.

After the campaign was over, an interested and organized public
remained. This group developed into a watchdog organization and
proved to be a helpful constituency to this advocate in related
causes.

While advocates are more willing to face open conflict than most
of the community leaders studied, advocates obviously need some
of the same abilities at negotiation and manipulation, for they cannot always be obdurate and intransigent if they are to use the various political and community networks. One woman, for example,
saved a special ghetto school for juvenile delinquents when federal
funding was cut off by a combination of the behind-the-scenes
work favored by most women community leaders and the direct
public campaigns so necessary to the advocate.

> I personally took it on . . . and we mobilized a campaign.
> The governor's, senator's, and congressman's offices were
> involved and we got them to commit staff time. We orga-
> nized letter writing and press conferences. And got stuff
> back from the warehouse and kids back in school. And I
> [got] funds from the mayor's criminal justice council. I
> spent weeks and months on it, and it worked.

This discussion of the advocate highlights the ways that skills of
women volunteer leaders are related to their interests—and their
place in society. Partly through already established family and
friendship connections and partly through connections established by experience, these women have access to key people with
needed information or power. These connections constitute a
major resource in developing skills in any aspect of civic leadership. Connections provide career options not available to other potentially able women. This network of friends and relations to draw
upon means that once in an organization a woman can benefit from
that position in ways other women cannot. She can rise faster and
receive more encouragment and information than others, for example. The acquired skills do not then exist separate from the contacts; the maintenance, expansion, and general use of the contacts
continues to be a major component in the skill developed. Thus,

even the most determined advocate has connections in the community power structure, as well as some type of charisma that inspire a public following and weld it into a citizen action group. The pattern of interests determines the range of network developed. The advocates, for example, have their connections to office holders and other politicians interested in reforms, disaffected agency representatives desiring some drastic changes, outraged members of special publics, media specialists and philanthropists concerned with issues similar or related to those of the advocate. Membership in such a network, however, is likely to antagonize important leaders in more conservative networks or else it is irrelevant in those conservative circles where such memberships can provide no exchangeable resources. The most political of the advocates move in different orbits from their more cautious or conservative volunteer colleagues and find working partners in the worlds of politics, professions, and journalism as well as in special citizen action groups drawn from a wide spectrum of society. Accordingly, advocates are known as specialists and not generalists. While they have some of the skills necessary for producing "the big package," they are not widely known or called upon for these skills by other volunteer leaders who are uncomfortable with advocacy tactics for social reform and suspicious of those who use them.

General Consulting

Some of the women in this study of community leaders are widely known and respected for their advice on virtually any issue other volunteer leaders wish to consider. These women are the specialists' specialists, as it were. But they are accessible to beginners and newcomers as well. They are known for their broad-based networks and their abilities to rally support from widely disparate community figures.

The special skill of generalists lies in their knowledge of the city and how to expedite fund-raising, organization building, or public relations within it. They are advisors—and sometimes masterminds themselves—for the big package or the big production number in fund-raising for university major gifts, political campaigns, and local charities. Miller (1950:216) discusses some of the characteristics of the generalist under the title of troubleshooter. His study of the Jewish leadership of Lakeport focuses exclusively on men, but his description fits the generalist presented here. The troubleshooter may or may not be a board member of the organization asking for help. The ability to offer assistance comes not from their holding formal offices but from their powerful ties in the community. And the troubleshooter has a real reputation for detachment, honesty, and principled conduct. Such a reputation takes time to build, particularly for women who may be invisible in the male world of the community power structure—as they appear to have been in Lakeport. But as their reputation grows, women who are generalists become prominent civic figures.

They often have a highly successful track record of accomplishment. Their interests cut across a wide number of substantive areas (from culture to health, education, and welfare to politics) and their skills are also varied. The widespread network a generalist can call upon allows her to come up with an idea, a person, or a tactical suggestion in almost any situation. This ability is developed systematically; the general consultants are well known for their files and records. They keep track of people, organizations, and services in an orderly fashion.

Since staff assistance is irregular (a career contingency to consider later), most generalists develop their own systems for maintaining and broadening their network. One woman keeps track of invitations and solicitations sent by various charitable organizations or events that carry the name of sponsors or board members on the letterhead. A file of these announcements can then be used to review the pattern of philanthropic interests over time: what programs other volunteer leaders are developing; what issues or areas are drawing the support of major donors; what donors are diversifying their gifts or concentrating on a narrow range of issues and organizations. Whatever the system, these women explicitly acknowledge the importance of broadening their contacts and meeting a variety of people who may be useful to know one time or another.

These women are named most often by all the rest of the women in these interviews—and by others as well—as the consultants to turn to, the women with the most influence and knowledge in the city, the volunteer leaders who have done the most for the city. Twelve of the women in this group meet these criteria: two of the twelve are growing into the role; three are gradually retiring. These are the women, then, who possess the skills referred to earlier as those of the broker, troubleshooter, consultant, and financial advisor. Such women help plan a campaign or fund-raiser rather than carry it through. One woman could pride herself, not only on finding the right woman for a job, as validated by the success of the resulting conference, but also on finding one who proved additionally valuable for her ability to create new networks. The ability to provide contacts adds to the luster of a woman's reputation and convinces others to seek her out, just for the consultation.

> The college administrative and legal processes program has an advisory council that is mostly corporate people. There is an aggressive young woman who is head of Career and Life Planning and she is developing internships for the students. She has been calling on me for a link to the private foundation and agency world.

The woman quoted above is a good link in this circumstance because she is one of the two generalists who sit on corporate boards as well as boards of philanthropic organizations and social service agencies. She also has special contacts to corporate philanthropy as well.

Some of the women are courted for their mediating abilities as well as their connections across different worlds. In describing these abilities, colleagues described particular generalists as being "able to get shrill women and very busy men together," or "she made lots of strange bedfellows work together and like it." These mediating qualities are often essential when delicate mergers are contemplated and much conciliation required. The advice of the general consultant is often wanted to show how to mediate commonly recurring problems in the volunteer world. Here is what Mrs. Harrison, herself a generalist and also a woman with a long career as a professional staff member in agencies using volunteers, had to say about a major figure among the consultants:

> I've turned to Mrs. Aubrey on many occasions, primarily for advice on the professional role in relation to the lay board and how that involves problems of leadership and expanding council activity. We would discuss the philosophy of contacts for volunteer work. And she became a sounding board for some of the planning. And she was the person I sought for guidance on which volunteers might be most supportive in development [i.e., help fund-raise] . . . and [for] her unique leadership capacity, her experienced knowledge of how to develop and mobilize volunteers.

The feeling that these generalists are major strategists is captured by the description one of their colleagues provides of her favorite advisor among them.

> Madeline Aubrey offers positive strategies, a way to tackle
> a problem or the decision that this is not the time and it had
> better wait. . . . Her contribution was ideas, involvement,
> and the real ability to keep in focus with the issue.

The generalist is often asked for help on delicate matters. She
may formulate strategy to handle the replacement of a board member or fill a vacancy in a particularly touchy situation when warring
factions want representation. Some delicate matters—such as firing
an executive director—may be unresolvable until one or more of
these knowledgeable and powerful women has been consulted on
the most appropriate tactics.

At least one of these women has become so powerful as well as
knowledgeable that her advice *must* be sought in many situations
(wherever her friends, supporters, or protégées hold important
directorships) or the project may not succeed. Were she to become offended or displeased with the scope or style of a venture,
she could suggest to other important figures that it was not worth
doing. Her sense of a project as impractical or not worthwhile
could then serve as self-fulfilling prophecy. In this manner, knowledge and influence can bring power. Here is how one generalist
described the power to punish in two other consultants that she
knew quite well.

> Mrs. Mainwaring would punish anyone who didn't come to
> her first on how to start a membership organization. She
> had a lot of ways to trip you up. She could do people out of
> a job on a committee or demote them. When she had the
> power, she would do it. Mrs. Lanahan is not a killer; but
> she doesn't forgive. If you borrow without reciprocation,
> she holds it against you [and she won't give you further
> materials, advice, or introductions].

The generalist just quoted also stressed that these are personal
idiosyncrasies among consultants rather than characteristics related to the specialty. They are only presented to suggest the power
consultants can have among volunteers because their abilities are
needed. Most of the women in this group are known primarily for
their helpfulness; that is how their reputations have grown, after
all. When they are not in sympathy with a project, they often withdraw without prejudice.

Formal recognition of their special skills comes when such women
are asked to sit on governmental commissions. Two of these civic
leaders have served on important governor's advisory committees

to consider delinquency and mental health issues; another three were tapped for a blue ribbon panel on education problems. One woman chairs a task force on city and county district relations. These appointments, together with trusteeships on prestigious foundation, university, or college boards, indicate that a woman is a capable generalist and that she has been recognized as a distinguished civic leader.

This picture of the general consultants indicates how well regarded these women are because of their skills and the advice they can offer. These women know how to do everything as well as who can be recruited for any task. They also know how to approach any task or participant in the most politic way, for they are long-time residents and know of political and family alliances, hidden conflicts, and where "bodies are buried" in the worlds of local government, politics, philanthropy, and business. The combination of the power or influence they may wield through their connections in various networks and the energy they can bring to bear on a project of interest can make these women formidably effective.

In addition most general consultants are known for their analytic skills, their ability to read and digest masses of technical material and find the gist of the matter at hand. Some of them are wide readers with some intellectual interests; but all are curious, eager to learn new things, and interested in how things work. "I really love to pit my brain against the obstacles. You have to twist and turn until you find a way out. It is like a scientist . . . dealing with people in society. How in the world do you change it?"

The generalists develop in the same areas as all leaders: three have focused on health, education, and welfare; one on culture; two on politics; the remaining seven cover all these areas. They are representative of the other leaders in that they share common experiences and the same range of social characteristics (see table 6.1). And, of course, all the volunteer leaders have some of the qualities exhibited by general consultants. While table 6.1 does indicate some differences between members within the group, there is no clear pattern suggesting that the social attributes of general consultants are different from those of their colleagues. Perhaps the difference between consultants and other community leaders is that the generalist has a good grasp of most skills other community leaders possess to a lesser extent. And general consultants have developed opportunities to acquire an overview of the city that cuts across substantive interests. Such opportunities arise when they

Table 6.1   Characteristics of General Consultants Compared with those
of Entire Sample

	Generalists		Others	
High SES	42%	(5)	47%	(27)
Extensive salaried work experience*	33	(4)	19	(11)
Never held a salaried job	33	(4)	34	(20)
Jewish	25	(3)	22	(13)
Catholic	15	(2)	21	(12)
Childless	25	(3)	36	(21)
Widowed	8	(1)	22	(13)
Divorced	17	(2)	12	(7)
N		(12)		(58)

*Self-supporting for five years or more either before marriage or after change in
marital status.

are chosen for service on boards of local united charities and private foundations (ten of the twelve have had such experience). This
board activity is honorific and signifies that the volunteer leader is,
indeed, one of the most widely respected and experienced among
her colleagues. In addition, the appointment gives the general consultant a survey of many different action and interest groups in the
city; for the soliciting board members and professional staffs present information about their services as part of appeals for funds.
The more she learns, the more valuable she becomes on the boards
of private foundations, where many suggested projects must be
evaluated each year.

As her reputation grows, the generalist develops a "clientele" for
her consulting service. As this clientele becomes more varied (for a
reputation for shrewd judgment and accessibility encourages a
wide variety of requests for help), she learns more about problems
or issues in the city. A characteristic related to curiosity or interest
in what is happening across a variety of fields is a general consultant's flexible attitude and openness to new experiences. This
woman, for example, was willing to listen to youthful protestors.

> When I was a college trustee, during our years of con-
> frontations, students could always talk to me. It got so that
> other board members wouldn't go to a confrontation if I
> couldn't go—they had no fear of eggs thrown at them if I
> were along. I was always interested in students, so they
> would invite me down. If you don't go, you don't see how
> generations change.

The qualities of interest and sympathy permit some consultants to be comfortable in interactions across race and class lines.

> I was on the board of a public agency and chairman of an interracial council. And I came to know minorities well—a tremendous advantage in the problems that arose recently on the board where I am currently chairman. I learned about the exercise of compassion. What people are really asking for, even poor devils in housing units, is to be listened to—and a little bit of hope—even when they have legitimate claims to make. A part of life you have to learn about.

Of course, there is a patronizing tone implicit in the sympathy for the unfortunate that is expressed above; the liberality of these generalists should not be overstated. Their sympathies are basically with the establishment; they believe in gradual reform rather than radical change; they live conventional, traditionally oriented lives and conduct their affairs with decorum. Yet they can serve as a bridge between members of their own class and others in the city who want reform. While consultants plan fund-raisers for cultural causes and participate in at least some "social" activities, they also play city politics in the integration of minorities and women into city institutions. Through these activities they maintain some credibility—and access—in a wide variety of interest groups and social worlds. They show their willingness to negotiate and conciliate in ways that, for instance, some culture enthusiasts in the social whirl—or advocates intent on social reform—may not.

As women develop skills in any of the specialties discussed in this chapter, they become knowledgeable about civic organization. In gaining an understanding of how various segments of their city operate, they also learn how to make them work together for various projects to benefit the city as a whole. In this process, women who become civic leaders are important agents in the task of unifying the city. Yet their role is never institutionalized and the nature of their contribution is always seen as entirely idiosyncratic. Accordingly, the development of specialties is not generally recognized.

This work, however, can lead to a new consideration of various salaried entrepreneurial activities that also depend upon the development of networks. Do these activities have the same consequence as volunteer specialties do, connecting various communities or groups? If so, in what areas? Clearly, salaried counterparts of volunteer specialists—public relations experts, political party or issue organizers, market researchers—have some of the same skills. Others—like journalists, small business entrepreneurs, police detectives and police officers on the beat, social workers, and probation officers—have some of the same need for networking and patrolling or scouting for potentially relevant information as do volunteers. How these aptitudes or skills are modified for the volunteer by work outside the paid work force, how the profit-making, bureaucratic, or philanthropic goals of the work may influence the outcome are questions that remain to be answered in future research.

Rewards and Problems

7

The Satisfactions of Volunteering

Implicit in the previous discussions of developing specialties is the pleasure, pride, and excitement women find in discussing their accomplishments. These women also speak directly about the rewards of volunteer work. Their remarks suggest the sense of constriction or limitation that even privileged women may find in their social position. Volunteering provides a socially acceptable release. The need for greater access to the world than even their special position can afford appears in the kinds of issues these women raise when they talk about the satisfactions they find in their work. Like women workers who cannot point to high status or remuneration for their work—secretaries, airline stewardesses, waitresses, for example—these women may focus on the rewards they *can* have from contacts with interesting people or places in defense of their occupation. Volunteers bring both a special sensitivity and defensiveness to this discussion, for they are always answering or anticipating questions about their continued commitment to unpaid work.

An additional problem for these women of the leisure class is created by their own, not quite explicit, sense of how different or special their own circumstances are from those of the less privileged. Volunteer work offers the opportunity to befriend others who would be inaccessible through usual social contacts. At the same time, these women can withdraw or set limits on newly developing intimacies as they wish. The contacts are "safe" accordingly, even though they provide an experience not otherwise available. Women show some sensitivity to these issues in interviews as the discus-

sions of "dear persons" will show. Their desire, however, to minimize class differences and to emphasize the democratizing aspects
of volunteer work make this topic one that is hard for women to
face directly. Instead, they focus on the opportunities voluntarism
offers to widen their experience.

Windows to the World

Gilded cages can be confining, even if luxurious, because any style
of life or position in society can be limited to a narrow sphere
through routine and habit unless one has some rationale for expanding or breaking the pattern. Careers which have this opportunity inherent in them are seen as "glamorous" because of it. Journalists, traveling business people, airplane stewardesses, even
social science researchers, are thought to have interesting lives because their work can take them beyond a customary social circle.
These careers suggest opportunities for meeting interesting people
or visiting interesting places. Routine jobs that tie workers to one
place where they see few or no people all day are the antithesis of
this glamorous career; and the work of housewives, even wealthy
ones, can easily be categorized as one of these routine jobs. The
problem of inserting variety and interest into an otherwise routine
and isolating life pattern can be acute for wives of busy, successful
husbands who are away for long periods of time and who consequently relegate all home care and child supervision to the wife
(Fowlkes 1980). Often the nature of this responsibility is taxing;
work on behalf of class and family is the price these women pay for
privileged lives (where there is property to manage, entertaining to
be organized, children to be reared, collateral relations to be attended). This work would make regular paid employment difficult
even if that were an acceptable alternative for traditional women.
A volunteer, even a civic leader with many responsibilities, can
have the flexible work schedule that many professionals and self-
employed people enjoy. With this opportunity comes the interest
and variety in daily interchanges that add excitement and satisfaction to life. At the same time, the work is demanding enough so
that women say it "keeps them on their toes," or that it keeps them
"from getting lazy." They realize, then, that some of the satisfaction
of the work resides in its process and structure. Most generally, satisfaction arises through opportunities to do or see something new.
As one woman put it, "It's the stimulation, activity, and intrigue"
that is so much enjoyed. Specifically, this opportunity appears as

access of various kinds: to friends, other social and occupational worlds, places.

The advantages of a traditional life style for women who are well off include security and comfort; but any domestic circle can become confining. One thing women in this position find gratifying is the opportunity to make new friends through their working relationships. If they are new to the community, their volunteer work provides a quick way to make friends. "I would not have had the number of friends in a new community as a professional person that you make as a volunteer." It also provides a common basis for establishing rapport with others in a short time. Volunteer work can mean "getting to know people quickly because you don't have to push through all the chaff. You have the common interests." As one diversifies in volunteer work, the range of friendships also broadens.

> One of the more interesting things about volunteering is that you are given the chance to change around and work with so many different kinds of people. Then the variety of things I've done, I have developed a broader sense of acquaintances [even though] I can't always remember the names and which board [we] worked [together] on.

The preceding comment by a university trustee and participant on many other school boards suggests that some of these friendships are at the level of casual acquaintances. Or friendship may be defined in terms of stimulating interchanges between strangers who meet over a common cause.

Some reminiscences suggest casual acquaintances are the satisfaction—with the added exhilaration and stimulation provided by an association which provides a convention atmosphere. Others in this study speak of enduring relations, characterized by great affection and respect, that were developed through the volunteer context.

Many friendships arise among women who otherwise would only have known one another casually. But sometimes friendships, whether close or casual, develop outside the usual patterns of sociability for these women. When they do, they have a special "hands-across-the-sea" character which informants are proud of or pleased with, so they speak of this opportunity as one of the satisfactions in their careers.

These contacts may arise while working together on boards, the arena where most of the volunteer leader's activities take place (see chapter 9). Women enjoy the fellowship and the sense of teamwork that comes from working in these settings. In this way, they are like the men and women who serve as college and university trustees and who report the same satisfactions (Wood 1985:58).

A satisfaction these women share with many who volunteer is the opportunity for the gratifications associated with altruistic work where the recipients are pleased and helped by the encounter. For most of these women, this experience is invariably associated with early stages of their career, where the greatest satisfaction came from the direct service ("There is nothing like a smile on the face of a client whom you have helped"). Later in their careers, the administrative and organizing work that replaces service is sometimes rationalized, at least in part, as helping others to serve. "There were satisfactions in bringing others along and giving them the opportunity to work for the smile on the face of the client."

Whether they graduate to leadership positions, as do the women in this study, or remain engrossed in one-to-one service, this kind of volunteer engagement is attractive enough to serve as an important way of securing commitment.

> When I was . . . in college, the YMCA representative came around to my beginning psychology class and asked if anyone [would volunteer] at the local . . . hospital. . . . I went and tried it and I was hooked forever. [It was] the quality, I guess, of a relationship which is essentially working on a one-to-one basis with somebody in which you are both better for it in the end.

Three major arenas for this experience are helping the sick, the aged, and the young. Working with very ill or disabled people takes a special kind of talent; for, as we have seen, some women wish to avoid "sad things." For those who do not shrink away, there are rewards. In this category are women who read for the blind and those who combine two areas, such as working with sick children. While some women feel constrained to leave service work as their leadership roles become more demanding, a few try to keep some time for the one-to-one service. In the field of service to the aged, the returns can be so gratifying that a woman may not wish to lose them. "They will tell you marvelous anecdotes. You miss a lot by not listening."

Generally, the most popular arena for one-to-one service is working with the young. Orphans, foster children, the handicapped, the underprivileged, as well as the children of their own milieu (in nurseries, public and private schools, children's clubs, and special activities) attract the service efforts of young women and mothers. As noted, some may embark on career lines in politics, health, education, and welfare through such early interests. But for many the focus is on the immediate interpersonal gratifications, what one woman called "psychic income."

> Our commitment was to tutor the first grade level on a one-to-one basis twice a week for a number of hours. I did that for four years. . . . I had to give it up because of this [presidency] and I hated to do it. There is a great sense of accomplishment at the progress with a child . . . and a satisfaction that comes back much greater than you ever give. . . . What do they call it, psychic income?

While the sense of accomplishment may not always be entirely realistic (one woman volunteering as a tutor asserted: "You can change a child's life in a couple of hours") it is clear that the response from those helped and the quality of the interaction as experienced by the volunteer give this experience a "lift" or a "high" that is much valued for its own sake as well as for the opportunity to help another.

Another kind of stimulation women enjoy from their volunteer work—and that sometimes involves the gratification of one-to-one service—is meeting people from across the class and race barriers usually separating well-off middle- and upper-class women from others. Incorporating these people into their routines of community service, women are quick to point out this range of acquaintance and friendship when the names of minority community, labor, political, and business leaders arise. At luncheons with volunteer leaders, listening to them talk to one another about current projects, I would notice that as names would arise, listeners would insert their claims to friendship with those discussed. All concerned would then chime in and assert or reaffirm the status of the discussed as a nice or interesting person worth knowing. Even people with vaguely alarming reputations are included here and such individuals are firmly placed within the general category of approval by being called "a dear person." Consequently, gang leaders, political activists, mental patients may all be called dear persons, as in the following: "When I was on the Mental Health Board . . . I was locked in with a man who was going to have a lobotomy. A very dear person." Servants or ethnics also fit this category of distance combined with friendliness. Duveneck (1978:117), a civic leader who published her reminiscences, mentions her cook named Wong Chong, saying, "This old Chinese was a very dear person."

Part of the reason that women community leaders may wish to make known the range of friends and acquaintances they enjoy is related to their "portfolio" development. As the worlds of community service change under the impetus of new consumer and minority pressures, these women have to prove that they are knowledgeable and flexible enough to survive in these contexts. The range of their acquaintanceship is part of that proof. There are practical reasons, then, for volunteer leaders to pride themselves on the ability to survive—and make friends—in mixed company. Another practical reason arises from the nature of board work where staff and/or motley constituencies are involved. Board members for hospitals, universities, or other organizations attracting public concern, particularly in times of social unrest and public dissension, have to be aware of and sensitive to undercurrents of disagreement and dissatisfaction. The better they understand other participants, the more likely they can engage in preventive action and avert open conflict. Or, if conflict cannot be forestalled, the better they can emerge from the public confrontations that occur. The ability to work with clerical and professional staff on boards is also much prized. Further, as community leaders noted in earlier chapters, sympathy for and interest in people with fewer advantages and opportunities can help create a bond of understanding as well as an esprit to weld disparate persons together in a common cause.

Sometimes this bond carries some overtones of benevolent maternalism, as in the following anecdote:

> [I know a young black man] who works with the [local ghetto youth group] to establish food stamp programs and children's breakfasts. I have helped them along. Johnny is an utter gentleman when he comes to see me. I am proud of him. I got a call from him the other day. "Mrs. Lanahan," he said, "How's everything?" I said, "I'm as busy as a bird dog." And he said, "Well, I'm going to add to it. I want you to serve on the board for aging we are starting here." I said, "Well, I'm terribly busy. Maybe you can get someone better," "No," he said, "I want you." "All right, Johnny," I said, "I will until you are established." That is where I stand with the blacks.

In this example, the satisfaction of the now elderly speaker comes from her ability to work with the black community and with young people and youth groups despite her age. The bonds of mutual respect and trust are affirmed across the distance created by differences in age, race, sex, and class. Yet the distance is also affirmed.

The young man is called by his nickname while the speaker receives the special courtesy of the more formal title Mrs. and her surname.

In the following example, the satisfaction of the speaker arises from her ability to socialize with working-class men. A somewhat younger woman than the first speaker, her style is not so formal, and she prides herself on a first-name basis of friendship across class and sex barriers. But the distance is reaffirmed in other ways, as she took pains to explain.

> I am the only one on the Zoological Commission not employed. So I have a lot more free time. I go to more things and get more involved. I know the [maintenance men and the keepers] and the other people who are employed. The . . . men have a luncheon every year and cook their food and invite me. So I have a very fine rapport. I am the only one of the board that they call by first name. . . . Of course they respect me and all that, but it's just on a more friendly basis.

In addition to priding themselves on their ability to transcend the usual social distinctions, women are pleased when their volunteer work gives them the opportunity to demonstrate tolerance and flexibility.

These remarks assume that the speaker fully understands the relationship she has with others of different statuses and interests. We do not know what they would say about that association. It seems likely, however, that most of these others—including the "dear persons" among whom the researcher might be included— are not sufficiently intimate for a really egalitarian friendship to develop. Yet the opportunity to make friends extends across the barriers of different classes and statuses. Women are also sometimes pleased by their contacts with much younger and more modern women in their own social worlds. The ability to work with younger people is a saving grace for many elderly community leaders.

Occasionally, the friendships formed may even have a tinge of the exotic, as in the following:

> I worked a seventy-hour week with the carney people . . . I did it because the man who wanted help was someone who had helped out at raising money [for the private school we started]. . . . These were all old carney people and they taught me how to get a tap [pitch] going.
>
> We became great friends. One of them said, "If ever you need anyone rubbed out, let us know." Naturally, I don't

know if they could really do that, and the suggestion is ter-
rifying. But it was their way of showing that they liked me.

While some of these friendships seem to have some patronization about them, other "hands-across-the-sea" friendships have
the quality of important personal relations in that informants may
wish to share family events. Staff are invited to a board member's
anniversary or a daughter's wedding party, for example. In the following account, a woman spoke of entertaining people from the
community at her daughter's debutante party—a meeting of east
and west, as it were:

> The people I met from the foster child agency I see occa-
> sionally, though not in everyday life. But when my daugh-
> ter had her coming out party, I invited them all and they all
> came. And [there is a] woman . . . at the agency I still see.
> And we have a warm, close relationship. . . . Not all my
> friends are Junior League.

This account suggests that while many friendships, here as any-
where, tend to become ritualized in their expressions of solidarity
once their base in working together disappears, some persist.
Others are reactivated for symbolic occasions (weddings, coming
out parties). Or they can be reactivated by a new need to work together, as in the following:

> I invited a former communist I had known in the depres-
> sion to a dinner party to discuss some of the issues of the
> effort to preserve open spaces for parks in the city. And my
> sister was there. She is not really interested in this sort of
> thing. She said she had been somewhat dubious about
> Manny Alvarez; but since he kissed me, she guessed it was
> all right.

The options, rather than the limitations, provided by these sociable excursions out of one's usual pattern are emphasized since
the focus is upon broadening rather than limiting one's sphere. Except for the provisos set by a few of the older respondents, then,
the wish is to minimize social distance in friendships. Once in a
while informants are caught up short by some of their working colleagues who point out that some of the sociability engendered by
common interests is quite clearly and obviously limited. "The
[female] labor leaders [mentioned to me that they] were always invited to the money-raising functions and the luncheons or dinners
with a price, but they were never invited into our homes." Similar
problems have been known to arise in the organization of commu-

nity fund-raisers. Prominent Jewish philanthropists have been courted and urged to give the first big donations that spearhead a campaign and signal less generous or innovative donors to join. However, these Jewish philanthropists are not included in the "select" social events, clubs, boards, or other more social relations that indicate acceptance in an inner circle of friends. Until the late sixties, for example, their daughters were not asked to join the Junior League, even though the Junior League regularly and successfully solicited them for its causes. These patterns are changing—and have already changed to some extent—both across the country generally and in Pacific City; but they have not disappeared. And efforts at any friendly overtures across the span of class interests have to be seen within that context.

While many informants in this study are not from that inner circle of combined social, economic, and political elite that participates in the power structure of the city, some are. And occasionally one can glimpse the chasm they unconsciously assume between themselves and others. Elsewhere (Daniels 1980) I have written about the problem of studying people of higher status than the researchers. This study provided many examples for that paper. Here I wish only to point out that friendship with someone like me can be seen as one of the rewards of community service. This is how one well-connected and active community leader spoke of her satisfactions from volunteer work: "It's a very broadening educational input from being out in the community . . . a fantastic opportunity to learn what is going on. It is a challenge . . . meeting new people at different levels of society, like you."

My sociologist's ear had picked up the term "different levels of society," so I kidded the informant about what she might have meant. I joked about how we sociologists talk about the equalizing effect of education; even though my social origins might be termed humble, I could now pass muster as an equal. My informant did not want to joke about class and social station. She became quite flustered, and reddened, saying she hadn't meant *that* at all but that I was a professional and so from a different world. When I saw I had touched a sore point, I stopped teasing; for I had not meant to confront or challenge her. The incident is suggestive, however, and corroborates the picture of the uneasiness felt by respondents in discussions of class and status. The discomfort created by open discussion may be a sign of the respondents' unwillingness to discuss their continued participation in a society stratified by social class despite the American creed of equality. The opportunity to evade these class differences is desired, but not at the cost of a radical examination of the entire social hierarchy. Many men and women in society and "from all walks of life" want the advantages of their position without the disadvantages it may entail; "wanting to have your cake and eat it too" is a well-known human foible. Therefore, it is not hard to imagine that women who want to transcend class barriers, yet leave them in place, must walk a delicate line. The possibility of a successful balancing act is also one of the satisfactions of volunteering.

It is important to stress the fact that even a partial opening of class barriers through the pressures of consumer, minority, and other civic interests has made life more interesting for those who found their lives confining. As one woman said, "The composition of boards has changed enormously and now they're much more interesting. They have broadened enormously and they're not just the usual [mix of] banker, lawyer, society lady." Some are grateful for the opportunity to make friends from social worlds they could not enter except through their social service; for it is not only upper-class enclaves that restrict entry.

A few are really surprised to find friends and allies where they had initially expected enemies. One woman had intensely disliked a political leader at first and had told him so. She said she didn't trust him but would work with him on a coming election issue. Fortunately he liked her direct, forthright manner. Eventually they became very close friends, even though at first he was everything she didn't like: a loudmouthed, voluble, flashy, Hispanic ward heeler with a pugnacious, lower-class style. Ultimately he showed his friendship in heroic acts of support in various community services and she found herself doing the same for him in his campaigns. Her perspectives on class and ethnic stereotypes began to change drastically after that friendship developed and it led to other strong and close friendships across class, race, and sex barriers.

Another prominent woman with a great reputation for taking people under her wing was famous for her ability to get along with young people. She could touch and inspire them and she could defuse their hostility and destructiveness, endemic or already rampant, in public meetings. Among her loyal followers and supporters, then, were college-age students and young professionals who came to her for advice. Her coterie also included ghetto, suburban, and working-class community youths of both sexes who also admired and respected her. The quirky, affectionate relationships that

continually developed between young people and this quite imposing dowager-like older woman were a source of amazement and curiosity to the more conservative and sedate members of her social
world. The older woman enjoyed not only the friendships but the
fun of surprising and even annoying those of her contemporaries
she considered too stodgy.

The satisfactions women report from winning access to new
friends should not be dismissed as just "slumming," even though
such an element may be a part of the fun of their work for some
women. A more complex relationship is suggested by the accounts
presented in this section: the satisfaction and sense of privilege
that arises from meeting a memorable person, a great human
being, an individual who captures one's imagination or touches
one's sensibilities. Such a satisfaction, of course, can be a rewarding
experience for anyone. The genteel language of many informants
permits some confusion over whether they are talking about someone from another social world who can, in some sense, be both categorized and dismissed as a "dear person" or whether a friendship
or moment of friendship is recalled because a woman was touched
and also touched another, consequently even changing herself or
changing the life of the other. It is this possibility of real intimacy
and the privilege of a glimpse into the feelings or thoughts of someone generally regarded as strange or even repugnant that can be
rewarding. Any or all of these facets of "hands-across-the-sea" are
involved in the satisfaction women may derive from their work as
civic leaders.

Another satisfaction that volunteer leadership makes possible is
the excitement of meeting and knowing celebrities—local or national and even international personages from the worlds of arts
and letters, politics, government, professions, and business. These
gratifications have been mentioned in preceding chapters, as when
a woman noted that she kept her husband happy about the low-
status political workers constantly passing through the house by
introducing him to important political leaders and elected officials
from time to time. The women working in cultural areas, of course,
meet prominent musicians, artists, and actors. The interest is particularly keen when the volunteer has a serious personal interest in
the area where the celebrity is a star. Or the celebrity aura may
simply attach to the interesting people with specialized talents or
knowledge that become accessible to women through their work.
Meeting celebrities may be one of the main rewards in a little package of benefits. Or it can be an added treat in some already exciting

activity. The importance of celebrity contact may sometimes mean a great deal to a volunteer as shown when there is a miscue of some kind and it doesn't occur as planned.

> The year we had [a movie star] as the MC, at the end of the program, someone slipped a bouquet of roses into the president's hand and said give that to [the star] . . . I was very hurt. I should really have given that bouquet [as is customary for chairman of the event]. [I told the president] and she said, "Forgive me, forgive me, . . . I just didn't think." I said it didn't matter; but I was upset about that.

Sometimes women are flattered by special attentions from celebrities, as when the aide of an important presidential cabinet secretary asked a civic leader to lunch in the secretary's suite with business and labor leaders to advise on a crucial matter in that particular region, but women in this study did not dwell on such affairs. Contacts with celebrities are reported in off-hand asides; yet a variety of contacts with celebrities is indicated by the photographs of famous artists, movie and television stars, presidents and senators, local congress people, and mayors displayed in their homes—all personally inscribed or showing the civic leader and celebrity together.

In general, while women don't stress the importance of meeting glamorous personages in the array of satisfactions derived from community work, it is there as a fringe benefit worth mentioning. Like the chance for "hands-across-the-sea" encounters and other unexpected friendships, it can widen the world and provide new perspectives.

The opportunities for finding new and unexpected friends may seem personally rewarding because of the quality of the friendship that develops. It can also be seen as an avenue to other worlds. The friends, then, act as gatekeepers who guide these women into a new terrain where they will then be able to manage on their own. Two such opportunities are mentioned by a few informants: access to business connections and access to politics.

Access to the world of business requires more than introductions; it requires some substantive learning and involvement as well. But just as important, it requires a gradual acquisition of self-confidence and willingness to move into areas previously difficult for, and even closed to, many traditionally oriented women. The volunteer experience can provide the right training ground. As noted earlier, a talent for business, and an interest in pursuing the access to business worlds that volunteer work encourages, are possibilities that open for women through civic work. But a few women in this study have always had such interests, combining service and paid work throughout their careers. Four women, for example, have been associated with major department store chains through some combination of family and marriage or early employment. The amount of time given in each world differs among these women, and for each of them it may vary over time. They may marry into the business and leave paid employment or remain or return in a partly employed status or, as family members, serve on the corporate board or in some paid advisory status. These women who are especially knowledgeable about money, not only in fund-raising but also in investment, production, marketing and sales, can be especially helpful to others. The more knowledgeable teach the less sophisticated how to read a financial statement or analyze a budget. Those with more ambition may learn about long-term planning, investment, personnel practices, and the interplay between business and governmental regulation.

Volunteer work is a traditional avenue into the world of politics in this country. One can approach the avenue directly by working steadily for a political party or a succession of candidates. A few women in this study have developed access in this way; but most who approach the political world do so obliquely through the realization that certain kinds of civic causes can only be advanced through political action. Again, as with business access, the entry may become a stepping-stone to paid employment or political office, or it may be used to develop a greater network of alliances and a larger store of information to use in further volunteer causes.

Women especially interested in conservation quickly learn that their goals require development of political alliances. Those concerned about public education also find that they must develop political ties to further educational goals. In either case the first access, both to an understanding of the importance of politics and to influential people who can provide entry to that world, arises in volunteer work. A woman comes to know "everyone at City Hall" through years of pursuing one civic cause after another. Or early experience in a neighborhood civic improvement project may provide the acquaintance with a labor leader that is so helpful in collecting the necessary labor endorsements in a conservation bond issue.

This access is reviewed here, as part of the satisfactions and rewards of volunteering, because of the opportunity it offers for a range of very different experiences, ordinarily beyond the traditional volunteer's ken. For the community leader interested in a philanthropic career, the access to politics offers many of the satisfactions mentioned earlier—acquaintance with celebrities and some knowledge of the world of power brokers in politics.

Another somewhat oblique approach (at least in the past) to the world of politics has been through the League of Women Voters. Participation in this organization gives access to the political arena —and to office (see Clusen 1979:112–32); but the recruitment pattern and nonpartisan stance of the League has offered some limitations to women interested in traveling this route.

The generally middle-to-upper-class backgrounds of the membership encourage assumptions that discourage membership from working-class women: for example, the expectation that local meetings can be held in members' homes implies a home where it is comfortable to have twelve to fourteen women at a time. The language for studying issues and developing a consensus assumes a middle-class, educated style in organization and presentation. Consequently, League membership may not encourage the development of a broader constituency than that already available in women's usual range of volunteer service.

In addition, the stance of nonpartisanship may encourage women to believe their activities are "above" some of the crasser aspects of politics. Their general tendency to avoid confrontation or even argument may encourage a somewhat unrealistic notion that issues can be or will be resolved through cool, rational analysis of both sides of an issue. The importance of power politics and special interests are overlooked.

Consequently, while women may have received training in organization skills (going up through the committees and chairs of the organization) and have learned how to do research (following legislative bills through committees, studying city charters and state constitutions), they may still be naive about politics. One woman felt she learned more about politics by working in campaigns and then running for office herself than she had through her years in the League.

> The League has prided itself on nonpartisanship, but it crossed the mayor in its recommendations against a bond issue he was supporting. Then, after his reelection, there were no active members from the League of Women Voters appointed to any city commissions. The officers went to see the mayor in some consternation. But the mayor told

them: "You don't cash in loser's chips at the winner's window." They should have understood [that hard political
lesson].

Notwithstanding these limitations, the League of Women Voters,
like the Junior League or the Volunteers Bureau, can provide a sheltered, structured workshop atmosphere for the woman interested
in familiarizing herself with political issues in the city.

Women who become volunteer leaders sometimes find that the
world opens to them, quite literally, in a way previously unknown.
And they relish this opportunity. The women mention the opportunity to travel, on their own and without any family accompanying them, as a special kind of treat that fosters a sense of independence as well as offering the chance to meet new people in new
places. Again, the glamour of a setting, as well as the celebrities
who may participate, is sometimes seen as part of the rewards in
philanthropic work: a famous country estate of an eastern financier
may be headquarters for a conference, a visit to Washington may
entail an invitation to the White House, a symposium or conference may be held in an exotic locale—the Bahamas, Puerto Rico,
China.

All the opportunities to expand horizons suggested by new
friendships and new access help women to construct a larger identity beyond the traditional pattern in which they were raised. The
opportunity to travel comes to be seen as part of the general opportunity to learn new things. And, as we have seen, able, active, energetic women dislike and even fear boredom and routine. They want
to learn new things, develop new skills, meet challenges. In this
process, they also test their abilities and develop self-confidence.

Learning New Things

As women enter new organizations, accept new offices, and meet
new challenges, they inevitably learn something new, like the skills
in fund-raising or public relations mentioned earlier. This process
is also seen as a reward and even a privilege by some women. As
one woman put it:

> I learned a great deal more from this job than I ever learned
> from college . . . you learn about groups and you learn
> about community. I took a management training course
> and that was useful. . . . But every day I was learning just
> by working with the staff. That to me was a great reward.

Part of the learning process, discussed earlier, is learning about one's own abilities, one's knacks, tastes, antipathies, and *capacity* to learn. This learning process is part of the reward system too. The reward here is the opportunity for self-growth and self-realization. This type of reward is prized by many in a society which stresses self-actualization and personality individuation. It is not surprising, then, that these women also prize it.

Another opportunity prized by these women—as well as others in the society—is the chance to build self-confidence. From Dale Carnegie (1936) to the present, the popularity of self-confidence building manuals attests to the general pervasiveness of insecurity about or interest in how to develop a "positive image" of self. While it is not unique to these women, then, lack of self-confidence is often a problem, even for highly skilled, well-regarded and well-off traditional women. Their place within the traditional family structure of their class does not engender the self-confidence they would like to have. As indicated in the hesitant and even self-deprecatory comments women made in interviews, some women continue to have problems about self-confidence even when they are demonstrably successful. The boost to self-confidence given by a growing awareness of how competent they are and how well-regarded they have become is often seen as a great reward, accordingly. Self-confidence also develops from having one's own sphere. This type of assurance may be especially important for women who are not sure they can be leaders but who would enjoy such a role. It is, as one woman put it, "the opportunity to do things that were not otherwise possible" that helps gain or regain confidence. Success in volunteer work provides the springboard to lever women out of confining routines. It also provides the opportunity to reflect back upon progress once one has escaped the confinement of domestic or social circles. In this reflection, women come to think better of themselves, and as one originally shy woman said, experience the reward of "personal esteem. I found out I could do something . . . and in this way I could get some self-identity and some confidence."

This sense of accomplishing something can be summarized or symbolized in the array of accomplishments that women can look back upon or review for themselves or others. A discussion of these accomplishments shows not only what women regard as rewarding but also how specific accomplishments are tied to the larger vision of community service that is at the core of the ideology of voluntarism informants espouse.

Accomplishments

In speaking of accomplishments that were the greatest sources of pride, some, as noted earlier, spoke of their families. A complementary response, also focusing on traditional expectations for women, reviewed altruistic efforts in helping others, facilitating the growth of organizations, bringing influential people together so *they* could accomplish something, organizing a task so that, for example, a book could be published or an art show could be mounted and exhibited.

One woman saw her moment of glory as the culmination of a lot of work to further what was, essentially, a family project. In mounting a great art exhibition for the city, this woman also asserted the importance of her family in producing the cultural heritage of that city.

> I guess the art show we put on [ranks as my greatest achievement]. We worked like crazy on that. It was such a success and so exciting to see it happen. It was worth everything. It was my happiest moment. The whole thing . . . was my mother-in-law's idea. She thought of the whole idea of the show and she knew the people who owned the paintings and wanted to see them all together.

The inhibitions common among these women concerning boasting, or even self-assertiveness, make it difficult for some to assess the full range of what they have accomplished. Some don't know of any particular accomplishment or say they can't think of any, despite their imposing list of appointments (which are both reward for and indication of accomplishment). Of course, personal achievement does not loom large as an explicit goal for every woman; it is then natural to forget a number of accomplishments when asked to review a long career. An added difficulty in making assessments follows from the nature of work that is never done independently of all others and requires considerable community participation to be successful.

Some women sidestep the issue by focusing on what gives them a *personal* sense of accomplishment rather than what difference their efforts have made to the community. They may see their own self-development as their greatest accomplishment. Or it may be pride in developing craftsmanship ("I was glad to succeed in writing . . . a lot of writers try and don't succeed"), or in putting forward one's very best effort. One woman expressed a certain grim satisfaction in forcing the city's power structure to take respectful notice of her accomplishments. But, again, her primary focus was on her personal conquest of obstacles rather than the substantial accomplishments in service accompanying that conquest.

A few of the older women, very traditional in their views of appropriate roles for women, said their big accomplishments dated from the war years. When it was permissible—because it was necessary for women to play an important role in the economy—they enjoyed, and were proud of, their participation. These women worked in the Red Cross as ambulance drivers, became nurses' aides, and developed war relief programs for refugees and the homeless overseas. A few were helpful enough to receive decorations from foreign powers or expressions of gratitude from local and federal officials.

Reviewing what satisfactions these women say they find in their volunteer work shows us both their efforts to escape the confines of traditional roles and the limits upon how far they want to travel. Some of the benefits—like meeting new people, associating with celebrities, visiting new places—can be assimilated without difficulty within the general expectations of what women of their class background and life-style may undertake. The philosophy and ideology of voluntarism provide the necessary framework to justify the effort, and the personal satisfactions that accrue are understandable and acceptable in the social circles where these women move. Other satisfactions, like those connected to development of competence in business and politics, are marginal as serious interests for traditional women, though acceptable if maintained as avocations.

These interests, like the development of self-confidence that appears as a possible consequence of a sense of accomplishment, are appropriate if they do not lead to overt conflict with traditional expectations of a woman's behavior. Except for women who are widowed or divorced, informants don't even expect satisfactions to include economic and social independence. The growth of self-confidence is correspondingly limited. The limited aspirations these women set for themselves and their loyalty to the traditional system in which women accept subordination to men may be incompatible with any strong movement toward independence and self-assertion.

Whatever the scope of satisfactions from their volunteer work, these women also indicate by their efforts to reach across status and class barriers what kinds of bridges in society they have been able to construct for the city—and the larger society. The friendships they have been able to create offer support for Domhoff's contention (1971:34) that leisure-class women mediate between their own class and other interests in the society to provide welfare and other services where they are needed. Reports of successful friendships across class lines indicate that these women are indeed engaged in this activity as they go about their volunteer work. Most generally, then, the satisfactions of volunteering reassure women not only that they are capable but also that they are accomplishing the work that the ideology of volunteering suggests they do.

8

Career Contingencies

A number of possible problems may arise in the course of a career. The range of potential difficulties and the likelihood that any will occur is not always easy to assess in advance. As noted in the introduction, careers are "running adjustments," as Hughes puts it, "between a man, his life, and his professional world." The careers described in this study are adjustments between a woman's own interest in a career, the satisfactions it offers, her sense of family responsibility, her social concerns, and her sense of what career limits are set and directions indicated by opportunity and propriety. The contingencies discussed here suggest the framework within which running adjustments are made. Problems arise because women have chosen careers containing some ambiguities about their legitimacy. Unlike physicians, for example, women volunteers have no well-recognized calling, depicted and idealized in novels and the mass media, around which a sense of the importance of their career can coalesce. Further, they have no coordinated system of expectations from clients or other professionals about what is expected of them. Consequently, each woman creates her own career line, idiosyncratically and extemporaneously, without seeing the common elements in this endeavor. The lack of an official base, the normative confusion over the appropriateness of volunteer costs as business expenses, the problems of building, stabilizing, and retiring from a volunteer career, and the potential for identification of career ambition with social climbing—all contribute to this ambiguity.

Working without an Official Base

The problems common to the nonsalaried workers concern their lack of various resources associated with stable employment in responsible or executive positions. First, they have no regularly available staff support. Second, they carry out their duties in a physical setting that combines a confusing mixture of home, social, and work-related responsibilities. The women themselves are not always sure whether they are gossiping or building a network of volunteer participants as they talk on the phone. They wonder if they are shortchanging their family or their volunteer task when they work at home and then rush from luncheon appointment to family errand. These confusions are exacerbated by their lack of an official base. They have no separate office world in which to insulate themselves from conflicting responsibilities. Finally, while these foregoing difficulties may also exist for home workers receiving wages or fees, they are compounded for the volunteer woman who may not *appear* to be working, who receives no financial return to justify her efforts. The leisure-class woman faces the quandary of how to manage a demanding work schedule while appearing as—and meeting the responsibilities of—a woman of her class. However she juggles her various responsibilities, she does so without the usual resources available to salaried executives. Employed men or women who rise to community leadership often have high-status positions with perquisites attached to be used at the discretion of the incumbents. Such paid workers usually have a variety of support resources that even the wealthiest women do not ordinarily enjoy: office staff, business or professional expense accounts for travel and entertainment, and space to store and maintain files. These assets can be used to "bootleg" volunteer work as well. Sometimes firms also assign staff to assist their representative on a local fund drive or other volunteer organization for the public relations benefit that is anticipated (Ross 1953:453).

Women who work without the staff supports supplied through paid employment, yet who are full-time volunteer executives in a variety of organizations, are not so fortunate. They consult on many community projects and are sometimes hard-pressed to keep track of everything. They have no regular staff who can be commandeered to type letters for them, send out mailings, xerox materials, phone and run errands. Hence, even the most distinguished community leader must look for ways to maintain her "business." For, in a sense, each of these women is an entrepreneur, whether moving from one organization to another, or rising through the hierarchy in any one of them. Various strategies are common: some women bootleg office assistance and supplies from their husband's business; others are fortunate to have excellent staffing for some or-

ganization they serve. These adjustments, however, are impermanent; other peoples' business offices may be unable to grant a
steady stream of favors. Further, women lose their staff when they
resign from a board or their term of office expires. In any case,
these services are not a "right" that women can expect on a regular
basis. Consequently, a few hire full-time or part-time secretaries,
although this pattern is fairly uncommon. (No nonsalaried working
women interviewed had a full-time assistant—and only two were
reported who do; the wealthier women have part-time assistants
who double as social secretaries and a few have part-time assistants on a temporary basis, as special projects require.) Most
women have "offices" in their homes consisting of a room, or a section of one, with desk and files. A few also own an electric typewriter. In general, however, each woman manages correspondence, xeroxing, telephoning, trips to the post office for postage,
and mailing by herself or with some family assistance.

The responsibility for all such duties, on top of the work of committee meetings and preparation for them, must be sandwiched in
among home and family duties. This integration requires women
to be extremely well-organized. Many of these women take courses
to learn special tips on the subject of efficiency and organization.
Some patterns of adjustment have become generally accepted.
There is a general understanding, for example, that these women
are to be called by other volunteer women only between 8:00 and
9:30 A.M. The rest of the day they are too busy and evenings are
reserved for family. Every woman carries an appointment book at
all times. These little books are used for appointments, but also
for notes, useful suggestions, reminders, and errands. Daily or
weekly schedules are then transferred by some to a larger schedule
to accommodate a longer time period; but most women seem to
carry a yearly book. The books, in addition, chronicle family, personal, and social events. For these women are also going to hairdressers, having lunch with friends, attending a matinee at the
symphony, arranging for a child's visit to the dentist, visiting an
aged relative in the hospital, squeezing in family errands or shopping, in addition to an average of three meetings a day and a schedule of "business" lunches. In this study, most women (except for
those retired or preparing to retire) had to be contacted well in advance of the desired time for an interview. Except when they had
cancellations, meetings had to be planned for two or three weeks
ahead and sometimes had to be rescheduled as their commitments

required. These fragmented, busy schedules require organization and tenacity. Requests from friends and family are harder to deny when one cannot point to the scheduled imperatives of a paid career. These women lack a stable base (an office to go to every morning) and an institutional or professional title (some official position with a salary attached). These attributes offer both a barrier and a rationale to ward off alternative demands on time. It is difficult to show how volunteer work is serious competition with social and family responsibilities. Justification of this alternative requires constant vigilance from even the most respected civic leader.

One problem in adjusting this schedule is a traditional woman's ambivalence about playing either the family or the volunteer role to the hilt. The need, and the desire, to fulfill family expectations for companionship, as well as service, motivates many of these women to choose a volunteer career over salaried employment in the first place. But they know this ambivalence about the priority of the work role consigns them to a somewhat pejorative "amateur" or dilettante status; for serious professionals in this society place their work commitment first.

The home as the setting for work and the public knowledge that this work has no financial remuneration compound the problem. Consequently, much of what volunteer women do does not "look" professional. Part of this appearance is deliberate; for volunteer women are often in the business of carefully constructing "spontaneous" events. The success of the large benefit depends greatly upon the sense of gaiety it can produce; the success of the volunteer group planning such events depends upon the bonds of friendship and commitment that develop among the planners. In addition, informal and facilitative interactions that women use to promote good working arrangements in the volunteer worlds do not fit traditional expectations as to what is important about work. Much volunteer work occurs within sociable contexts. Despite the many studies in industrial relations that demonstrate the importance of the informal patterns of relations in organization management, the importance of the sociable event is still questioned. Businessmen's lunches may be understandable as part of the workday, but ladies' luncheons and teas are more suspect. The notion of what goes on in a luncheon is gender-stereotyped as frivolous or irrelevant to business affairs. Yet much of the work preparing for formal meetings (in committees and on boards) requires this type of informal preparation.

Since women do much of their work in their homes, it requires use of the phone. It is coordinating work in any case, drawing various segments of the public into some project. The telephoners are tapping widely divergent sources and people (both salaried professionals and business executives as well as volunteer colleagues) on varying schedules. The volunteer leaders catch them when they can by phone. The stereotype of women, endlessly chattering on the telephone, obscures what they accomplish with this working tool. They are not only coordinating activities, they are engaging in the encouraging, calculating, supportive activities that "sell" the activity to others. The telephone is also an important link for women without an official base. They can maintain and strengthen relations by telephone when the opportunity to meet at work, in and around the office, is missing. The phone becomes an important tool for checking on what tasks remain undone and what organizing problems remain to be solved. In the absence of office contacts, it is also the means by which the committed reassure the faltering workers and persuade them to continue.

This persuasive stance underscores another problem for leaders in the volunteer world. Their traditional stance requires them to cloak their identity under their husband's; hence, they have no clearly recognized public status. Their lack of a "handle" to their names (like doctor or associate director or manager of the X firm) contributes to the confusion of some who, upon speaking with or meeting these women, hear or see only a stereotypical "lady" whose primary status is that of wife. In outward appearance, these women are indistinguishable from others of their class: they dress expensively and discreetly, are beautifully or carefully coiffed, and show the genteel and ladylike manners one might expect. If they are then mistaken for silly, superficial, or time-wasting women by people unaware of who they are, it cannot be helped. It is in this area that women of the leisure class face some of the disadvantages of their privileged position. Their allegiance to their own class and its system of values makes it difficult for them to openly repudiate or disavow their membership. The dilemma is one of wishing to assert one's identity as an able, professional volunteer against one's position as a member of a class. The solution to the dilemma is generally to say little, make no fuss. Accordingly it is difficult for their reputations and skills to be acknowledged beyond the circles where they are already known. The career, then, is not easily transferable to other locales.

Facing Up to the Costs of Volunteering

Serious volunteers have many of the same work-related expenses as do the salaried. But, of course, volunteers receive no remuneration to offset these expenses. Community leaders realize that society sees their work as marginal in part because the society fails to officially recognize their work-related expenses. The irony of community leadership is that volunteer work can sometimes cost a great deal to perform. The higher a woman rises, the more expenses she may incur. Many of her expenses are not considered tax deductible under current law; much of her daily work-related expenses for food, clothing, and transportation are treated as nondeductible— the same way as that of salaried workers, for example—and expenses are increased by her own reluctance to charge legitimate expenses against the organizations she serves. The reluctance to request reimbursment or file for tax deductions is partly related to volunteer ideology about the importance of altruism, the sense of noblesse oblige, and an acknowledgement of affluence. However, reticence in discussing expenses or reluctance to claim them is also related to confusion or hesitancy about asserting the legitimacy of costs as work-related. One issue to consider, then, is how or when to request tax deductions for volunteer expenses. A second issue is the actual costs of contributions, entertainment, travel, and organization building or maintenance.

A working professional or business person can claim expenses incurred in working for some not-for-profit groups as either charitable or business-related tax deductions. Full-time volunteers are much more restricted in what they can claim.[1] They may not claim as business expenses meals in their own geographic area, for example. When lunching with any of the women I had interviewed and had come to know as friendly key informants, I would often joke with them about my relatively greater ability to pick up the check—in terms of what percentage of the bill would be offset by tax deductions. I gradually learned that such jokes were ill-timed. Many women became uncomfortable when reminded of the value differences, implicit in the distinction made for tax purposes, between paid and unpaid work.

Women who combined salaried careers with their volunteer ser-

---

1. See Publication 526, Charitable Contributions, IRS, U.S. Government Printing Office, 1982:381–543/718 for an explication of the issue.

vice were, of course, able to take a greater variety of tax deductions for their expenses. Their perceptions about the necessity of keeping track of expenses changed when they moved from a solely volunteer to mixed volunteer and salaried career. Women with husbands in business or professions where charitable in-kind contributions were deductible could sometimes make the expenses a deduction from a husband's income. "During [my most active period] I spent several thousand a year. Much was picked up by my husband—his office supplies and help. Then his office would claim an "in-kind" contribution." Many costs of entertaining (and so facilitating esprit) are not deductible—whether one is a volunteer or salaried worker. In political campaign activities, for example, there are restrictions on the amount of political donations. Three informants, active in politics, recognize these limits.

Part of the problem is that some of the costs are very hard to keep in mind. None of this is deductible or else it is too much work. As one informant put it, "It's expensive in the sense you can't put your finger on it. There are . . . expenditures you don't want to bother committees with [for reimbursement]"; and as another informant said, expenses "don't come all at once so they don't hurt too much." In all, twelve women do not keep track of all or part of their expenses because of difficulties in doing so. These women come from both the rich and the less well-to-do segments of the sample; but they share a common problem. The ideology of voluntarism is that all citizens should do it, that it can be done without great cost. One inference to be drawn from their position is that it shouldn't cost a lot to volunteer, therefore expenses are nothing to be accounted.

In addition to all these difficulties connected with assessing expenses, some women are ambivalent about setting a price tag equivalent to their service. They are supposed to be engaged in altruistic work without thought of gain. Altruism brings its own benefits. They feel they get so much in return; it may be to their "personal advantage," as one woman remarked. In all, seven women, besides those twelve who couldn't be bothered, said they didn't need or want reimbursement. One of them strongly asserted: "It is a great reward working with people who care as you do. Nobody and nothing owed me anything. I did it because I wanted to and if I didn't want to I didn't have to."

Two of the women in this group seemed surprised at the notion that some costs were an expense. "I never thought of entertaining as an expense, to be honest. It was a way of entertaining myself in the place of bridge. The financial side was not significant."

In sum, twenty-one women do not record all or part of their expenses. But a goodly number (46) of these women were able to describe the expenses of volunteering in some detail. Their basic distinction seemed to be between the costs of the contributions given to some cause and the costs of facilitating some charitable activity. Obviously, donations in small (checks for individual memberships) or large (major gifts) contributions are the costs that come to mind most easily; for these expenses can be considered as either charitable or business deductions. They are more likely to be deducted accordingly. And twenty women focused on these contributions when asked about their expenses.

If one considers the informants prominent enough in their community to be widely known for philanthropic work (and listed as sponsors of causes in the organization's programs and brochures), by conservative estimate there are at least nineteen women in this study who give major gifts (at least ten thousand and, more generally, fifty to one hundred thousand dollars a year in contributions). They are joined by fifteen women who give at least one thousand dollars a year in contributions to any one organization. Five women mentioned both the requirement for such contributions from leaders in an organization and the expectation that they will give more over time.

When asked just how they discovered the rules on how much they should contribute, women found it difficult to explain. The rules on giving are not all that clear-cut; it may take time and experience to learn their nuances. Some potential givers will be affronted if donation requests are made too explicitly and too directly as a quid pro quo for some honorific appointment. Here is how one spokeswoman rebuked a junior colleague for overweening zeal.

> Two or three years ago [the organization] had a very aggressive president who decided that every member of the advisory council [of elder stateswomen and past presidents] should be assessed five hundred dollars a year. I spoke to that lady and told her in no uncertain terms that it wouldn't wash. [Another powerful women philanthropist] had called me up. She was so outraged I had to cool her out.

Either through family indoctrination, gradual socialization, or snubs administered by powerful women like the one just quoted, women learn how to give and ask for gifts. Sometimes these women speak of the difficulties they—and their husbands—face in coming to terms with great expenditures. But some of these women are matter-of-fact about the opportunity given them by their wealth. They can give generously because they have become affluent—as their husbands prospered or when they themselves have come into personal inheritances. Or they have wealthy husbands who have always been generous despite their wives' lack of personal fortune.

Some of these heavy spenders also focus on the issues raised by those who discuss the "outlay" expenditures of volunteering: the expenses of working without the salary other workers receive. In all, forty-two women in this study mentioned the range of their volunteer expenses in some detail—from gas mileage to wear and tear on their clothes. While they might not be willing to make assessments of all these costs for deduction purposes, they were aware enough of the outlay to describe it in the interview. A review of these details shows how community leaders spend money to facilitate the work of organizations and services to benefit various segments of their city. Their estimations suggest three categories for analysis: entertainment; travel; and keeping an organization afloat or building it. These expense categories also reveal some of the implicit dimensions of their work: heartening the faithful and encouraging the not yet committed through entertainment; travel for participation in broader and broader philanthropic networks as a career progresses; shoring up the structure and physical location of community organizations so that services may continue.

Twelve women focus primarily on the costs of entertainment in describing their major expenditures (and fifteen women mention entertainment as one in a mixture of the important categories of expenditures). They may keep track of these expenses for tax purposes as in the following.

> [Expenses] are high. I was trying when my income tax came to figure it out—well over one thousand dollars for one organization—just in incidental expenses. I take people to lunch, and furnish wine at parties. . . . Like I just put nine minority people on the board. So I helped because they can't afford expensive lunches. You can't equalize this volunteer work . . . unless you make it possible for people who can't afford expensive lunches once a month.

The issue of whether or not volunteering is possible for any but the privileged in society is one constantly debated in volunteer circles. This community leader is only one of the two (although I believe others do it) who specifically mentioned earmarking some of her expenditures to minimize income disparities between volunteers. She has also spent money to facilitate volunteer activities ("furnish wine at parties") as do others. Four women specifically mention the importance of liquor to grease the wheels of social interaction. Sometimes they may spend money on special gifts to their hardest workers as well as on food and liquid refreshments. Sometimes they focus on the entertainment expenditures that build both community and organizational esprit.

One quandary for a successful community leader can be that the higher she rises the more travel expenses are involved, particularly if she sits on regional and national philanthropic boards. Even if deductible, some women feel they cannot afford the costs. Out of gentility or, perhaps, embarrassment at appearing to be in straitened circumstances, they feel disinclined to ask for reimbursement. They may refuse positions or resign them for this reason, yet never state that explicitly.

> I'm going to get off that board as soon as I can. At one point the organization was sort of falling apart. And we had to meet in airports. Everybody flies in and it gets expensive. Frankly I'm not really comfortable about flying to the other end of the state or making phone calls to the east every day. Because I'm a volunteer, it's not an office expense in any way.

And so they may voluntarily limit their aspirations. As one woman said: "I structured myself in refusing certain things."

Such a position accepts the notion that volunteer leaders should pay for the privilege of serving. Four women talked about the costs of airfare as just part of the costs of volunteer participation. And another three commented on the steady, if slow, drain of money from local travel. Expenses are greatest when they involve not only one's own travel but sponsorship of the less well-to-do ("I would take extra people to conferences and pay their way").

Although travel costs may create a barrier to the development of some types of careers, they are not a serious limitation for women who focus their energies in their own locality. And, since most women in this group espouse traditional values, they are inclined to accept limitations on their own geographical mobility without much question. Accordingly, the expenses of travel do not loom large as a problem in the development of volunteer careers. It is not surprising, then, that only seven women in this study thought to mention them.

While at least half of the women in this study have experience in organization building, only five talk about the financial costs. These women may supply rent, furnishings, and all overhead expenses in opening a business that is the prime support and information dissemination system for an organization. Or they may bankroll a new organization until it gets on its feet. The costs will include purchase of postage and mailing lists, telephone expenses, xeroxing, and typing. Or they will include underwriting such projects as decoration, redecoration, and cleaning for the organization facility. This woman discusses the part donations for political "good will" can play in developing or safeguarding an organization.

> There was a noticeable rise in [campaign] contributions to incumbent [Pacific City council members] when the new museum building was under consideration. [The women supporting the project knew] the city had to accept maintenance responsibility and approve the project [even though volunteer leaders had successfully managed the drive to raise the construction funds].

Another woman explained how increasing the size of donations to a faltering organization may keep it going. "I spent a hundred dollars in tickets for the fund-raiser and gave additional as the ship was sinking. On the auxiliary I paid the highest dues and now I am a life member." Here, as in the evanescent costs of entertaining, women pay, and sometimes handsomely, for the privilege of working for nothing.

In accepting these responsibilities women also show their acceptance of informal leadership responsibilities. As Whyte (1937) points out in *Street Corner Society*, leaders in any informal group accept a system of obligations to their followers. When the corner boy leaders in his study were unemployed and could not treat their lieutenants, they worried and even became ill over a sense of failure to meet responsibility and the consequent threat to their leadership. These women are sufficiently well-off to meet the costs of leadership without such worries. Part of the general socialization process for volunteer leaders, either from their families or from their participation in community service activity, teaches women to shoulder the costs of leadership.

These expenses bother some who see them as contributing to the picture of volunteers as a special, privileged class. They don't wish the "price of admission," as it were, to serve as an excuse for inaction. And so some (4) women from both well-to-do and merely "comfortable" circumstances stress that it needn't cost much to volunteer. In the main, however, many informants (27) were quite matter-of-fact that their kind of volunteering costs a lot. They mentioned yearly sums of five hundred dollars to seven or eight thousand—with vaguer allusions to thousands, and hundreds of thousands, in major gifts. The remainder (29) of the informants hedged somewhat: they were not sure; they didn't keep track; the subject was of no consequence. But the costs of volunteering are the costs of "doing business"; the greater the sense of noblesse oblige, the greater the costs.

The ability to pay for some organizational maintenance, as well as start up costs, to offer as well as solicit contributions and emergency funds, promotes the institutionalization of services. In this way, the expenditures these women incur create the ambience in which they work as well as the more direct promotion of civic causes. These expenditures create the comfort, success, and aura of stability for their workplace.

You Must Move On

While women are divided on whether or not the costs of volunteering are significant, they all understand the conditions imposed by the instability of civic leadership. One of the problems created by the impermanent and marginal work position of the woman volunteer leader is that she is generally moving from one position to another. This condition is hard to avoid, given the fluid nature of the organizational structures in which she works.

A few women stay in key positions (on boards) for a decade or more, but it is understood that the usual tenure is—and should be—much shorter: three to five years is a reasonable term of office, either in one or rotating through several executive positions. Board membership may continue for long periods, but executive positions are expected to rotate with some regularity. The importance of this movement is built into the structure of many organizations serving a particular community. As situations in the city change, the volunteer leadership should change. "New blood" is needed to face new public relations and fund-raising problems, to inspire the rank and file, to assess and revise organizational goals.

Of course, salaried workers on temporary assignments, politicians, and professionals holding limited contracts or in limited-term offices have similar problems and face many of the same issues. However, they are highlighted for the volunteer leader who has no rationale of stable paid employment to fall back upon. When she is between jobs she may feel more ambiguously at liberty than paid workers who must have—or are expected to seek—new employment.

Community leaders express the need and even the desire to move on, explaining the value of this movement for both the organization and for their personal growth. These women develop a plan for relinquishing one set of tasks and taking on another. Sometimes this movement is part of an overall career plan; at other times women spend time and thought trying to decide how and where to move and what they would like their future to hold. Toward the end of their careers, this planning includes how and when to retire from volunteer work. Despite their understanding and acceptance of the rationale for moving on, throughout their careers many find it difficult to meet the expectation that they will leave important jobs easily.

Volunteer community leaders are, however, spurred on by the ideology that you should move on and find new employment when you have learned all you can or have completed a term of office. This ideology fits with the exigencies of volunteer organizations where rotating offices are the general pattern. Even where rotation of officers is not mandatory, it is expected. Sills (1957:48) notes that volunteer organizations try to avoid stagnation of leadership. Their publications urge membership to look constantly for new members and to rotate the office of chairman. Aside from any value placed upon democratic process and avoidance of oligarchy, rotation serves to create a wider leadership to work for the organization and to seek out new publics and participants who can help spread the word to further reaches of the community. This advantage can outweigh economies or efficiencies produced by long-term leadership that might prove more important in profit making enterprises. In recognition of this value, bylaws of many organizations require limited terms of office. The rules spare members the necessity of unpleasantness in ousting an entrenched (or a nonperforming) officer. Many in this study think that these rules are a good thing. As one woman explained it:

> The nice thing about the League was that I stayed there through being president, but then you are off the board. They have the rule that once you have been the president, you no longer serve. And that makes it easier for the next president.

Often women simply refuse to work further in the organization: "They asked me to be president again, but I had done that." Movement may be rationalized as in the best interests of both the individual and the organization when a woman has exhausted her ingenuity. Or a woman may assess her usefulness as too limited and refuse a position on that account. Too much time may have elapsed, and too many connections and contacts may have atrophied since the last position held for that old experience to be useful.

One woman amplified the argument for new blood, pointing out how valuable it was for the organization as well as the new officers.

> When they couldn't get a president to serve, they went back to a president from four years back. This is a sign that an organization is really dead. You need to cultivate new and young people to bring in new ideas and their new circle of friends if an organization is to grow and flourish.

The idea that you must move on has been sufficiently entrenched for some so that they say they can even relinquish something they love to do without a murmur. One woman had invested enormous time and energy in improving services for the aged. She had developed a program about which she spoke with considerable pride. Yet she showed no regret in announcing that the consequence of her own efforts was to do her out of a job. Such action fits with the complementary ideology about the necessity for moving on—that volunteers fill gaps in social service and point the way for business and government to institutionalize services once they have been created. Good volunteer leaders, then, pave the way for this institutionalization as well as for other volunteers. In this way, they reaffirm their own support of career mobility.

Knowing that you must move on is a spur to career diversification and planning. Some women wait till the end of one position before worrying about the next. Women who have reputations as civic leaders can usually pick and choose when the moment arises. Some women begin planning early to vary their interests so that one involvement can be developing while another phases out.

> A former president said to me, "Once having been president of the Junior League, you have no place to go." I thought, I'll always have a place to go. I am never going to do one thing because if you do you feel it is so important or you are so important that they can't get along without you. If you have three or four things you know they can get along without you.

In general, then, moving around and trying different jobs helps to assemble the package of skills and experience that enlarge a civic leader's portfolio. Careful selection of opportunities as they become available allows a woman to be acclaimed as successful. Women have a variety of plans for how to make this ascent. In the cultural field they may do it through proficiency at decorating, entertaining, and budget management to maximize profits on fundraisers. Women may cease finding anything challenging in a line of work or even a whole area of substantive interest. Consequently, they may turn, as one woman did, from culture to politics. In general, volunteer leaders move out of areas where women predominate to the fields controlled by men. Developing careers, then, can progress from cultural interests (with their pejorative overtones of frivolity) to the "serious" interests of politics or business.

Some women see their careers going through progressive stages they regard as inevitable, though in some ways regrettable. The transition often regretted is from service to administration.

> We found that our members who were good at the ground-level stuff [service to clients] didn't stay there long. . . . You start out thinking you will do the wonderful dirty work and no phone calls, no organizing, and no meetings. But our [civic leaders'] talents really lie in administrative work.

In general, though, women believe that progression through training and experience is required in development. From this perspective, it becomes easier to leave one set of tasks and take on others.

While women can review their careers and find the pattern in retrospect, the problems of how to decide what is the next best move in career development often cause considerable worry. Women cast about, in a dialectic between whatever inner promptings develop out of the growing realization of interests and antipathies and the array of opportunities offered them. This career pattern, like those for most of the women in this study, shows how progression takes one out of helper, subordinate positions after one has developed leadership skills there. The wider circles of influence present new challenges—and risks. The woman quoted next mulls over the alternatives given to her as she moves away from women-centered activities toward the rough and tumble of politics. Perhaps her resistance to planning, though it poses problems for her, is a response to the difficulties to be faced in moving from one arena to another.

> I really never have thought what I would like to do in the future. I am today oriented. . . . What am I going to do

with the rest of my life? Certainly not the PTA. I am getting too old and the children are growing up. I have been asked would I run for the school board and I think not. I value my sense of freedom. . . . Running for public office changes you . . . I think you should recognize what you are and what you can and can't do.

This woman moved into a citizen advocate role, gadfly to local governmental agencies; but she did eventually run for—and win—elected office. Other women say they want to change direction but find no opportunity sufficiently challenging. They may continue, then, with what they did in the past and wait for something new to present itself. Sometimes a plan never does appear; and not all careers are seen as continually evolving. Some women enter and retire from interests serially as organizational demands seem to require; other women stay with their interest or series of interests until exhausted, bored, or ready to retire from all active public life. Those wishing to retire sometimes see the opportunities for individual growth in their civic work as exhausted.

In a demanding job the phone rings all day and night. It gives me great peace that every morning now my phone doesn't start ringing between eight and nine. In the last years I have become more introspective and interested in the personal search level. I am less and less willing to have my private life circumscribed by organizational activities.

The problem many women face is how to make manifest their own waning interests and energies so that they may retire, gradually and gracefully, from demanding careers. Some assuage any sense of guilt or ambivalence by asserting they have "paid their dues" and given enough time to the city. Others see themselves as just too old to carry burdensome responsibility any longer. A few women end their careers, both symbolically and officially through such ceremonial events as retirement parties.

The description of a retirement party shows how these occasions celebrate and mark the accomplishments of a career—as well as how modestly the guest of honor receives these attentions.

Want to hear about my retirement party? I got invited to a surprise party for someone else and I said I had two friends coming to lunch that day so I won't be able to make it. My friend said you can't do that because it's really for you. So I asked my friends if they would come to that and we trotted down. All the agency advisory members were

> there from [the three or four major agencies I had served],
> including the new chairman of the county children's ser-
> vice. There was one nice statement. I said little.

Whatever the problems of change and retirement, they are eased
or exacerbated not only by the array of other alternatives open, but
also by the temperament of the individual. Some women fight with
themselves to relinquish something ("I was chairman for eight
years and now I must let go"), and others look forward to the end
of responsibility with relief. Despite the prevailing ideology about
needing—and wanting—to move on, some women believe relin-
quishment is hard. They tend to doubt that expressions of disinterest in decision-making powers are genuine. Perhaps they believe
that the ideology about desiring to move on—even combined with
adherence to the notion that volunteer service should be altruistic—is insufficient against the reluctance individuals feel to relinquish power. In any case, the following woman had difficulty per-
suading others she was just as happy out of a powerful position
as in it.

> I had a little letter from the last chairman. She said "I imag-
> ine you are having the same mixed emotions I did when I
> resigned: phew, it's all over, plus it's a little hard to let go of
> the reins." I don't think it would be hard for me to change
> course. I could go either way with relative ease. I do love to
> read and garden and do things with my hands. I could go
> an entirely different route and be quite happy. I am pliable.
> Generally it is harder for men with busy business lives.

In her response to the doubts of others, this woman can fall back
upon a rationale not so available for the gainfully employed; traditional women—whether or not they are involved in volunteer work
—are ready to retire to the sanctuary of home life.

The variation in temperament is also seen in the different responses to becoming a venerable and trusted advisor. The term
"mother hen" is one often used by these women. Most use it affec-
tionately or admiringly to call attention to the nurturing and advice
elder stateswomen can provide. And women will speak of themselves in these terms when they are frequently called upon by
younger women to consult or give talks for their organizations. But
some women resist this term. They will leave an area of expertise
and want no reminders of their passage from the seats of power.
Perhaps they also sense a patronizing undertone to the use of the
term that mentor, for example, would not have. The absence of any

institutionalized value to the work of a "mother hen" makes the transition from leadership roles to occasional advisor difficult for some. It may be difficult to wait in the wings until asked for advice—when no established understandings exist whereby the newly initiated "touch base" with the old guard. If a newcomer does not wish for "mothering," there is little an older, more seasoned advisor can do from the position of bystander.

The ambiguities of the advisor's position point to some of the paradoxes of the volunteer career. It is something one chooses to do for its intrinsic interest or value, without external pressure to be gainfully employed, but it suffers from the problems of activities marginal to the economy. Since it is not well-institutionalized or understood as a career, participants find it difficult to insist on their legitimacy if questioned. Trained to adopt traditional, ladylike behavior, they are hesitant to insist on their rights or proclaim their accomplishments. If they *do* insist or assert their prerogatives, there is always the danger that they will be resisted and their claim not honored. In consequence of these ambiguities and the dangers of asserting any status, rights, or privileges attending the career, women do not envision the shape and direction of volunteer careers as a generic form but as a personal or idiosyncratic accomplishment. They receive no encouragement for any other view; no increments of salary or fringe benefits, no change in formal title or responsibility heralds their increasing stature. They must turn to a review of their accomplishments, combined with their own sense of increasing self-mastery, to gain a sense of what they have achieved.

As a result of this absence of the usual reassuring markers of progress, those women who are serious workers and who become civic leaders take their sense of accomplishment as much from the progression and direction their careers have taken as from any one achievement. The lists of offices, successes, and honors lose some of their meaning when seen only as a string of events. They are also the record of experience in, and increasing knowledge about, the community. However, this record is hard to read, except for those knowledgeable in civic affairs or the history of community organizations and social services in the city.

This ambiguity contrasts with the consensus surrounding salaried occupations. For example, the understanding of professional and business careers comes, in part, from the ways these occupations are formally connected with the larger social system. The participants are also members of their organization's or profession's pension plans; in the course of work life they share a working career formally recognized through office interactions of clients, colleagues, and those higher or lower in a bureaucratic structure. Wherever they go they are identified as members of their occupational group and understandings about that group color interactions they may have with family or friends as well as those in the same occupational circles. This mixture of requirements, perquisites, and expectations changes over time as a worker advances along fairly well-established career lines—making more money, supervising more underlings, achieving higher rank, garnering awards or other recognitions of special ability.

The parallel record for volunteer women is not so readily nor publicly available. When these women win an award or are honored at a fund-raiser, and when their obituaries are published, some review of their record appears in local newspapers. These accounts, however, (particularly the obituaries) only establish a leader's accomplishments as a career after the fact. The idea of career remains ambiguous.

The honors (or the obituaries) at the end of a woman's life reveal the difficulties of building a career in the absence of shared occupational ideologies and formal placement of work within an accepted organizational framework. The difficulties are compounded by women's participation in the displays of status, the networks of class, and the activities of a leisured wife and attentive mother. These circumstances show how the ambiguities of the career affect the understandings others have of its significance. The ambiguities also affect the individual's course of action.

The advantage of this ambiguity is that the career can be tailored to the individual wishes and personal talents of women with resources and capacities to move through the community developing services. The disadvantage is that a clear picture of a career and a sense of recognized, cumulative accomplishment are difficult to achieve. This disadvantage is especially clear at the close of a career.

Some of the specific issues surrounding retirement from office show the difficulties to be surmounted in following the principle that one must move on. Sometimes they are not successfully resolved. While the ideology about the advantages of, as well as the necessity for, mobility is well understood, women sometimes face the conflicting demands for serious commitment to an organization versus the necessary distancing to avoid overinvolvement. They know, for example, that some organizations cannot survive unless a really desperate expenditure of effort is made. Thus, even though everyone recognizes the need for "new blood," a former president may return to leaderhip in time of crisis. She may feel especially responsible if she helped build the organization in the first place. Once such a long-term effort in an organization has been expended, it is hard to relinquish proprietary interest, if only to rescue that organization when it founders.

The line between retiring and trying to keep control beyond a legitimate term is often hard to discern, and women wish to avoid any confusion over whether they have left graciously or have been ousted. They realize this problem and wrestle with it. "I will be president up to June. There is no possibility of a second term. Maybe that is best because I could make a career of it and I know that is darn unhealthy." These women understand that the organizations they serve must be responsive to changing pressures, interests, and needs. The stamp of one person's personality (or "vision" as some of the women like to put it) may distort or divert an organization that has to be sensitive to these changes—if the impress remains too long. Women may also lose their "touch" if they become too tenacious about one organization. If a woman becomes known as a zealot, she, like the advocate, may lose some of the general accord or trust that gives her entry into so many parts of the community. Making a career of one particular presidency, then, can be unhealthy for the organization and also for the careerist.

The ambivalence created by the desire to stay and the knowledge that one should go are well expressed by the woman who said: "I might go back if they asked me but I believe it is time to pass the baton." It is hard to relinquish an important position which offers unparalleled opportunities to be in the thick of things and to participate in important decisions affecting the life of the city and involving large sums of money. Such positions include policy-making for major publications, building projects, and complicated mergers of museums, schools, hospitals, or libraries. The shrewd, capable, and well-connected woman will surmount ambivalence over leaving by using her network to broadcast her availability and the type of work she would now like to do. Over time, her movement through assignments adds to her experience, visibility, and knowledge of the city.

For those less fortunate, the times of change—or waiting—between jobs can be wearing. It is particularly hard to give up an excellent appointment when you have nothing commensurate to turn to. Most of these women have experienced some of this feeling of being out of things. They miss the day-to-day contact with an organization's problems, and they are no longer privy to inside information, so they know how others feel. It is often lonely at first, after the telephone calls stop and the hectic pace abruptly ceases at the end of a major presidency.

> When I was on [a very prestigious and influential] board, there was one important man in the mayor's office who always flew to my side at parties because he was interested in what the trustees were doing. He won't come near me now. So I can understand how hard it is to retire.

Some women feel they can manage to continue a commitment after leaving office by playing a role behind the scenes. "The only thing that kills me is that I can only have one more term as president. It's not as easy after you leave office, but you can stay in the underbrush and still do a lot of work that way." Unfortunately, not everyone agrees that this "underbrush" activity is so helpful to the next set of officers. When the woman quoted above left the presidency at the end of her term, other women who knew her and her organization commented on how difficult it was for the next president to set policy and run the organization because of this woman's attempted interference. Another woman told me the year she spent as president of a school board was made miserable by the prior president who couldn't let go of the office. The woman telling the story felt forced into a series of untenable positions where she had to support actions she really wanted to oppose. In another interview, a mutual friend reported that the past president of the school board insisted on naming the nominating committees year after year. When she came to complain that the organization was throwing her out after ten years, this mutual friend coldly responded that it could easily have thrown her out several years earlier and perhaps should have done so. A common tactic for managing interfering former presidents is through the counsel of such mutual friends. The ex-president is "told off" by someone seen as a neutral observer who represents public opinion on the subject. In this way the ex-president is "cooled out" and made to realize that she has no constituency to support her actions. Then the new president may pursue her own course in peace.

These problems appear for both men and women and in either unpaid or paid work, wherever the transfer of power has to be arranged. Male presidents may also have to be removed after too long a tenure on a volunteer board. In Pacific City, one very powerful civic leader led a group to oust a male chairman of a board and then assumed the chair herself. Business corporations in such varied industries as steel and movie production create news when old guard founders of the business are confronted by new management interests wishing to assume control of the operation. In each case, the newcomers emphasize the needs of the organization, attribute the failure of the past to the limited or failing vision of the old guard, and stress the importance of serving the organization by an infusion of new blood and new direction.

The battle for control can be equally sharp in profit and nonprofit corporations; but in the philanthropic world, women may wish to temper their judgments and be merciful to the old guard. These community leaders sometimes look at the hard core elderly women who cling to their board positions with some dismay; but as with those who understand the plight of women rotated out of their important positions, they try to sympathize and even accommodate. They can, for instance, offer honorific titles as a substitute for the powerful positions once held.

In fact, many of the positions available to volunteer leaders are ambiguous, providing titles rather than real power. Wealthy women who wish to have notice taken of them but who do not wish to work or are not capable may have such titular awards in return for handsome donations. Or, in honor of past achievements, respected elderly and failing women can receive these appointments. These elderly women, after all, only occupy honorific positions when they sit on boards.

> We have a grandfather clause. Anyone who was on the board when the bylaws changed [to limit future terms] begins a full term at that time. That is so as not to be unkind to older members. Let time take care of the problem. One recently died. And another resigned; her whole life has been spent on the board. But she retains full board privileges. She is too disabled to get around. But we wish to avoid any unpleasantness or unkindness. Once a month I write a letter or call her up so she will know what's going on.

These elderly women are a reminder to some. They provide an object lesson in the perils of resisting the ideology that one should change positions and retire gracefully when necessary. The problems created by those who resist retirement or the passage of office highlight the difficulties of any shifting, constantly reorganized, and entrepreneurial type of career whether salaried or volunteer. Entrepreneurial careers are organized on the contest model: competitors challenge the already successful. In the volunteer as in the salaried world, younger people are sometimes impatient to replace their elders who may seem to have lingered overlong in key positions.

Both women and men may resist movement off important, prestigious boards, especially when alternatives in the volunteer or salaried work worlds do not seem attractive. But traditional women are uninterested in salaried careers and are restricted in alternatives and new opportunities for career development. There are relatively few exciting positions accompanied by power and prestige in the volunteer world. Traditional women must compete for them with paid professionals and male community leaders as well. Return to traditional volunteer jobs is always possible, but by comparision, a routine volunteer job or even a trustee position of limited power and influence will seem quite tame. For a time, these women have tasted some of the excitement and carried some of the influence of real captains of industry, what the men who are movers and shakers in the community power structure possess. Like elected politicians, these women have been in limited-term positions where successive terms are difficult to achieve. Unlike most politicians, these women have no opportunity to use the power base they have developed to prepare a stable salaried job after their incumbency. The ideology suggests that new jobs will be equally challenging; but in a sex-stratified society like ours, there are not yet so many jobs for women that are equivalent to the real "plums." If a woman is genuinely interested in one field, such as art or music, it will be a wrench for her to come to the top position available to a civic leader and realize she must start in a new substantive area if she wants another position of power. Her alternatives are to accept lesser positions in the field where she rose or to diversify as a general consultant and advisor, making it known that she would like appointments to governmental and other commissions as they may arise.

Some women follow the first alternative and accept lesser positions. For those who came to an important position early on, it may mean that they are no longer promising leadership material. As a few mentioned, rather ruefully, their careers have gone downhill since they were presidents of the Junior League or the League of Women Voters or one of the prestigious cultural boards in the city. These positions have given them prominence in civic affairs, facilitating appointment to other important positions on blue-ribbon commissions and advisory groups. If these opportunities did not then provide a springboard to other offices and avenues to civic leadership, the initial prominence was over when office ended.

Some women are resigned to this eventuality and accept "early re-tirement." They can leave office without any loss of face; for the tra-ditional roles for women are open to them and offer socially accept-able options.

Of course, this picture is gradually changing; more options for salaried work and career independent of family are now becoming acceptable for traditional middle-class and upper-class women. However, top positions equal to the leadership roles women have developed through civic work are not yet so readily available, even to well-connected women. Nor is it yet clear whether the career op-tions for their daughters will be so much greater.

For the present and the recent past, it may be tempting to argue that the most astute and talented women continue in volunteer leadership and so those who retire early or content themselves with subordinate positions show only that initial confidence in their ability and perseverence may have been misplaced. Alternatively, one may argue that the contingencies of this career make it difficult for women to pursue it uninterruptedly and single-mindedly. There is insufficient social support and validation for all except the most determined, resourceful, and fortunate. Women with sick children, husbands who move frequently, or elderly and dependent relations may find the impetus of their career disrupted. In any case, the am-biguities of working conditions, career direction, and social sup-ports create a difficult context within which to shape a career.

The Ambiguities in Definitions of Ambitions: Social Mobility or Social Climbing

One interesting difference between the work worlds of voluntarism and salaried employment is the role permitted individual ambition. Part of the American dream is that people can rise to new status and occupation from humble origins. And the persistance and abil-ity necessary to make this ascent is correspondingly valued. While excessive competitiveness and self-assertiveness is deplored, the "self-made man" who becomes a great tycoon is an important part of American mythology. Especially in a race-stratified society like ours, there is admiration for minorities who have succeeded against all odds. They are a "credit to their race" if they achieve power, position, and wealth through some combination of discipline and talent.

Women are in a more ambiguous position with regard to ambi-tion. It is not so clear that they are a credit to their sex if they

achieve positions generally open only to men. Women like the recent democratic vice-presidential candidate Geraldine Ferraro walk
a careful line between showing their ability to succeed in a man's
world, like politics, and in the world of the wife and mother. However women demonstrate competence, the question is often raised
of what they may have sacrificed in middle-class understandings
about femininity, family life (if they do not have one), and family
welfare (if they do). Women who espouse feminism at least have an
ideology to answer the doubts and fears such questions can encourage. More traditional women find the question of personal ambition very difficult to face. They see such ambition as "natural to
men," as did the woman who believed that men find it harder than
women to abandon energetic business lives. But they do not see
why it should play an important part in their own lives. Women,
after all, are primarily engaged in the business of nurturing others.
They care for their families, they receive vicarious satisfaction from
the achievements of husband and children, and they gain satisfactions from altruistic service to the community. They are expected
to understand and discuss their own motives within this framework. So, as we have seen, while some women do speak frankly
about their own ambitions and their desire for leadership roles,
many equivocate about or deny ambition and interest in leadership.

These hesitations and ambiguities are present especially for the
majority who are not working women with salaries. The full-time
volunteer leader does not have the rationale for personal ambition
that a working woman in a position equivalent to a man's may have.
There is no model or context for vertical mobility when not engaged in an already established profession or work field. There is
no sense of orderly progression through career stages, no incremental achievement shown in promotions and raises. Thus women
who choose nonsalaried careers in volunteer service have neither
the reassurance provided by these external validations nor the support for the pattern of achievement and upward mobility implicit in
the value placed upon them.

Another problem that can provide difficulties for the ambitious
volunteer leader is the problem of divorcing a sense of ambition
from social climbing. Even if ambitiousness is not a pejorative term
and an undesirable value for some women, interest in social climbing and the desire to gain membership in an exclusive group, to
win honor and praise through association with socially prominent
people are denigrated by virtually everyone. The snubs that must
be endured, the fawning that is required, the attention given to

people of little intrinsic interest but great wealth and social position have all been noted disparagingly by novelists like Marcel Proust and Edith Wharton. The women in this study are sensitive to negative connotations attached to social ambition. Such ambition is concerned only with personal aggrandizement and is not a "worthy" motive for determined and persistent activity. In their view, too much activity looks like an effort to push beyond "natural" class barriers. From that perspective, class has nothing to do with economics or power in society. Rather it is simply a combination of wealth, birth, family, and association which should not be challenged. Like an effort to penetrate another's friendship or family circle, a concerted effort to push into where one does not already belong is unseemly. Only two women in this study said they had been social climbers, though they were no longer as interested in such activities. They said they were unusual women to admit their interest and said few would speak so frankly; and they were right. Yet almost everyone saw others around them as social climbers. Informants would damn each other with the term while disavowing it for themselves. This widespread system of derogation seemed to be used against those a woman didn't like; but this negative category also serves to symbolize some of the vicissitudes for these women of rising to community prominence through a volunteer career.

Volunteering and charitable works are traditional routes for social climbing; and everyone interested in these matters in any city can quickly learn which activities are more or less exclusive, what avenues lead from the less to the more exclusive, how long it takes, what one must do, and what the odds are for someone intent on passage up the ladder, given his or her particular combination of antecedents, skills, wealth, and sponsors. But what is the relation between charitable work and social advancement? The problem of how to answer this question is compounded for volunteer community leaders who have no "legitimate" account to give for their immense efforts. They are working within a value system based on cash for value; concern for social responsibility is not a legitimate full-time occupation in that system. Their problem is compounded by the fashion of cloaking social climbing aspirations under the more acceptable rationale of charitable concerns. Despite the numbers of social reformers who have come from their ranks (women like Jane Addams and Margaret Sanger, for example), traditional women are suspect—in their own as well as in others' eyes. They have no need of work; for they are well-off. Furthermore, they accept the view of the home as the primary focus of interest as long as husband and children need them. In a society emphasizing the cash-nexus economy as ours does, and where the interests of women for an independent life have not yet been validated in the same way as those of men, it is hard for many to understand the determination of these women to have careers. After all, they don't need the money; career ambitions are luxuries or ornaments for rich men, perhaps, but not for their wives.

As yet, our society gives little credence to the notion that women may show the same range of ambition, assertiveness, and desire for autonomy found in men. Traditional women, particularly, are not expected to desire personal achievement. In response to this expectation, as we have seen, women often describe their civic accomplishments as secondary to family and to the sense of personal reward they feel from offering service. If they do show such an interest in achievement, they can be dismissed by assigning their behavior the pejorative (and trivializing) label of social climbing. These women, then, are caught in the dilemma of how to find an avenue for ambition that will avoid pejorative overtones. They may also, of course, have mixed motives and feelings about their work. The desire to meet and know more socially prominent people *may* be an element of some weight in their concern for community improvements. It is mixed in with the desire to meet celebrities and people in fashion, to make contacts in the political networks of the city and be "in the know." For all these reasons, then, social climbing is a "hot" topic.

The anxiety that even raising the subject of social climbing can cause, and the eagerness with which women dissociate themselves from the topic, was shown to me by an incident early in my study. I met a thoughtful and intelligent respondent who ultimately became a key informant and chief advisor on many aspects of the volunteer career. We were getting on famously and I was particularly impressed with her ability not only to provide rich answers to questions but also to understand their underlying purpose and to point out additional issues. I was so pleased with the progress made from these very first contacts that I burst out thoughtlessly with what I thought was a mildly teasing remark. "This study promises to be so interesting and rewarding," I said, "and you are so helpful! I think I may stick around and try social climbing for a year or two." My new friend's manner changed. She seemed taken aback and a trifle constrained. "But seriously," she said with a rather thin smile, and returned to a topic we had been discussing, as though my comment needed special encapsulation to under-score its irrelevance to the discussion. Perhaps she wanted me to understand that there would be a limit to her helpfulness—that it would certainly not carry me that far. In addition, her discomfort showed that she did not want her serious civic concerns framed by ideas as frivolous or pejorative as those surrounding the concept of social climbing. The topic was especially sensitive for the women in this study, like the informant just described, who were from the middle-class or upper-middle class. Even the most well-connected women belong to a relatively new society. Pacific City does not have as many old guard families nor as much entrenched society as might be found in cities of the eastern seaboard. Consequently, few could claim such impeccable antecedents as to be entirely above any suspicion of wanting to improve their social position. Thus it would be easy to confuse ambition directed toward civic improvement and social striving—particularly within a value sys-tem that does not seriously consider the importance of ambition and desire for public recognition among women.

The ambivalence about personal ambitiousness seen in the readi-ness to use pejorative labels like "social climber" or avoidance of the topic altogether makes it difficult to engage in any overt expres-sions of striving or eagerness to get ahead and accomplish some-thing like building a hospital auxiliary from scratch or helping to overcome the opera deficit. Such desires always have to be "framed" in terms of altruistic dedication, zeal for a cause, and eagerness in community service. This requirement often makes it difficult for women to openly state a desire for a leadership position in an orga-nization. And as noted earlier, many women do disavow such a de-sire—or explain they are mavericks when frank enough to admit it.

Throughout this chapter we have been concerned with the career contingencies facing women who rise to volunteer leadership. A theme that runs through all the contingencies discussed—lack of an institutional base, invisible or unrecognizable expenses, the need to change jobs, ambiguities in the legitimation of ambition—is the absence of an appropriate, socially validated understanding of this work as a *career*. Without such validation, working at home is suspect, expenses are not legitimately deductible or reimbursable, positions cannot be institutionalized, and motives cannot remain unassailable. A serious contingency of the work, then, is that there is no assurance it will be taken seriously by others.

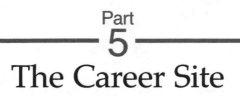

Part
5

The Career Site

9

The Nonprofit Community
Board as the Context
for Career

The context within which much volunteer activity occurs is the not-for-profit trustee board: the governing body of an organization, association, or service devoted to some philanthropic activity. This board structure represents the spirit of volunteer effort in that all members are supposed to be selected and serve because of their abilities, resources, and motivation in some service. The general understandings about such boards, both from the public and from participants, is that these structures can synthesize and direct the spirit of citizen participation.

The organization of activity within the legitimizing structure of a governing board (via a president or chairperson, secretary, treasurer, or committee heads delegated specific responsibilities) is adopted for a wide variety of goals. It is a format taught to children (from primary grades onward), as part of democratic principles of government, through the institution of class officers, club associations, and other forms of student government. And it is used in many kinds of philanthropic and political activities as well as corporate business.

Volunteer women are trained to use this board format, in school and other youth associations, as are other Americans; but these women also become familiar with the format as they are recruited into philanthropic activity by family and friends. The assumptions about the propriety as well as the usefulness of this structure are thus commonly shared by the respondents. The citizen's action committee, used by the advocates in this study, for example, is formed to change, dispute, or fight some aspect of the established order. Organizations as diverse as Friends of the Earth, The Black Panthers, and local antibusing committees in various communities have all adopted the format (see Conrad and Glenn 1983:169–81 for a discussion of different types of boards and culturally diverse voluntary organizations). The same format, however, can be used for the most conventional and traditional causes favored by the establishment. Women who work for culture boards, private schools, and historical preservation projects work within this structure. Their board work may be regarded as a convenient cloak for a club of privileged elite who wish to control some aspect of education or a cultural pursuit in their hometown (Ostrander 1984). The board structure is flexible enough to adapt to such cross-purposes.

However the structure is used, service on boards requires a special array of understandings and skills. The careers of women who become leaders among volunteers are shaped by their work within that structure of board organization. It provides both the framework for aspiring leaders to receive training and the showcase for their accomplishments. Boards provide the channel through which women raise money for building funds to improve churches, hospitals, educational and cultural institutions, to organize and provide health and welfare services, or to spur social action on a political issue.

The board provides a framework for all who work within it—men as well as women—but women who are without an alternative salaried career are particularly constrained and challenged by this structure. They may become especially sensitive to the distinctive aspects of this work: the shaping of talents and energies to meet the requirements of a project. The task requires discovering and securing the allegiance of new talent as well as getting board members to work together. The expectations of what board structure requires and permits give direction to the way volunteer women envision their task.

Corporate Boards as Legal Entities

The corporate form of organization (with a board of directors and a staff of varying size and specialization) has grown from a format initially developed by medieval religious orders (Davis 1905). In its modern form it extends across religious and secular, profit and nonprofit, governmental and private ventures. The modern corporation (Berle and Means [1932]1968) has become an important focus of concern; for corporations control vast assets and governmental agencies are concerned with regulating or overseeing these activities for the public good.

Although there is a considerable literature on the organization and management of large corporations, there is relatively little known about the part boards of directors play in them (Whisler 1982). One important question in the regulation of corporations is assessment of the powers of boards of directors; for they have, as Zald notes (1969:97) "formal and legal responsibility for controlling and maintaining organizational operation and effectiveness." General statements about the powers and responsibilities of directors are available (Mace 1971), but these powers are difficult to assess; some boards are docile instruments for the chief executive to guide while other boards make it clear that they set policy—and hire and fire the executive. Boards of welfare, philanthropic and cultural services, traditionally dominated by the upper classes, are likely to keep control; and it is in this area that we find the women presented here. Unlike the men, who serve on both business corporation and philanthropic boards (Hunter 1963:231–36; Baltzell 1958: 364–83), these women are limited by their background and position in society to nonprofit boards; only two serve on boards of business corporations as well. As a result of this limitation, women directors or trustees do not have the influence in the business community that men who are well connected in the corporate world may have. But they do have great commitment to their work. Further, they have time, energy and, in many cases, money to devote to it. Finally, they have developed specialized experience as directors of nonprofit boards through their years of training.

This experience is what women discuss in explaining the place of board service in their philanthropic careers. Of course men—and gainfully employed workers—also have philanthropic careers. Ross (1952) studied businessmen in a Canadian city who rose from minor canvassing jobs through fund-raising campaign hierarchies to positions on the executive committee of a board. In contrast to full-time professional volunteers, the requirement to participate in philanthropic careers, as well as how to do it, is made explicit for the businessmen; and the importance of this participation for furthering one's business career is clear (Ross 1952).

The context affects board members, whatever the gender composition of the board. Nonprofit board meetings can involve more debate and individual participation than would business corporate meetings; for nonprofit board members can argue about goals or priorities since ownership and responsibility are not clearly defined. The issues Whisler and Hirsch (1979:10) find, in their study of the culture of boards, are: "Whose interests are to be served and what are those interests? How do we know what we are supposed to be achieving and, then, are [we] achieving well?" Board meetings can be noisy and intense if members represent diverse backgrounds and constituencies. These differences between business and non-profit boards are reflected in the characteristics of members. Business corporate boards remain strongholds of white, older males —with only small percentages of women and minorities despite affirmative action efforts.[1]

Women in this study begin their career as board members through becoming leaders in organizations of like-minded women; board composition reflects the constituency and is, accordingly, homogeneous. As they progress, women take on more varied, difficult, and prestigious assignments where they come in contact with more diverse elements of the city.

Recruitment and Development of Board Members

Recognition of the importance of board membership in the volunteer career is quite explicit. Some boards, like that of the Junior League are organized to offer training in board management, even if this activity can sometimes be time-consuming enough to conflict with the ability to offer service. Other boards, by their structure and the nature of their activity, also offer good training grounds. As one woman put it: "There are certain organizations that are very valuable for young board members . . . because they can't do too much damage, and they can learn a lot about how a board is run . . . I learned a great deal about such things in the [Girls Club]." These organizations have to be distinguished from the more powerful boards in the city. "University . . . and foundation boards . . . need

1. Although a great proportional increase in the number of women directors has occurred between 1970 and 1980, the actual numbers are still small. For example, in 1970, .05 percent of the directors of the 1,000 largest industrials were women; by 1980 this number had risen to 2.3 percent. (March 1981:5, Summary of the Profile Analysis of Corporate Board Women and Their Corporations, U.S. Human Resources Corporation, San Francisco, California.) Nonprofit boards have a few more women and make conscious efforts to include people of various ages, ethnic and religious groups, as well as geographic enclaves in an effort to represent broad community interests and maintain community support. In 1980, for example, in a survey conducted by the Council on Foundations, 13 percent of the board members were women in the independent, company-sponsored, and private operating foundations. In this same survey, 4 percent of the board members were blacks or from other ethnic or racial groups (Boris et al. 1981).

. . . sophistication about the way a community works and how
money needs to be watched over." From this perspective, then,
board members can "try out" in positions on boards of relatively
little consequence to the larger public. Word gets around once a
woman has distinguished herself at several assignments on boards
and has shown her leadership. As in other worlds, successful volunteer leaders have fads in popularity. "People are really like lem-
mings. Once I had begun doing things . . . then they all wanted me
to do things [serve on boards]." Since popularity may be fleeting,
women have to be careful how they use these opportunities. As the
foregoing informant continued, "A very dangerous time. But I was
not toppled because I don't take on too much."

An invitation to board membership is an indication that one is
a recognized leader—or is in training for leadership positions.
Therefore women consider these invitations very carefully: how to
get them and how to rank them according to such dimensions as
board effectiveness (including political clout, social cachet, and
general prestige in the larger community), learning and interest
potential, and place in an already existing array of personal and
volunteer responsibilities. A woman explained how a great volunteer (from an earlier day) had explained the principle of selec-
tiveness to her.

> Dorothea Jameson who revolutionized [a cultural organiza-
> tion] said to me: "You must not divide your loyalties or you
> will become ineffective." So when I was invited on to the
> opera guild and the museum boards I turned them down
> [because I was interested in education issues and already
> working on boards in that area].

A cautionary note to these generalizations is also provided by
women who understand the necessity for and limitations of diversification in career interests: too intense a focus on one interest or
organization may leave a woman stranded emotionally and occupa-
tionally when her term of office is completed. If one overextends, it
is always possible to be embarrassed—and even to find one's career
hopes thwarted—because one takes on more than one can accomplish. As one woman said, "If you are unreliable, you can get off
Madeline Aubrey's list [a very powerful community leader] just for
skipping around."

A reputation for dependability and judgment is essential, particularly when a woman has no professional credentials or other
work experience to speak for her. In practical terms, this reputation

is symbolized by the job that is *always* done well. Most projects require doing groundwork: reading over background materials and making preliminary investigations. As one woman said, "You are on stronger ground if you take board membership seriously and read the bylaws and understand the board/staff relations. If you do your homework, you can really be ready to use your instincts right." Without that preparation, a project may fail, as the following informant learned early in her career as a board member:

> You've got to do some homework, you just can't fly in and wing it. I tried to pretend once and it fixed me. [The director] asked me to do interviews and to write them up. I was lazy and didn't look in on the topic enough. And I hacked it. But that was good for me. Mistakes in judgment pay off the next time.

The secret of success in groundwork seems to be to start at the bottom—"go through each department and never begin at the top." The problem is always how to learn as much as you can by observation, preparation through study, and research in the organization.

Selection of New Talent

While women who come well recommended through family connections may never face the problem of how to demonstrate the competence to be invited onto boards, many women rise through the levels of board membership by the demonstration of ability. This process is difficult to make explicit; and the difficulty is compounded by the generally favored tendency to approach potentially touchy matters obliquely rather than head on. A newcomer may find this pattern difficult to counter for she may find the charter members won't give any information about the selection process and they won't explain that it is not proper to ask.

> I asked several of my friends [on the board] who recommended me, but they won't say, [using such ladylike evasions as:] "It must have been several people"; "I don't remember now; it was so long ago." "Everybody wanted you."

The entry point for board membership can never be clearly delineated because the prevalent value system discourages explicit interest. Aggressiveness and ambition for "plums" are tinged with too many negative connotations, like social climbing and pushiness. Those who are already in the establishment do not like to feel beleaguered or opportuned. Such characteristics are also generally regarded as counterproductive in the general task of developing concerted action on the board. Miller (1950) and Ross (1953:276) note the same perspective about the rise of men in the philanthropic power structure of the community; they mustn't seem too eager. Miller (1950:219–20) says:

> Rewards must flow from a clear recognition on the part of the prestige-bestowers of the honorable nature of the actor's work. To *demand* prestige is to negate the whole tenor of the action, since in terms of the formal structure the individual's actions are selfless.

As one elder stateswoman in this study put it:

> You have to quiet ambition a good deal in voluntary organizations because if a fellow volunteer detects your ambition to rise out of the ranks, most of them become very wary of you.

While overly ambitious newcomers are viewed negatively, whether women or men, the problem presents special difficulties for women volunteers. Without opportunity in the business or professional worlds, it may be hard for capable, assertive women to contain their eagerness to assume positions of authority and their impatience with the less capable.

A mitigating circumstance for the ambitious is that the shortage of capable, willing hands in the volunteer world is perennial; women of executive ability with time for volunteer service are always needed. The patrolling behavior of men as well as women civic leaders, looking for this talent in the world of women volunteers, has always been an important activity for the leadership. The Junior League and the League of Women Voters are regularly "cased," accordingly, to see what talent is developing there. Scouts look for women who are reliable—who will take responsibility in their committee tasks and show independence and initiative in fulfilling them. Women who also write clear reports, speak well, mobilize others and delegate tasks to them, create new projects or come up with new ideas for the management of ongoing ones are the new talent. The woman in the following statement was noticed by a prominent male civic leader in this way and then placed on an important board. "Gerry personally chose everyone on the board. He watched the League of Women Voters like a hawk. When he thought there was somebody promising, which was where I fell— he came and invited me to join the board." These bush league organizations are so useful to talent scouts because the leadership within them actively undertake the responsibility of training their replacements. One prominent community leader recalled how she had been appointed to head a major committee in the League of Women Voters when several of her committee members were wiser and more experienced. The woman who appointed her explained the importance of giving younger people the leadership experience, both to develop talent and also to help the League by providing new skills and perspectives. In turn, this civic leader did the same thing.

Recruitment is an issue throughout a leader's career. When president, she has to consider just how to arrange the composition of a board for greatest effectiveness. Her concern has to be understood within the context of knowledge that board members have about one another and of board work more generally. Zald (1969:100–106) outlines the variations in the powers and functions of boards of directors to show what opportunities and restrictions they can expect. First, board members with special or technical expertise may receive greater attention to their proposals from other participants. Second, board members with external bases of power (personal wealth, constituencies or networks through which to gather support, information and other resources, family connections to other powerful people or business interests) have more leverage within boards. The right mix of those with various types of talents and resources or power in the community makes a board effective. The belief in the efficacy of this mix persuades the board members to cooperate with and, if necessary, be conciliatory to one another. An understanding of the significance of the mix also helps women select and recruit members when they change the composition of boards or create new ones.

Getting the Right "Mix"

One aspect of leadership prized by respondents is the ability to find the right people to make a successful board. Here is how one president accounted for her success.

> I thought it had been a narrow group and needed a broader base in the community. And I worked on bringing in new members. Half of that [symphony] board are members I have brought in. . . . I introduced a couple of Junior League people who were good at fund-raising. The new president, I got her in. She is extraordinarily knowledgeable about

> music. And there might be a few socialite presidents I helped keep on [by encouraging them and helping them with] the grub work of getting ads and signatures for the anniversary program.

Implicit in these remarks is an estimate of what kind of mix a symphony board requires. Some of its members should be fund-raisers; others should have a real interest in the substance (music). Still others should provide the cachet of names from high society.

In assessing what a board needs, these women pride themselves on foresight beyond that of other board members, including both businessmen and young turks of the community.

> I made the board more cohesive. . . . I try to get people talking to feel a part of it. That sort of thing bored the older businessmen. . . . They were interested only in the main function [to maintain solvency]. I perhaps overbalanced with the younger, arts-oriented. [John is an example of that group.] Now it is going the other way. But John really was convinced that we would need the other after I pointed out how I turned the board around to bring on people like him.

The ability to make a board most effective by choosing the right mix of members has to be accompanied by the clout required to persuade others to accept an appointment. Prominent women volunteer leaders possess this influence, combined with their judgments about what talent a board needs to operate well. Wise judgments—and the clout to act upon them—are particularly important in building a new organization. Women often speak of the greatest service they have done for an organization not as what they have done for it but who they found to serve it.

Getting someone who is already busy to serve in yet another capacity is not always easy. Even when successful, it uses up some of one's influence to ask such a favor. Accordingly, women of great reputation allot their store of this kind of influence carefully, even though they realize they must use it in order to be successful. The more good "mixes" they create, the more it redounds to their credit. But the possibility of disaster and consequent coolness, or just exasperation between old friends when a friend is cajoled against her will and the project fails, is not dismissed lightly. In political terms, one might say that volunteer leaders use their "chips" wisely, trying to give and receive them to maximize a stock of influence.

Temperance in these matters can be overweighed by enthusiasms for a cause and a hunch that some candidate resisting nomination is really the best person for it. When they care enough, women will pull out all the stops, using entreaty, reference to old ties or favors owed, promises of help or assurances that the tasks will really not be burdensome. Whether they are or not, once the candidate is "hooked," her understanding of the responsibility and her desire to keep an unblemished record for her own portfolio will keep her at it. The ability, not only to call out rank-and-file troops, but to put the board leadership firmly in place, is a great political asset. And some women do use their stock of favors on behalf of political campaigns. More often, however, they turn their efforts to a civic organization developing to meet some new or previously unmet need. A board formed to create an association to protect children or improve their education, an effort to save an endangered open space, or a local bond drive are the kinds of things women have spoken about as motivating them to stretch their own energies and those of their associates.

In seeking help from colleagues and friends, women also look for names of important people who can lend solidarity to the enterprise and encourage others to participate. These names represent people who are peripherally involved in the organization but wish it well. Their public support gives the enterprise an air of legitimacy, a shorthand way of saying the right people are involved and that others should also offer support. Those important people are listed as sponsors or advisors on an announcement or letterhead.

Many organizations combine these honorific and advisory functions in the array of talents expected of the working board. The civic leaders realize that some representatives of wealthy and influential families are needed to secure establishment support; but they may not be the best or most useful board participants. Others who are knowledgeable about the service or program, who have some special public relations or political contacts, or who are useful in organizing board activity complete the membership. The trick is getting the right combination so that all the responsibilities of the board may be met.

This aim is complicated by requirements for affirmative action in board membership. As one president (of an important hospital board) said:

> I am determined that our board will arrive in the modern world with an understanding of governmental regulations

[about public meetings, affirmative action,] and [the necessity for expanded] community support [including minorities on the board] and the rest of it.

Board members have to realize how times—and their responsibilities—have changed. Women sometimes talk about this change as breaking up "the club" that board membership once provided.

> Some old members . . . saw the interaction as not quite so warm as it used to be [when it was] more of a club where they would have lunches and discussions with friends. Now the board is much more mixed in its membership and the people are there for a purpose—a major breakthrough.

These changes reflect practical concerns to broaden the base of participation in an organization's activities. Organizations devoted to cultural purposes (opera and symphony boards, for example) do not face the same pressures for a wide spectrum of community representation on their boards as health and welfare organizations. Yet even prestigious, independent culture boards show an increasing concern for a wider base of participation in the community as individual wealthy donors can no longer meet the deficits in operating costs. The boards accordingly come to include more volunteer women and more middle-class business people to guide public relations and fund-raising policies directed to their constituents and fewer socialites who do not really work.

Many boards have always been hardworking, whatever their exclusive and "social" character. They have always required a mix of talents because of the range of tasks to be covered. Here is how tasks are allotted on one such hardworking, if socially exclusive, women's board.

> We have pre-meetings [to] decide on the agenda for the regular meetings and try to figure out where pitfalls may be found. . . . Each board member serves on one or more committees. There is finance [that's the internal funding of operations] and the executive committee, the joint conference, community service, public relations, and development [that's where money raising is]. Then there is house and grounds, building, long-range planning, and accreditation. . . . There is really too much work for one chairman so they are getting together with co-chairs [on each committee]. . . . Each meets once a month on a regular schedule all year, and there is 85 percent attendance at meetings.

Such hardworking boards show how the appropriate mix of members functions once it is in place. This level of activity does not arise and continue without effort on the part of the leadership.

Learning to Work with Colleagues

When a board is already assembled once a woman comes to office, she learns how to work with it, just as she learns how to work around those board members she finds less than useful. One newly appointed president of a powerful board—where she served as the first woman president—developed a strategy of assessing strengths and weaknesses in her colleagues.

> I knew I was being given a board. There was a list of committees and members were asked what they would like to serve on. But I thought I'd talk to each member personally. Maybe I'd find talents that could not be found on a piece of paper. And I did. I met with every member. . . . Then I knew what I had to work with. . . . Some I lean on and some I don't respect or include. They know and complain about it. But there are only some . . . who . . . have a basic understanding of what this institution is about.

The position of this woman on a board with conservative, wealthy, and influential males highlights some of the problems that any board member has in managing the need to work with people of widely disparate abilities and levels of commitment. As she points out, arguing and direct confrontation are counterproductive. "There are a lot of hangers on [among board members]. I'll listen . . . and I don't argue. What good would it do? I don't want to pull the board apart." This approach to managing board relationships shows how the generally accepted tactics of conciliation and indirection, described earlier as part of a common perspective, become part of the array of specific tactics for managing relations on boards. Women with a traditional view of appropriate behavior for women—including emphasis on mediation and supportiveness—are most likely to find these tactics comfortable and easy to use.

The array of tactics and the rules governing board member interactions described here focus both on the strategies available in a company of social equals (all women boards) and those where women work with men who are seen as having higher status. Informants say they give particular attention to those delicate situations in the second category where women are both less powerful in status and also in a numerical minority. And, of course, general principles, like those of indirection and conciliation, apply equally well in both settings.

Some of the problems of working relations require special tact and appreciation of the delicate balance of power that has developed on women's boards over the years. Here is how one elder stateswoman gave advice to a junior colleague on management of board politics.

> [The President of the Arts Society needed help.] There was a very aggressive lady who wanted to be the chairperson of something. And [this Arts Society] has its own "kitchen cabinet." There are three or four very strongly social ladies [prominent in society] that have the veto no matter what you do. . . . I was glad to see [this young president] understood there *was* a kitchen cabinet because they could behead her before she moved very far on anything. Now this tough lady wanted to get in. And I told [the president], "Just refer the matter to your kitchen cabinet." So [this president] was taken off the hook.

This analysis of how to manage board relations fits with observations of others who discuss the importance of frequent consultation. Diplomatic board presidents, then, learn which members may be troublesome if not provided with constant attentions.

Managing difficult and powerful colleagues can resemble those Japanese martial arts where the force of opponents' thrusts are used against them. By stepping aside, for example, one can cause an onrushing attacker's impetus to dissipate harmlessly. Similarly, the shrewd board member sees how to engage a potentially destructive participant in harmless, or even useful, activity by letting her have her way. In one major culture board, this strategy was illustrated by the advice a senior generalist gave those who consulted her on their problems. The stumbling block was the hard feelings created among the key fund-raising committee members by one prominent woman's wish to do everything. The senior generalist was brought in as the "big gun" to oppose this woman. Instead, the generalist said, "Just let her do what she wants. If she wants an automobile parade, let her do that." In this view, giving her her head was the only possible strategy for managing a rich, spoiled, willful woman. Letting her work full steam, without opposition, would entirely occupy all her time and energy. The other women could then work on their own projects. As there is always more work than can ever be done in the volunteer world, any amount of ferocious energy can be used up this way.

Sometimes the strategy is used to require warring factions to reach agreement.

> The one big argument . . . that really amused me was over what color uniforms the auxiliary would wear, and the ladies were all squared off in two corners, practically . . . I was anticipating something like that—disagreement about something [not] worth fighting about . . . so what I did was to appoint a committee on uniforms, and I put the most vociferous of the two opposition groups together and asked them to come back . . . with a recommendation that we could follow. And it worked very well.

The ability to see quickly what is and is not worth fighting about and to defuse polarization is a generally useful organizational strategy. Women's special talents of indirection and conciliation so useful in this context are what Janeway (1980) has called "the powers of the weak." Every leader realizes the importance of keeping *all* volunteer colleagues sufficiently committed to keep working. These women must show sensitivity and ingratiating behavior toward their peers and juniors as well. The problem of motivating and inspiring workers to continued and even greater effort is always present in volunteer service.

Women also stress the importance of planning carefully at the start of a new venture. This careful planning includes conferring with key people and getting to them in *the right order* and at *the right stage* in the procedure. In this way, those who should have their *amour propre* attended to will be gratified; potential trouble will be averted. The ongoing and interlocking system of friendships and partnerships requires a board member to avoid embarrassing another or causing someone to "lose face" through public confrontation. Not only are such situations likely to lead to enmity, they also cause dissension or weaken the working consensus necessary to keep a group's purpose viable. If you can forewarn people about emerging areas of potential conflict and sound them out in private, you may gradually accustom them to accept whatever position is required for consensus.

> You don't get along well by embarrassing people. That's the last thing in the world you should ever do, if you can possibly avoid it . . . . Group process is really a way to arrive at a consensus. . . . You can't force your own opinion . . . you alienate half the people when you do that.

A related principle is that it is important to smooth things over. The development of consensus—and the maintenance of the ambience in which a consensus can develop—is the guiding purpose that focuses all these principles or strategies. Sometimes that may mean ignoring something which is annoying, as when a woman remarked that one irksome contingency of her work was doing another's assignment and then writing that person a thank you note. Sometimes this concern can be systematized in a list of values, as in those recommended by the following community leader:

> I had a list . . . something I called "pointers," that were little things . . . about how food at the beginning of a meeting is a very important way to get people feeling comfortable with each other. And . . . people are very uncomfortable, when they don't know who else is in the audience, about opening their mouths about anything. So you must start out by making clear who the others are, and why they are here, and something about their backgrounds. . . . So everybody feels they are talking in front of people who would understand what they are talking about.

The understanding about the requirements to propitiate are complementary to the understandings about the necessity for indirection and for not seeking leadership too eagerly or quickly. As noted, colleagues may become wary of rapidly rising stars in volunteer leadership. Although some women do succeed through sheer ability, even without skill at diplomatic strategy, they pay a price. Here is how one woman explained it.

> I think the major problem anyone encounters is envy. Always the women who want to do what you are doing and aren't capable of it talk behind your back and you can't fight it. . . . You have to establish yourself very slowly and work quietly and slowly.

These complaints from a conservative Republican community leader who built her reputation in the cultural area have been echoed by radical feminists in the women's movement. Freeman (1972–73), for example, complained that women would turn upon and attack any woman who rose to leadership status through movement activity. Her complaint is often paralleled by blacks who become upwardly mobile and are attacked for leaving their race behind (Drake and Cayton 1945; Cruse 1967).

Some leaders incur enmity because they adopt strategies alien to other working colleagues on boards. For example, one prominent civic leader organized brilliantly successful benefits. She could do the grubby and the creative work of decorating, as well as the purchasing and general managing of the business affairs necessary for profit making. Yet she had many problems working with others because of her direct and forthright manner; she didn't have the conciliatory interpersonal skills so prized among women volunteer leaders who serve on boards. Here is how another volunteer leader described her.

> I wouldn't cross her. And I'm not sure I'd go out of my way to work for her again. She rules by dividing. And she can take a lot of your time; she can get your bowels in an uproar. So I just say "yes, yes" to her. I don't let her embroil me. But she is a very talented woman and has been badly treated [kept out of some prestigious boards].

Women must negotiate when they cannot insist. Gittell and Shtob (1981:24) note how community organizers in lower-income and minority areas shift their priorities and goals when they are dependent on external funding. "They are now more likely to express a preference to use the political system and eschew confrontation and conflict."

Tactfulness and sensitivity are also useful for women who often see themselves as making something work rather than being the prime mover. Successful women talk about how they manage not only to avoid conflict but also to build consensus. The issue of consensus can be framed within an understanding of how board members must work together.

> What I want to do with a board is to try to keep it, no matter how disparate it is, together, to keep the opportunities open for discussion and support of differing points of view, but to recognize the moment when, if you allow anything to get rammed through, it will destroy the board and the board's self-confidence. . . . If you start losing members on account of their position never being understood or their being cajoled into something they don't believe in . . . I don't approve of it.

The interpretation of their skills as helping rather than forcing something to happen can resolve any ambivalence about leadership that traditional women may have. This view is particularly helpful when they can see their action as averting trouble and forging new alliances—as when a woman can mediate between other board members representing conflicting interests. These skills are important to any executives—whether male or female—who work with others who are powerful in their own right: high-level public administrators, politicians, and impresarios are examples. Traditional women, without the trappings of privilege and authority associated with important occupational titles, have the greatest incentive to understand and employ these skills of mediation and persuasion.

One volunteer leader taught these principles to some minority youth who had been chosen as their community representatives to serve on a board with civic leaders—including important local businessmen:

> My role [in this organization] has been one of, really, conferring with the youngsters. If they think something's gone wrong, they'll call . . . and say, "Can we come see you?"
>
> Occasionally I'll . . . tell them that they're much too hard on the businessmen . . . for instance, they'd love to have [the businessmen's group] take a stand on . . . issues. Well, it would be the death of the group if you had to do that, because the businessmen might be . . . on the other side of whatever issue the young people thought was important. But the personal relationships between them mean that the businessmen are willing to . . . assist in . . . areas where they might not be willing to go on record as supporting [a political principle].
>
> I just said, "Now, you kids don't want to destroy a very delicate relationship you have by your inability to understand these businessmen and how they function and what they can take from you." . . . For instance [the youth can] take advantage, and should, of . . . coming to know somebody like [a bank president] and they will go to them [outside of the organization] and say, "We have a project. Would you help us?" They never would know [these businessmen] otherwise.

The ability to formulate the advantages of negotiating tactics, and the benefits of this approach for the relatively powerless in the society, can bring together interesting coalitions. If, as we saw earlier, militants can teach Mau Mau tactics to conventional middle-class women, these women can, in turn, teach their ladylike skills of sidestepping rather than confronting, using mediation and persuasion through personal influence and persistence, to Mau Mau specialists. This ability, not only to be skilled at negotiation but to persuade others to try it and then show them how to do it successfully, explains how many women community leaders widen their spheres of influence and come to be known and prized for their special abilities when serving on boards.

Acting as Catalyst

Of course, conciliatory skills *are* very useful, particularly in situations where confrontation is a risk—or a danger. The mediator with such skills can represent the board to a larger community as well as help create consensus within the board. This great civic leader attributed her influence on one board to these skills.

> Martin told someone I had great influence on the board of regents because if there were students or teacher problems, I was the only person who talked to these people. So many votes changed on that account. That pleased me because that was what I tried to do. I was not a star, but a catalyst between all these different forces in the university.

The mediator role is peculiarly appropriate for women who are not clearly associated with any stable institutional position, even when they serve on boards. In this view, the career contingencies of a volunteer position possess the advantages as well as the disadvantages associated with a socially recognized, permanent, unofficial status: the position offers the freedom to choose one's own responsibilities. Since they often say they like to work behind the scenes, and thus do not need special credit for their accomplishments, traditional women are personally—and ideologically—prepared to develop a role that permits disparate activities or interests to come together. These catalyst activities can encourage a modest stance. As one woman put it: "I am not particularly creative, but I am good at putting together people and operations." These skills are a special asset in managing working relations within some of the most powerful and prestigious boards in the community where males dominate.

Learning to Work with Male Colleagues

Some civic leaders think women do things differently. These differences are highlighted in the boardroom. One woman said, "I serve on many boards that are half men and women. And women are softer and more negotiating in their approach. They come to the same solution [as men] but they do so in a warmer manner . . . more comfortable to us because we are more humanistic."

Tactfulness and sensitivity can attract the sympathy of influential male community leaders who act as patrons or supporters of talented women. Thirteen women refer to this type of patronage or protection specifically. Men can engineer appointments. Or they can run interference when the going gets rough, serving as assistants to a woman president.

Women could also use their natural talents and personality characteristics (as well as stereotypical expectations about the behavior of women) to charm more powerful (male) board members into accepting suggestions, as did one informant who was one of only two women on a powerful civic board. She told me the other board members seemed to like her particularly because she kept them amused; and she was clearly a woman of great charm and wit, as her interaction during interviews showed. One tactic used by the relatively powerless is to assume the role of the court jester. The fool (Daniels and Daniels 1964) often has opportunity to make otherwise unacceptable suggestions. In this case, the civic leader felt that she became the darling of the board—though not likely ever to be made president.

Occasionally, women mention leading the way for men to follow. In one instance a woman forced a confrontation on a difficult issue and won. She feared her outspoken opposition to a racist policy would estrange her board colleagues. The majority were prepared to accept this discrimination, whatever their own views, in order to keep peace with those colleagues upholding discrimination. She felt her direct confrontation of the issue forced them to adopt a nondiscriminatory policy. In this instance, confrontation was minimal and victory seemed to have no negative consequences for her. But women volunteer leaders often fear and dislike confrontation so much that they will not risk it. Even if it seems worthwhile and fairly safe, confrontation can create too much personal discomfort.

Occasions of determined opposition are thus mentioned rarely. Only five informants report them, and they say they choose issues carefully; for a reputation for good judgment is important to maintain. Even men can be discredited and ignored if they show consistent poor judgment. "I don't fight little things. I'm not crazy. There is one board member who has gotten so far over to the right [politically] that no one listens to him. He is fenced in."

These observations neglect the possibility that some reforms will not occur without confrontation. The advocates who worked for integrated schools, for example, found confrontation necessary, though difficult. Even women with reputations for being abrasive and tough say they have to nerve themselves to confront others.

In general, women make their mark on predominantly male boards by being super achievers, as did the following informant. "I've brought in the most money—$100,000 in cash plus buying five new [community services]. And I've brought in two new members who will give money. [But] the association is a one-man show run by the senior [male member of a prominent family]." The place this woman holds in a predominantly male board illustrates the dictum expressed by Whisler [1982:4].

> Those who attain high achievement status . . . in . . . corporate boards [are] usually white Anglo-Saxon males. . . . Individuals who do not have one or more of these personal characteristics are going to find it necessary to furnish out extra and convincing proof of their eligibility to serve on the corporate board.

Traditional women are not inclined to question this pattern. Since they have more time to devote to volunteer work than do male board members, they may believe they *should* do more, try harder. "Volunteers expect more from me than they would, say, from the chairman of the board. . . . He can always say, 'I'm doing the best I can and if you don't think it's good enough, I'll be happy to leave!'"

Implicit in this view is that men are both busier and more valuable additions to the board than women. The contributions of men—their experience, contacts, and resources in the business world—make them desirable enough board colleagues to overlook most defects. These arguments provide the rationale for accepting a system of priorities wherein the volunteer service performed by women is not of the same significance as that of men. If women are snubbed by men on powerful boards to which they have been invited, they bear their injuries quietly. One woman mentioned, in confidence, the trials borne by a friend who repeatedly complained that the times set for board meetings were terribly inconvenient. Apparently she was not important enough to her male colleagues for them to be accommodating. Men sometimes ride roughshod over the wishes or feelings of female colleages in other ways, forgetting to include them in key meetings, treating them in a cavalier or even rude fashion during public meetings.[2] Nevertheless, women volunteer leaders recognize the power of the gentleman's club and

2. Capek (1986) reports on the difficulty women trustees of New Jersey Colleges and Universities have in feeling they are taken seriously, even where professionally employed in business, education, and foundation administrations.

they prize even restricted admittance. The maverick volunteer leaders who speak up to defend themselves and their rights may face serious career obstacles. One woman was reputed to be kept from board appointments partly because of her willingness to oppose the leading men of the city when she worked with them on civic projects. She was not afraid to say "screw you" to a great cultural benefactor, for example.

Assertiveness, even in the service of a worthy cause, can create problems. While those who resist any change to the status quo and those who want drastic change can both use the board context for their ends, they are limited to their own partisans in the range of influence and action they command. Those eager to expand their influence and transmit their message beyond their own group must take a more neutral or even conciliatory stance toward those with different priorities (Thorne 1975). The women concerned with building and extending civic spirit and service choose their causes and their tactics accordingly.

Women who play strong advocate roles are more limited in this circle of influence. They concentrate on divisive issues like fighting the city council for childcare, slum clearance, or integrated schools. Consequently, others do not see them as generally desirable board members. An interest in conciliatory or adversary work thus affects one's eligibility for the array of board memberships available. The requirement of successful board membership and the lure of acceptance from the more powerful (and male-dominated) volunteer boards combine to reinforce the tendency—already well established by training and outlook—for women to channel their energies into the conventional philanthropies. Their careers require them to emphasize indirectness and conciliation once they arrive.

The board context will evoke such behaviors from either men or women who wish to influence its activity. However, men (or women) who become business executives or organizational chiefs of any kind may face counterpressures to be assertive and to use confrontational tactics. These counterpressures often arise in the area of board staff relations.

Board-Staff Relations

Tension is always endemic between board and staff, for the lines of authority and responsibility can be difficult to keep clear. New exigencies and new permutations of idiosyncratic personalities and skills in the array of board and staff members suggest new divisions

of labor and resource allocation. At the same time, the daily responsibilities or special skills of staff members—and their generally longer term of office than board members—tend to create
situations where the practical problems of managing an organization consolidate not only management but even some policy-
making powers in the hands of staff.

These problems are always potential in any organization where
an executive staff and a board of directors work together. They are
aggravated, however, in organizations where salaried staff serve a
board composed wholly, or in part, of professional volunteers. It is
difficult to resolve the question of whether the appropriate model is
one where the board are owners and the staff are employees or
whether the model of collegial relations between participants united
in serving a common cause should prevail. The board members are
sensitive to any imputation that they are *not* professionals because
they are unsalaried. They feel that executives, particularly men,
may patronize or even snub them. The staff, particularly women,
feel that board member volunteers may be insensitive to the pressures of the workday and demand attentions at inopportune times.
Further, board members may be insensitive to the requirements of
staff for salary and career advancement. Board members may expect salaries to be kept minimal in the wish that everyone connected with the enterprise contribute to it; staff members who are
not rich may find this expectation unreasonable. All of these possibilities make maintaining the balance of power between board and
staff a delicate issue.

Zald (1969:104–6) suggests that highly paid executives will have
more leverage than less affluent board members, and executives
presiding over large or technically complex organizations will have
more information and thus more leverage than board members
without it. But boards composed mainly of people with special resources in expertise, money, or constituencies have greater leverage with executives and staff. A correlate of the foregoing is that
boards serving organizations dependent upon them to raise all or
most of their funds rather than upon the regular, small contributions of a large rank-and-file membership also have great leverage
with staff. Similarly boards of newly formed organizations and organizations in crisis are more dependent upon board initiative;
thus members have more leverage than staff at such times (Zald
1969:108).

The balance of power is especially delicate when board members
have the amount of time and energy of professional volunteers to

focus on the goals and management of the organization. What may appear to board members as useful development of new programs or seizing new initiatives may seem meddlesome and obstructive to an executive concerned with ongoing programs. Experienced board members and executives approach one another warily over such matters. Sometimes executives can take control.[3]

As Zald notes (1969:110), there is a wide range of expectation, from executives who are Machiavellian toward or even openly disdainful of their boards to those who are obsequious. The problems at the extremes are clear: an executive risks even a sinecure if he or she is constantly high-handed to the board members who hire and fire. And the overly obsequious executive may also run dangers of dismissal—particularly if seen as too weak to function without constant board oversight and management of administrative tasks. In either extreme, the proper duties of staff and board are unclear and the confusion of functions can lead to all kinds of difficulties (such as problems of meeting corporate obligations under law, effectively maintaining public relations, and the constant jockeying for power in the internal management of the organization).

If the organization has funding problems and depends on the board to raise or contribute money, these problems can be magnified. The problem, even for a powerful director, is complicated by the necessary division of labor between staff and board. The board must raise money for the organization even if it does not entirely control its direction. The delicate balance of power is particularly clear on culture boards.

> Up till now, the pattern of all theatres, when a board starts dictating, then the theatre goes down the drain eventually. Our director has set up his theatre so artistic leadership has the last say. But how can this realistically take place when the community board has to take responsibility for raising the money? That is a predicament yet unsolved.

The authority of both board and staff is related to the results each produce. Very powerful directors of theatrical companies maintain their power by producing box office sensations. Boards are power-

---

3. Zald (1969:98, n.3) cites an example of how boards can be guided and even manipulated by executives in social service agencies. The board is "informed" of every decision before it is made; but board opinion is not seen by the long-term executive as influencing his judgment about policies and practices. Instead, the board is "educated" constantly and persistently to come to conclusions approved by staff and told how to vote.

ful if they can deliver the money required for operating expenses and ambitious new projects. The division of labor is generally, but not always, clear-cut. If executives become too high-handed or demanding and have too many expensive flops, boards can withdraw support or fire the director. When the board becomes too powerful, as the woman just quoted explains, an organization can deteriorate.[4]

However, autocratic direction from a small board becomes increasingly difficult today. Symphonies, for example, are now too expensive for one millionaire—or even a small group of benefactors—to maintain. Accordingly, powerful patrons have to accommodate considerations of public relations and modern management, as well as artistic vision, in order to maintain a competitive position in the national network of symphonies. This change in the balance of power reflects what Zald (p.107) has called "life-cycle problems."[5]

The volunteer leaders are not likely to be passive board members directed by an executive, even though they value a conciliatory manner. And they are likely to surpass executives in social status and wealth even when not gainfully employed themselves.

Of course, the ideology expressed is that joint cooperation in the service of the community characterizes both volunteer and staff. As this board president saw it, volunteers claim to offer assistance

---

4. Toffler (1965:198–99) offers an example of a ballet company that folded rather than change its name to that of its major patron. The company director feared the change meant that he would also lose final authority over artistic policy. Such fears are quite realistic when an organization is captured by a powerful patron.

> All through the forties the Detroit Symphony . . . had been the bauble of a chemical millionaire . . . who covered its deficits and called it, candidly, "my orchestra." When anyone complained about its programming or quality, he reacted with the hauteur of a medieval pope. "I like that kind of playing music," he is reputed to have said, "and that's the kind of music Detroit is going to get." (Toffler 1965:76)

5. Hospital management, for example, has shown shifts in the balance of power between administration and boards (Perrow 1963). Hospital care in the 1870s developed as hygenic, responsible service through the efforts of upper-class women who formulated the policies governing these early hospital organizations (Starr 1982: 155). Now, authority in hospitals has passed from trustees to physicians and finally to administrators in response to changing technology and hospital requirements (Starr 1982:178). Some hospital boards in this country, however, are still run entirely by women who exert their influence on policy making and management (Moore 1961).

that complements the functions of staff in hospitals. For instance, she could patrol the wards and clinics to learn about problems that might be resolved through board policy. "In my hospital work I came . . . once a week and spent the day. The patients would tell me things they wouldn't dare tell the nurse. . . . I could get their confidence and see also what could be done to improve the service." Volunteers can even function as department heads, doing staff work, in times of organizational crisis. "I'm not supposed to; but there was no one else. . . . The administration . . . sent me in as utility outfielder. . . . [They] trusted me. . . . I set up systems and got our list . . . and files in order. I wrote letters and did soliciting and wrote foundation proposals." These perspectives are from board members. We have no information on how the hospital staff feel about patients reporting problems to a board member or how much the administration really did trust a board member acting in a staff position. The tensions between gratitude and resentment for both staff and board members are a condition of the work (see Conrad and Glenn 1983:108–20 for a discussion of the delicate balance). There are, however, indications that staff and board members of organizations can provide real assistance, training, and encouragement for one another.

Positive Relations

As the ideology of volunteer leadership stresses the importance of good professional-staff relations—and as informants expect such relations in the normal course of events—few (12) discussed them at any length in interviews. But I observed five close friendships and working alliances between staff and board members. Executives and board members invited me to lunch and other informal gatherings where management problems, and current and future plans for the board were discussed. In the course of these and other meetings, women told me how they regarded one another; I could also see how they worked together and how they helped one another on board and purely personal matters. Common themes arising from both interviews and observations stress the assistance offered by staff and the importance of the friendships developed with them. Staff sometimes "look after" board members. Board members also look after staff. They may have to guide their executives and give *them* the authority to meet their responsibilities. One strong board member helped a weak executive in efforts to balance the budget while encouraging her male colleagues to support her.

>The superintendent was always saying "yes, doctor" and "no, doctor" [without looking] to see who it was. One day he reported on the coffee shop . . . it was losing money. So I said, "Why not charge five cents more for each sandwich?" "Oh doctor," he said in horrified tones, "the doctors wouldn't like it." Our board, which was entirely a lay board [mostly businessmen], burst out laughing. [And they supported my suggestion.] And we said, "Charge five cents more for the sandwiches and balance the budget."

Board members may show their concern by efforts to get promotions and opportunities for their career development for good staff members. A board member may intercede with the executive, for example, on behalf of a secretary who should receive a higher salary or a promotion.

In an atmosphere of cooperation, the enthusiasm of staff adds to the fun of the work. In large organizations, board members and staff may both learn and socialize together. Sometimes this pattern is institutionalized in the joint visit to annual national conventions. This socializing may be part of the work of the staff; but making the work fun for the staff, making the staff actively participate with the board members toward some common goal, can be seen as one of the positive achievements toward which a board member can also strive.

Where long-term partnerships have developed between staff and board members, friendships become close and often extend beyond retirement. An executive continued to visit a former board member incapacitated by ill health, for instance, keeping her informed about current events in the philanthropic world and providing a steady trickle of presents, notes, and telephone calls. Or an aging executive is well remembered and regularly visited by her circle of former board members. One woman named an executive director as "my best friend, almost," and said, "My children adore him; he [played a prominent part] in my daughter's wedding." These close friendships are part of what is seen as the enriching experience of volunteering.

Problems

A good number (27) of the informants mentioned, even if only very generally, difficulties arising between board members and staff. Some of these remarks were mild indications of ambivalence, as in the following remark by one woman, which includes—as an aside

—reference to the time-wasting capacity of staff members. "When I was president I went four times a week and always stayed quite a few hours because I had such a good time. . . . Sometimes, of course, it was not working, just chatting and gassing—like the staff do." Or what I have called ambivalence may be seen in the patronizing attitude toward staff exhibited by the following woman. "The [presidency] is sort of like being nursemaid and mother superior. You check in every day and see the staff are happy. . . . It's a glorified housekeeper [role]." Another approach to the matter of strained relations between various sectors of the community-volunteer effort is to note them—and then assert positively that they are resolved through good will. "If there are professional standards, you can work together."

But some informants (10) accept the conflict between board and staff members as an ongoing problem. As in the earlier discussion of the advocate-lobbyist, women may have to fight the resistance of staff professionals with medical or other credentials to any challenge of their professional authority. The resistance can be frustrating. Here is how one board member used a crisis in the service to introduce volunteers into more active participation in the organization.

> At one time professionals didn't want volunteers working with these kids. They felt the kids were too sick and the issue was too touchy. [But when there was a strike] there were not enough counselors to run the cottages. . . . And then I got a phone call asking me to help and . . . if I knew anyone . . . who was capable and not scared of this sort of thing. They were forced to use a volunteer to work with delinquent kids. And they found out it was not serious . . . and counted on them afterwards. A fluke.

Most generally, staff tend to resist direction from volunteer boards, even though staff often must depend on the volunteers for fundraising. As one woman remarked, "In [fund-raising], you really have more to say than the professional staff. . . . Some are eaten up alive in having to be nice to me."

One of the reasons staff do "have to be nice" to volunteers is that often both do the same kinds of work in fund-raising. Accordingly, each knows that the other must have the kinds of background, experience, and achievement records to command respect in this field. Volunteers, then, can judge the competence of staff and feel free to comment about it. Political campaign committees often have structures—with paid staffs and volunteer directors—facing similar fund-raising problems. One volunteer leader disparaged the staff she was given to work with on a campaign.

> When you get into a campaign, you find out how incompetent the paid workers are. I made some suggestions to . . . a young man heading the regional campaign and he thought they were *fantastic*. My lord, he should have had a dozen ideas like that. Marcia [another volunteer leader] had more ideas than any of those slobs.

The staff professionals may not always accurately assess either the experience or the power of the volunteer leaders. Sometimes women may tolerate patronization for a long while before deciding to call a staff member to account. To avoid these misunderstandings, women see they must constantly assert their rights, or reaffirm their position of authority, not only with staff but also with others who just assume staff will make the decisions. "The [publisher's representative] said, 'You girls will never publish that book. Your lawyers won't let you.' I said, 'They work for us, not the other way around.'" Women also argue for expanding the responsibility and authority volunteers should expect to receive, warding off encroachments by staff. An issue always latent in staff-professional relations is: who is to have control over the agenda of meetings and, as a consequence, control over organizational policies and priorities? This issue is also implicit in allocation of responsibility for reports. If the board members construct their own reports, they take more control over the formulation as well as ratification of policies. Board members who are committed to volunteer careers are likely to see the advantages of elaborating their role in the management process. At the very least, they expect the option to be open. Occasionally board members have to be quite firm with staff over the allocation of responsibility. "I asked about [one section of the documentation] and we were told, 'We decided it wasn't wise to show that material to the trustees.' I was really furious. So they gave it to us."

One strategy by which women exercise control over staff is related to the women's concern for groundwork. Those who do their homework and follow through on issues and understand their context are able to give effective supervision and direction to staff even in the face of passive—or active—resistance. The key to this effectiveness is not only careful preparation but the ability to show persistence in the face of obstacles. One woman's battle for a botanical garden took ten years. A high-ranking city employee asked her,

"Why don't you just give up?" Yet eventually the project was successful despite bureaucratic opposition. This tenacity is supplemented by attention to detail, along with new and renewed efforts to bring others to accept the project.

The characteristic of persistence in careful organization is one that informants focus on when describing their general working style—not just their relations with staff. One woman sums up this careful preparation and dogged follow-through in describing her own modus operandi: "I believe in having meetings, discussing, letting everyone say their bit, assigning everyone a job, and checking on them like crazy." This style cannot help but be difficult for executives and staff to accommodate unless they are accustomed to working with volunteer women board members; salaried professionals usually do not have enough time for this detailed attention to their philanthropic work.

These problems reflect the ambiguity surrounding unpaid work as well as the pejorative aura attached to the woman volunteer, no matter how professional she is about her work. The care she shows in checking and the interest in detail can be interpreted as interference; the comportment and gentility of an upper-class woman can be seen as condescending. In turn, these women can see the defensive resistance or reserve of staff members as patronizing or arrogant. The constant potential for struggle between staff and volunteer is summarized in the following appraisal and review of working conditions. "I suppose . . . the continuing problem . . . a volunteer faces in dealing with those who feel threatened [concerns] status. 'I'm a professional and you're a volunteer and you had better get out of my way.'" But not all of the jockeying for control is aggravating. Sometimes board members are amused by the clever indirection used by staff to manipulate board decisions.

> We have a policy of grounding all our wires. Then the crunch began, tightening budgets. So some board members suggested maybe we could give up grounding wires. At the next meeting I got this staff recommendation for [putting unsightly telephone poles] on . . . the great beautiful drive to the museum. The board members were in a huff. [Another board member] and I got to laughing because the staff fixed it this way. Nobody [else] on the board realized the sequence of events; and the staff got to keep [all] the wires underground.

Alternatively, the clever indirection may come from the board member manipulating staff decisions. Sometimes a board member may see that subordinate staff are caught by conflicts between the executive and the board members and be sympathetic to the subordinate's plight. In one such conflict, Mrs. Aubrey, the board president, wanted the minutes to show that a dispute between her and the executive had taken place. When she found that this item was omitted she called the secretary to find out why. The secretary said that she was *sure* Mrs. Aubrey didn't want the minutes to say anything about the dispute, that it really wasn't advisable. Mrs. Aubrey insisted, but said that she was sympathetic to the position of the executive's secretary. Mrs. Aubrey said, " . . . she knows I am a decent person." Mrs. Aubrey wanted it clear that she would make trouble for the executive, but not for his secretary.

If the staff person is terribly powerful, as in the case of some executive directors, there may be no room for jockeying. Potential board members may not wish to put their energy into an activity where they can foresee no opportunity to affect policy.

The problems presented by the too-powerful board and the spectres raised by fears of capricious, high-handed interference in the management of an organization are also well known in community service organizations. One extremely powerful women's board in this study had a reputation for riding its staff hard enough to cause a relatively high turnover rate in executives. Board presidents may take steps to minimize such disruptions to the organization. "The administration was terrified of the board when I took over. I promised that nothing I know you will not know [I will tell you everything]. . . . I think we have trust now." These problems of control may be exacerbated by social distance when board members belong to wealthier and more influential segments of the community power structure than do staff members. Efforts to minimize social distance cost time and effort when a board president works to treat staff hospitably. "I felt that if [my pre-benefit party] had been catered the staff members' wives would have been very uncomfortable. So I did it myself; but I was exhausted at the dance. I was up from six in the morning working that day. But it was worth it."

Yet, even with the best will in the world from those who feel themselves socially superior, it is not surprising in a democratic society that some staff people may resent treatment just *as if* they were equals. Derogatory views of society *grandes dames* may be used to justify the professional distance or the delimitation of board activity that staff members sometimes wish to enforce. Through trial and error, sometimes through confrontation and tests of strength, boards and staffs work out a modus vivendi. Male

board members may be helpful, for example, in pointing out to ob-
tuse executives that a woman president of the board may be just as
important as if she were male. Then the woman leader, as in the
following instance, can smooth things over.

> At our recent meeting when I asked John [the executive] for
> some information I was told: "You don't have to know."
> Roddy [another board member] cut right across and said,
> "Who do you think you are? Why do you think you can talk
> to Mrs. Aubrey that way?" And he laid it on the line so that
> John was really quite shocked. . . . So then I smoothed
> everything over later and told John we had to go to lunch.
> . . . And now everything is fine. . . . After all, the chair-
> man of the board and the manager of the [organization] are
> what you need to make [the enterprise] go.

This anecdote suggests the uses of a male as a public front for a
powerful woman community leader who may choose a low public
profile so that she can privately smooth over difficulties arising between herself and an executive. This strategy reasserts the importance of the traditional posture for women as behind the scenes
rather than in the spotlight.

Although women recognize the risks of bringing internal difficulties out into public view—even if only in a full board meeting—
sometimes a volunteer leader will create adverse publicity for the
organization in order to train and, possibly, discipline a recalcitrant
executive. The woman in the following case had policies she wished
implemented and she was determined to make the executive do it.
She successfully managed confrontation with staff, forcing the
executive director to his knees, as it were, without assistance from
other board members.

> The general manager would disagree with the commission
> and not pay any attention to their requests and advice. So I
> would take the battle out in public and invite general scru-
> tiny. Finally the general manager came to me and said,
> "There is no one who could hurt me more than you can,
> Mrs. Jackson." So I said to him, "Well, all right then. Let's
> get some agreement in private about these matters." Now
> we get along very well.

When various tactics for persuasion don't work, board members
may contemplate even more drastic measures; and a number (22)
spoke of thinking about firing their executive or actually doing it.
Those that are just thinking about it may abandon the notion after

weighing the costs and benefits. "The program is not entirely a success. I don't think the director is as good as she might be. And I wanted her fired, but the other members would just not do it. Still it is a good program and it is . . . a monument to the city." Where a director has determined supporters, the discontented board member may console herself with the thought that this support stems partly from the good results the director has been able to produce in the past. Even where too much control by the executive is a danger, his efficiency may warrant toleration.

> At the board meetings everything was decided by the executive committee controlled by the director. So the kinds of decisions relegated to such meetings were: should we have box lunches or buffets? That type of unimportant little thing. So the membership of the board stayed away. Board meeting attendance is a good criterion of how healthy an organization is. . . . Yet this executive director was pretty well entrenched because he did have a good past record and the organization itself had an excellent record.

Sometimes the problem concerns a faithful executive who is no longer adequate now that the organization has grown in size and complexity. Such an individual has to be "retired" gracefully. And women do talk about problems connected with effecting graceful retirements.

> They called me in to chair a committee when Magda Levenson was getting close to retirement to recommend to them something of the future structure and to move Magda out. We moved funds around and jobs . . . and we really pushed Magda into retirement. It was not as pleasant [as we might have wished].

Generalists, like the woman just quoted, are also consulted when it is the too powerful executive who must be retired. "I made an effort to ensure that the board behaved in a moral manner in conducting the inquiries [about] the failure of the executive to give adequate opportunity to set policy to the board."

The preceding consultation suggests that "graceful" retirement involves concern about the proper care in making a case against an erring executive. Arbitrary personnel decisions without careful investigation and review processes can create adverse publicity for the organization, eroding community support and ability to raise funds. Board members may wish to avoid charges of high-handed and unfair action.

Board leadership also has to be wary about arousing internal antagonisms and creating splits, as Zald notes (1969:109). Boards are not necessarily unified in their views of organizational policy and management; coalitions and factions may arise accordingly. Members may represent important constituencies from external groups and oppose other board members and administration on behalf of these constituents. Executives may exploit these differences to collect the power of the organization in their own hands.

Whether executives become powerful through this exploitation or through the indifference of board members to their responsibilities, there is always the possibility that executives, left to their own devices too long, may abuse their powers. Sometimes the nature of disclosures about an executive's use of power are so explosive that a director may be forcibly retired. Some staff problems are very difficult to resolve: the problem is hard to identify or the board is reluctant to act against a well-established executive, even though the problem is identifiable. It may require considerable time and effort by the concerned and even alarmed board member to remove that executive.

> The administrator was given every chance to get help. He pulled himself together for a while, and then things got worse again. The board wouldn't believe me. Then he came to work drunk early in the morning. I happened to see him there. I said to the board, "You've got to make a decision."

All the foregoing difficulties in board and staff relations are exacerbated when the executive resists dismissal and prior presidents have not been able to bring themselves to do the firing. Three informants complained about how this dirty job (i.e., filled with confrontation and conflict) had been left over for them by weak predecessors. One of them described how difficult the process can be.

> Luckily I'm my age and very tough. I knew we had an incompetent executive. Do you think anyone would fire him? I got him to resign. And then he wrote this [public] letter saying I had forced him to resign . . . when I heard this I felt as though it were a blow to my solar plexus.

Implicit in her remark is the desire to avoid open confrontation. The question of just how much power these women have makes them uneasy. First, they shy away from the explicit display of power, as their remarks about leadership and criticizing others have indicated. Second, they are not always sure just how much power they do have in their ambiguous position as professional volunteers who are board members. These questions can make women acutely uncomfortable when their power plays become public, as in the foregoing. Even when they have the edge in a conflict, they may need reassurance.

> I didn't know how the meeting would come out. So I called a parliamentarian. . . . This was an old problem to her. She said, "I suggest you have the votes. Then just have faith you won't lose them. At the crucial moment, don't sell yourself short for not having faith that they won't vote."

In this kind of encounter a board president weighs not only what the conflict requires for immediate successful resolution but what it will cost her in terms of the long-term equilibrium of the board— and the organization it oversees. She also considers the consequences for her own reputation. Although some conflict is endemic between board and staff, it is not surprising that only a minority of informants report such activities; and the few instances are well remembered and commented upon by the protagonists—and other observers as well.

Most women give some thought to their reputation not only because they wish to avoid conflict or unpleasantness but because they do not have the institutional supports of stable, salaried careers. Like other entrepreneurs, the volunteer civic leader has to build on a reputation based on "delivering the goods" in context after context. In addition, these women also operate on what has been termed the "contest model" (Stigler 1963); they hold their positions just because they can meet repeated challenges. Like the prize fighter or the bull fighter, these women must show they can deliver better than challengers. These challengers—new candidates for board positions—come not only from the pool of volunteer leaders but also from both professional and business circles of men and women in the community. Especially for prestigious appointments, this competition can be keen, even though not formalized as it is in sports contests. Consequently, women have to be extremely careful, not only about the work they do but the reputation they acquire while doing it. It is no wonder, then, that women board members say they dislike confrontation, are interested in mediation, are eager to make alliances and conciliate opposing forces. It is ironic that the qualities women cultivate as part of the traditional expectations for women of their class are also the qualities that fit them for survival in a special type of entrepreneurial career.

Professional Volunteers on the Board of Directors

The tensions that may arise for board and staff, between policy-making and administrative bodies, develop a special character when the board is composed solely or in part of professional volunteers. This work is the volunteers' central focus for employment; consequently they may devote more time and develop greater commitment to it than their salaried professional counterparts.

The history of philanthropic work in this country shows the continual strain between the struggle to make some aspects of social service professional and salaried while maintaining the place of volunteers.[6] Board and staff relations are colored by this history of past conflict and disagreement. The problems of coordinating staff-volunteer efforts continue in community organizations today. The delicate balance between the rights and prerogatives of each group is always tested as the personalities, resources, and working conditions of staff and board membership change.

These ambiguities contribute to the uncertainty about the "true" worth of and "real" motivation for women's participation on boards, particularly if women are seen as serving on boards as a way to fill time, for aimless sociability, or for social climbing. The stereotypes of volunteers, and the marginal importance sometimes accorded their efforts, provide a background—even for committed participants—against which their activities can be perceived by themselves and by others as frivolous. A recurring theme in the interviews, then, is the effort to deny these stereotypes by explaining the real work that members do: the recruitment and development of new board members, monitoring the interactions of board members with one another and with the staff.

The stereotypes and the efforts to deny them should not distract our attention from the women's part in the city establishment. Their board activities play an important function in maintaining the institutions—the parks, museums, schools, cultural institutions—

6. The problems of how policy setting and division of work responsibilities should be assigned appeared early, from the development of the first friendly visiting societies and their employment of staff to manage the flow of work (Huggins 1971: 121). Lubove (1965:12) points out that the enterprise absolutely depended on volunteers, even if growth and rationalization of the enterprise required paid staff. These volunteers also served as trustees who raised funds and recruited new workers and supporters. And yet, staff resisted the influx of volunteers who might threaten the standard of service (Lubove 1965:44) and wanted these amateurs under careful supervision (Vandepol 1982). Volunteers countered that paid professionals lacked their own spontaneity and zeal (Lubove 1965:13).

that serve the city and make it a viable place to live. From their efforts to explain what they do, informants also tell us about how the city establishment operates: how the women of the upper class are selected and then participate on the philanthropic boards of their city; and how these women describe their behavior when they eventually become the organizers, recruiters, and leaders for these boards. In this process, they tell us about their style of management, their ever present concern with the development of consensus that marks their pursuit of civic service, and some of the differences between themselves and their male colleagues.[7]

The women on the major philanthropic boards of Pacific City have a different agenda from their husbands; without business interests of their own, women can feel freer to concentrate on civic responsibilities.[8] As we have seen, however, they generally avoid any social concerns that might set them on a collision course with established business interests in the city. Within these limits, these women develop and use their skills to create or maintain useful services for the city. They also create networks of talented women as potential board members. These networks are composed mainly of like-minded women—and women from similar life-styles and circumstances. The most important positions on these boards, when they go to women at all, are likely to go to women who are from the upper class or sympathetic to its values. The women see their values as stressing a prudent concern with conserving what is best in civic philanthropic institutions and building new institutions where previous arrangements are inadequate to current needs. They see themselves as working with all elements in the city. Yet, they see themselves as a special group as well, tied together by common experiences, family relationships and friendships, common school and club memberships—the special group of serious workers among the women of the leisure class. The values they hold and the way these values influence approaches to work inform and color their functions as board members.

7. Scott (1984:18,fn 23) argues that the history of women's voluntary associations in the United States shows a gendered division of labor. Women's associations have been characterized by the grass-roots creation of institutions to benefit the community.

8. Benét (1972) points out how aggressively male corporate executives may pursue their own business advantage over the objections of other board members, and even at the risk of provoking charges of conflict of interest, while they are trustees of a major university. Apparently, they do not permit a concern for consensus and the best interests of the organization they serve to dissuade them from using a nonprofit institution for individual profit opportunities.

In this chapter we have seen how women use what Whisler and Hirsch have called the culture of boards in their volunteer service. We have also seen how the effects of traditional expectations for women (such as their ability to conciliate) combine with experience in the women's worlds of volunteer work to create what might be called a special set of understandings about how women do—or should—operate within that culture.

The board is their workplace; like the career itself, it is imperfectly conceptualized both by the workers there and by a more general audience. It is not a discernible, publicly recognized work site; and the picture of the work done there is clouded by the latent tensions between board and staff members and aggravated by the pejorative stereotypes of women volunteer board members. Some of the problems of invisible careers, then, involve not only this issue of just where the work site is but also who are its most legitimate occupants. Professional volunteers must constantly work at assuring their place in this setting.

Conclusion

10

The Invisible Work in Constructing Career, Class, and Community

My aim has been to encourage a serious reevaluation of the "work" of volunteering, particularly that of the leadership who envision and organize the activities of volunteers in their communities. These women work hard, and persistently, on important projects that benefit their city; they belie the notion that all volunteer work is casual and intermittent. For these women, at least, it can be a taxing full-time and even lifetime occupation. In their serious commitment to this occupation, women develop careers as do salaried workers. Their careers, however, are not generally recognized and most of the women don't think in such terms themselves. They see themselves as volunteers who, though they are committed workers who may be needed by the organizations they serve, have leave to depart at any moment.

The invisibility of careers affects the way women think about and conduct their work lives. The voluntary and invisible character of their work means that it requires specific kinds of effort and skill not usually required of paid workers. The women must shape their own activities outside of institutional supports, negotiating and rethinking strategies that will allow them to be effective in ambiguous and sometimes marginal positions. In one sense, their work is always marginal; for women can make tremendous personal contributions with no clear evaluation by others and no explicit consideration in the society of whether that contribution, whatever the evaluation, is something generally desired by the population.

The marginality of their contribution reveals some of the problems occasioned by the discontinuities between the overt and covert dimensions of this work. The overt dimension—what people say they think of the work—involves the public attitude toward volunteering as it is expressed in published sentiments and in recognition of the tangible products of that work. This dimension also reflects the philosophy of voluntarism as the workers themselves understand it and the way women see that philosophy complementing or encouraging a traditional role for women in modern American society. Volunteering is part of family expectations, especially in the privileged class. The role women play in volunteering fits in and around regular family responsibilities as well. The expectation that the work is complementary to their main responsibilities—to husband and family—encourages women to accept roles in society with fewer (or a different system of) rewards than those available to their husbands. Further, since volunteering is supposed to be an altruistic activity, it is not as important either to specify the work or to insist on bringing all aspects of the work out for more public inspection.

The covert dimension involves the ambivalence toward both women and volunteer, nonpaid work in American society today. That ambivalence encompasses both respect and contempt for the work women do in creating the ambience within which philanthropic work and fund-raising can flourish. The ambivalence is highlighted by the stereotype of "society" parties, social climbing and, most generally, the recognition of one latent consequence of philanthropic work among middle-class and upper-class women— the work of wives in producing or maintaining social status for husband and family. Even though most women disavow these potentials in volunteer work, they are aware that they exist—that the covert dimensions to the evaluation of work are based on some observations of socialite life-style. Many women develop the defensive stance or ideology of volunteering accordingly. The two major themes—the altruistic commitment of workers and the democratizing element in the work—explain or justify individuals' commitment to voluntarism and the significance of their activity in it despite the absence of a cash return for service rendered. This response denies the significance of the socialite or idle, time-wasting component in volunteering. Instead, it stresses the altruism of workers irrespective of class and the importance of their work for community welfare. This oversight permits women to overstate the continuity between their own volunteer work and the unpaid work of women in other classes. The ease with which women of the privileged classes can make connections to the city political and business leaders, the resources they may use to advance volunteer projects, the opportunities they have to become renowned in their volunteer work comprise a particular set of assets related to their class position. The oversight also permits women to avoid any assessment of possible serious conflicts of interest over community projects that their philosophy does not cover. They do not know if other groups in the city think differently about community and how it should be organized, for example. Their philosophy permits them to recognize some problems in society while still accommodating the basic inequalities that exist.

This study of invisible careers has shown how women organize and justify their volunteer work within the framework of the tensions created by these overt and covert dimensions. The dimensions correspond to the overt and covert expectations of what women can or will do, how they should or will behave. Overtly, a woman can stress the importance of volunteer work as part of what she does for her family and community—but always as a complementary or subordinate interest to the family. The rewards are expected to come primarily from the satisfaction of altruistic impulses and secondarily from the development of new interests and friends in the community, new or growing self-confidence from seeing one can do a job well. The covert problems that women may have to face concern how to reconcile personal ambition with the alternatives open to traditional privileged women: how to manage the hidden work of constructing or maintaining class position for the family while denying the significance of such work, how to find autonomy in work while accepting subordination at home, how to maintain self-confidence while facing self-doubts and uncertainties about the value of unpaid community service.

Women manage to rationalize or justify their volunteer careers in the face of these problems in various ways. They see the advantages of their life style and are willing to pay the price that comes with the status of a pampered and indulged subordinate. They focus on the flexibility their ambiguous position affords to create connections and build bridges between groups for better public services in their city. The larger problem—how to incorporate and evaluate this invisible work out of which invisible careers have been formulated—remains to be considered. These three themes inform the conclusion: the conflicts and paradoxes in public views of volunteering; the individual assessment of a volunteer career; and the significance of this work in American society and in the division of labor most generally.

Public Ambivalence

The lip service offered to voluntarism (by the associations devoted to the promotion of volunteering, by newspaper articles and obituaries in praise of those who devoted their lives to community service, by introductions at public benefits and celebrations in honor of community leaders) provides a uniformly positive and praiseworthy picture of this activity. The idea of citizen participation is said to embody some of the best elements in the American ethos; the spirit of America appears in the volunteer. However, these public affirmations conceal or ignore the divisions in modern society created by the separation of public and private life, visible and invisible responsibilities. These divisions are related to the distinction between paid and unpaid work and the value accorded to each.

Public life is a primarily male world where the "important" affairs of a society occur; private or family life—where women predominate—is the backstage or preparation for these important affairs. The people in public life carry visible responsibilities that they are paid, appointed, or elected to fulfill. The business of public life, including business and industry as well as politics and government, is regulated by institutionalized patterns of recruitment, selection, and succession. A general understanding exists in society, if only through the media, of what this business is and how important it is.

Women's "backstage" contributions to public life, by contrast, are incompletely understood or recognized. The view of womens' service to the community as only peripheral is nowhere more evident than in community studies. The contributions of women to the shape and direction of community life have been largely unassessed. Where they have been recognized, as in the work of Warner and his associates, they were interpreted in terms of their supportive, prestige and status-enhancing functions for individuals or families rather than as contributions to the political and economic life of the community. Writing of small town life, for example, Vidich and Bensman (1968) provide only a rudimentary notion of how women participate in the economy of the community through gardening and preserving. In general, as Lyn Lofland (1975:145) remarks in a critique of community studies:

> [Women] are part of the locale or neighborhood or area—
> described like other important aspects of the setting such
> as income, ecology or geography—but largely irrelevant to
> the analytic *action*. . . . They may participate in organized

groups, but such groups are tangential to the structuring of community life or to the processes of community government (for example, in Robert and Helen Lynd's *Middletown*, 1929, or Gans' *The Levittowners*, 1967). When the researcher's lens pulls back for the wide-angle view, they are lost in the ubiquitous and undifferentiated "he." When it moves forward to close, detailed focus, they are fuzzy, shadow, background figures, framing the male at center stage.

Part of the problem women face is that the type of community work they do is neither seen by the researchers nor themselves as real work, so it is difficult to get the activity into focus. As Wadel (1979: 374–75) points out, activities associated with informal community relations have characteristics that make it difficult to associate them with work: (1) they tend to be ad hoc and sporadic; (2) they have a "personal" character and their value depends upon who performs an activity and how, as much as what gets done; (3) they have a "private" character in that much of what goes on is not open to public view; and (4) the activity is hard to divide into means and ends because so much attention and commitment is lavished on the performance, indicating that it has an intrinsic value, irrespective of outcome. These characteristics are essential components of community volunteer work, yet they are mystifying as well. Neither researchers nor informants associate this pattern of working conditions with formal work.

The difficulty all community studies have with spotting influential women may also be a consequence of the tangential quality of that influence in both national and local community spheres. Women are likely to be in the group of indirect power-wielders, or influentials, who do not always wish to advertise their position. Since most past community studies have been conducted by men, it is the worlds where they have easiest access that are the most sharply defined and thoroughly analyzed (Lofland 1975:158–62). Thus, even where women's activities are not seen as trivial they are presented without much detail.

Although women increasingly have made inroads into public life, and a growing interest in feminist thought and scholarship has begun to show how and where stereotypes obscure all the work women do, women still belong mainly to that world of support, privacy, and invisibility that makes the frontstage of public affairs possible for men (Margolis 1979). Traditional women and men accept more of the stereotype than do those who participate in the feminist movement; but many parts of the traditional picture of the division of labor between the sexes remain in place. The separation of work and family and the subordination of family or private interests to work or public interests continues. The problems of working women are, everywhere in the industrialized countries of the world, exacerbated by their difficulties in managing both the private worlds of home and family and the public world of salaried work (Cook, Lorwin, and Daniels 1984). Whether professional or working class, women face the problem of managing childcare and household arrangements without public concern for these matters as social rather than personal problems (Kahn-Hut, Daniels, and Colvard 1982).

The problems that working women face everywhere are part of the underlying problem of how societies treat the home work of women, whether paid or unpaid. It is not generally regarded as difficult or skilled, although some of it is absolutely necessary for the survival of the family members. Women are, of course, often praised by their families and friends for doing it well. But the absence of institutionalized forms of approval—of specific indications of the value of this work—appear in discussions of divorce settlements (Weitzman 1985). The plight of displaced homemakers creates an increasing concern for assigning dollar equivalents to the services women have performed for husbands and families to permit an equitable distribution of community assets upon dissolution. The concern continues to this day, despite some inroads on traditional inequitable patterns, for the pattern continues; women are still at a legal, social, and economic disadvantage when their rights to community property are considered and enforced.[1]

Even for the privileged women in this study, the weight of this distinction between what is valued in the public domain and what is overlooked in the private world—or attended to only sporadically and unsystematically—is a contradiction always to be resolved in one way or another. Even though volunteer careers take women into the community, their work is seen as private. It possesses all the characteristics associated with informal community relations that make it difficult to differentiate this service from the more personal services given to family members. The problem of how to value volunteer workers remains unresolved. In response,

---

1. Recently (8 August, 1985, page 1) the *New York Times* reviewed the impact of New York's five-year-old divorce law and concluded that it has been unfair to women.

women sometimes dismiss the issue of the social value of their work as insignificant, or they may just strongly deny that any problem in evaluation exists. These efforts reveal that at the very least, however comfortable they are in a personal resolution to the contradiction, these women recognize that their participation in public affairs, no matter how important or honored, does not carry the same social weight as does the work of the salaried men and women in public life. The women from volunteer careers in public life face the uncertainties and confusion that come from carving out careers in an area where respect for their accomplishments mingles with ignorance over how they did it, doubts about motivation (citizen participation or social climbing), cynicism about what most unsalaried workers really accomplish (civic improvements or frivolous and time-wasting activity). The doubts remain manageable when women are powerful, wealthy, healthy, at the top of their careers, and supported by family and friends. The tenuousness of public regard for a volunteer civic leader's position becomes clearer when circumstances like aging, illness, divorce, or widowhood make it difficult to maintain that position. As women note, the aging are pushed aside, treated with condescension or even contempt in ways that aging curmudgeons in established, prestigious professions (doctors, tenured professors, and lawyers, for example) do not necessarily face. When they choose to maintain their social and occupational role, it is often argued that we are too tolerant of aged professionals in this society, hesitating to challenge the licensing or certification of even those practitioners who may have become dangerously incompetent. Women civic leaders who hold their positions in a competitive setting have no public understandings about their sinecure to support them if they appear to falter. In that case, any of the negative aspects of the stereotypes about women's work can have full play against them: they are doddering dowagers, meddlesome do-gooders, or interfering autocrats who haven't the sense to realize they must step aside. As women in this study note, the force of these negative views is effective in isolating even the really determined woman who wishes to continue as a leader in civic work.

These problems of public ambivalence appear most clearly for those women who, through death or divorce, suffer reversals in fortune and seek to exchange a volunteer career for a salaried one. While a few extremely fortunate women (in my study, perhaps two of the seventy) may find highly paid positions on the basis of volunteer experience, most cannot find an equivalent, paid position.

Those women forced out to work by changing circumstances are lucky to find a position as staff for organizations where they were once board members. Such positions, as many have noted, carry neither salary, status, nor professional opportunity commensurate with what women possessed as volunteer leaders.

Individual Expectations and Perceptions

The mixed responses and conflicting understandings of what a volunteer career is worth in a cash nexus society, how a woman's work should be evaluated, and how the activity of leisure-class women should be assessed—all these color the understandings of the women who have risen to volunteer leadership positions. Although they have shown a range of abilities beyond the average person, and have demonstrated their skills in a variety of accomplishments, these women work within certain limits. Some find these limits galling, but most accept them with little or no question. For those who accept the limitations readily, the traditional notions of proper behavior for women and men offer the main prop. These ideas—such as the man is the head of the family, men are the leaders in the world, women are well-treated in the traditional order, women work best by indirection and conciliation—complement the traditional ideas current in the upper classes about the value of the status quo and the necessity for the order it provides. Women in or close to the upper class are aware of these ideas and generally support them, ignoring or discounting any discrimination they face from men. Instead, women focus on the amount of indirect influence (or power) that they can wield. However, even the most traditional women face obstacles and contexts which they find frustrating. They face occasional snubs or even intimidation by some salaried (usually male) professionals, condescension from men with whom they serve as board members and others who are family members or friends. The higher women rise in their civic work, the more likely they are to run into such reminders of their ambiguous status in their work world. Most women resolve the problem by restricting their work to areas where they are already known or respected, working primarily through women's groups and moving into male-dominated civic activities with caution, and then doing so only rarely. Some women make the transition, as generalists, to become widely respected by politicians and others in the city establishment. They move easily between men's and women's circles in nonprofit organizations. Still others (a very few) build constituencies and join the rough and tumble of politics, as advocates for a variety of causes, and stay to outface detractors.

The women who find the restrictions galling are more likely to complain, assert their rights, fight the traditional system, even if only periodically and in a limited way. All protest, however, including the most sustained, is relatively limited. The few advocates in this sample who have fought the established system consistently are renegades from an upper-class perspective, but even they want to operate within the political system. They are reformers not revolutionaries.

The very nature of the work all these women do, the skills they acquire and the goals they seek push them toward mediating and conciliating positions. Their image of themselves is that they wish to—and do—exert influence rather than direct power; they persuade rather than coerce. The requirements of the work and the exigencies created by emergencies, however, can lead women into more assertive postures. When these occasions arise, women realize anew the ever present difficulty of their position, the requirements for tact and delicacy in balancing personal ambition (or zeal for a cause, or the desire to do a professional job) and traditional role expectations. Women manage this balancing act through the code they live by (as mothers and wives first) and their philosophy of voluntarism (as an appropriate and altruistic adjunct to their family lives). The fragility of this balance appears in some general grumbling over how women are treated, in the bitterness the women feel toward the system when confronted by divorce or widowhood, and in the wistfulness of those who wished they had been able to seek paid employment earlier in life.

These regrets also reflect the tensions arising over the individual wish for autonomy and the traditional expectation of subordination in women. It is hard for women who have had some independent success through volunteer activity always to assert the primacy of their family roles where their own wishes take second place to those of husband and children. They say they resolve the conflict in various ways (reasoning with family members, bargaining, insisting, enduring while trying not to complain). It is clear, however, that this issue, like the problem of how to reconcile ambition and traditional role expectations in their work world, is always potentially volatile and difficult to resolve completely.

The difficulty of maintaining a balance between autonomy and subordination is exacerbated by the mixed public messages women receive about the value of their work. The difficulty in placing a dollar value on their work, of finding salaried job equivalents that would recognize the experience and skills acquired in volunteering can undermine the self-confidence of even the most successful.

The women in this study are reluctant to consider their place in a class as well as a community structure; they are hampered in their own efforts to understand the sources of whatever uneasiness they experience from these balancing acts. Their responses indicate that they don't see class as a particularly significant issue in civic service. Perhaps they deceive themselves about their own privileged position and the way their resources aided them in their careers, whatever their individual talents. They may also wish to ignore (at least not discuss with an interviewer) their views on how class hierarchies are maintained. The uneasiness around discussions of social climbing, class differences among volunteers, distinctions between Jews and gentiles, all suggest this interpretation. In any case, these women are firm about denying class distinctions in their work. In their own discussions, for example, they see community and civic work as the same thing. They speak of themselves and their colleagues as leaders in "the community" even though Pacific City is very diverse and contains many and sometimes overtly conflicting communities. The obscuring of the distinctions between communities—and which communities these civic leaders best represent—permits these women volunteers to obscure the importance of their own particular location, as noted in the introduction, at the intersection of philanthropy and "society," but also at or near the top of the economic hierarchy. In their insistence on minimizing the significance of class in the structure of opportunity for volunteer work in the city, women obscure the limitations on the amount of community spirit that they can construct to overcome differences and create community solidarity in a city. They also obscure their own work in the construction of class.

An important element in much of their volunteer work is development and maintenance of organizations that initiate upper-class children into the activities and responsibilities of their station. The independent (private) schools, the organizations that prepare the young for their own volunteer work, and the maintenance of cultural organizations are all examples of the volunteer activities which are used for these purposes. While these volunteer activities are pointed out as benefiting a wider public, they are part of the pattern that channels interests, energies, and resources into support of the established class structure. An unfortunate consequence of this system for these women is that it also reinforces a pattern of male dominance in which women's efforts are always of secondary importance, even when not completely invisible. Since women accept this system, they themselves discount the larger significance of much of their own work. The work of constructing and maintaining class is especially denied since it contradicts the picture of constructing a community that mitigates class differences.

The Significance of Volunteer Work in Constructing Community

If the work that privileged women do is not quite as democratic nor as unifying for their communities as these women believe, it is nonetheless of considerable importance. This work does create connections between interests and across classes when the regular institutionalized patterns of access are inadequate. Furthermore, the civic leaders provide opportunities for others to be creative, make contributions that benefit their respective communities as well as the city at large. Finally, these women, like their colleagues in other classes and other communities, provide the ambience, as well as the channels for actions, that affect the quality of life in the cities and towns of our society. When they divert their energies elsewhere, much of what has been termed "municipal housekeeping" (Blair 1980) doesn't get done. That our society is willing to accept this work as volunteer effort or else live without it reflects the ultimate value of this contribution to the quality of life around us: the members of society would like to have it, but there is no systematic provision for it and the governing bodies won't pay for it. In the future, perhaps, we shall all have to take responsibility for the quality of life in our cities, for the review and study of our social institutions and services to see how well they meet the needs of the citizenry, and for the creation and manufacture of new institutions and services when these are seen as necessary. The civic leaders who have done this work in the past leave us a legacy of approaches and techniques to use in facing new problems as they arise. We may need to consider their advice carefully in order to apply it. In the future it may prove difficult to persuade their daughters to make this work the full-time occupation it has been for the mothers.

Lessons to Be Learned from a Study of Invisible Work

As Wadel (1979:365) notes in his discussion of "The Hidden Work of Everyday Life," work is a socially constructed category, continuously changing, with new activities included and others excluded, just as the way we characterize work and distinguish it from nonwork changes continuously. The hidden work in that construction contains those activities we are less aware of or that we do not yet call work. Wadel (1979:373) points out the difficulty in naming these activities as work when they occur in formal organizations. They often occur "simultaneously with 'ordinary' work." They are also not considered "necessary," for people think the formal organization can manage without them. "Thus, when people, for some reason or other, stop their ordinary work to . . . chat, they—and their employers and their colleagues—are likely to feel they are 'stealing' time away from work." Consequently, such activities are extras, they are part of informal organization, perhaps, but they are not work. Yet it is important to conceptualize this activity as work, for much of it is necessary for the proper functioning of recognized work.

Much of it is also necessary for the functioning of social institutions outside the economic sphere where work is generally thought to be—for the functioning of family, neighborhood and community, for example. Much of the work that women volunteers do falls within this category of hidden work and contributes to these other institutions as well as to the economy.

In both economic and noneconomic institutions this work is an aspect of all social relations. It supports and maintains personal and private relations on the one hand and the collective activities that help maintain class, community, democracy, and other social institutions. The work these women do is particularly important in the maintenance of class and some aspects of community; but it shows how this work is done and how it can be organized and developed for other workers and other settings as well.

The underlying importance of this work is in the generation of social values. By insisting that some service must be developed, some social and groups' needs attended, volunteer women assert common values that all should uphold. By creating situations in which citizens become mindful of their responsibilities to others, and are then moved to donate money or to offer service, volunteer women also create commitment, even fervor, as well as channel interests and energies in the participants. An important aspect of hidden work, then, is the embodiment of social values through the activities involved in the work.

The core of much of this work is the social transaction. As Wallman notes (1979:11), work is about social transactions as much as material production. In their concern for building networks, creating an ambience, forging disparate board members into a team, the women in this study show how important it is to understand the social transactions which are an important part of their work. Perhaps because their options are limited by the absence of the institutionalized rewards of paid work, the volunteer workers are especially sensitive to the distinctive aspects of this activity: the shaping of talents to meet the requirements of a project, for example.

Everett Hughes, throughout his analyses of workers and their work (1971), emphasized the importance of understanding the relationship of work to the moral order. In the tradition of Durkheim, Hughes pointed out that the division of labor was a pervasive system of organization, ordering the lives of everyone in a society and giving those lives meaning and purpose. The careers of volunteer workers tell us about how that meaning and purpose can be formulated outside the formal division of labor. In examining those careers we also learn something about the contributions of the private worlds, where the informal and the transactional aspects of activity predominate, to the public worlds of work. Career volunteers show how the links between private and public interests are created, how important hidden work can be.

Appendix

Respondents for this study of Pacific City women in civic leadership were chosen through the reputational sampling method. Three women acknowledged widely as volunteer leaders (so identified in local media as holders of many distinguished local and national awards and as officers and advisors on many prestigious boards) were the first interviewed and helped choose the remaining sample on the basis of their long experience in community service. Additional choices came from the women these leaders had selected. A desire to find workers from both the welfare-reform and the cultural interest branches of volunteer work determined the sample range.

Focused interviews (Merton and Kendall 1946) permitted the discussion of selected topics rather than requiring answers to a predetermined set of very specific questions. Interviews varied in length from one to four hours, sometimes requiring two or three appointments to complete. For ease in discussion, interview notes were dictated on tapes immediately afterward for later transcription. Since informants received assurance of anonymity, specific details of events and places—as well as all names—have been changed in the text in order to protect confidentiality for the women who participated in the study. The size of the sample was limited by the time available for study rather than any preconceived notion of how large a group would represent every interest and career pattern in the city. But the selected sample of women appeared frequently in responses made by other informants—both male and female—to questions about the most important volunteer women in the city. Members of the sample also appeared in public commemorations for community service. They won volunteer-of-the-year awards, were chosen for blue-ribbon commissions by elected officials, were courted by political candidates for their endorsement and by charities seeking major public figures willing to be honored at fund-raising banquets. All these indicators suggested that the desired group for study had been approached.

The first aim was to select informants from the two major areas: (1) culture, and (2) health, education, and welfare. Later, the possibility arose for refining these categories in terms of specialty areas: in culture, support of galleries for modern and oriental art as well as the established museums and libraries; chamber music as well as symphony and opera; garden clubs and historical preservation. The health, education, and welfare category expanded to include advocates for school integration, ecology, and child welfare as well as workers in such established institutions as hospitals and private schools. Respondents came from a mixed work background of volunteer/paid careers, volunteer to paid careers, and paid to volunteer careers, revealing the importance of volunteer-staff relations as well as the interest in changing from volunteer to paid status developing for women in this study. Many women spanned several interests in their careers and so they presented the contingencies of work in more subspecialties than there were informants. As the study progressed, the importance of interviewing women who moved into the worlds of politics and political advocacy for special causes emerged. Women with these interests were selected for interviews, accordingly. In addition, opportunities arose for informal discussions with many more women than could be systematically interviewed.

At the time the systematic data collection ended, there were still twenty or thirty possible informants—many of whom were contacted by telephone or encountered at local gatherings. However, none of these women represented any radically different career line; the general outlines of career contingencies for this sector of the volunteer world had appeared through the information already collected.

Some of the women chosen were not really top-level leaders but attained position through some family connection or particular attribute desired by some prestigious board. In one case I was warned away from a woman by a key informant who said the potential interview would not really be appropriate. I disregarded the advice because of the prominent name this prospect bore—and because I suspected my informant of snobbery in her dislike of the flashy manner and insignificant origins of the woman involved. Yet in the course of the interview the advisor turned out to be right. This informant sat on boards, participated in important civic and charity functions, yet had little sense of the groundwork of preparation and management involved in these activities. Her prominent name had provided her entry.

In some cases, informants had been promising leaders earlier in their careers and had risen to major positions in the community but had not continued. They spoke about formative years and early training in detail, but drew a blank on the issues of women taking over new responsibilities in mid-career. In other cases, the stature and effectiveness of an informant was ambiguous and difficult to assess. The number and variety of activities led to the suspicion that most interests were superficial. And yet examples of organizing ability and a record of their achievement (as indicated by appointments and awards) required a suspension of that judgment. In all, about six or seven women are in this amorphous category. They do, however, resemble the rest of the group in many ways; more important, their differences from the other women help sharpen the sense of what characterized the rest of the group studied. Further, these women do have careers in this world of community service even if their motivation and performance give them the appearance of stereotypical charitable ladies.

Bibliography

Acker, Joan R. 1973. "Women and Social Stratification: A Case of Intellectual Sexism." *American Journal of Sociology* 78 (January): 936–45.
———. 1980. "Women and Stratification: A Review of Recent Literature." *Contemporary Sociology* 9: 25–39.
AJL Newsline. 1984. "AJL Today: Facts and Figures 1984." New York: The Association of Junior Leagues, Inc., December.
American Council of Life Insurance. 1982. *Factsheet on Women.* Washington, D.C.: American Council of Life Insurance.
Amory, Cleveland. 1960. *Who Killed Society?* New York: Harper and Bros.
———. 1947. *The Proper Bostonians.* New York: E. P. Dutton.
Andersen, Margaret L. 1979a. "Affluence, Contentment and Resistance to Feminism." *Social Problems and Public Policy* 1: 139–60.
———. 1979b. "Corporate Wives: Longing for Liberation or Satisfied with the Status Quo?" *Urban Life* 10: 311–27.
Baltzell, E. Digby. 1958. *Philadelphia Gentlemen.* Glencoe, Ill.: The Free Press.
Bellah, Robert N., Richard Madsen, William M. Sullivan, Ann Swidler, and Steven M. Tipton. 1985. *Habits of the Heart.* Berkeley: University of California Press.
Benét, James. 1972. "California's Regents: Window on the Ruling Class." *Change Magazine.* 4 (February): 22–27.
Benét, James, and Arlene K. Daniels. eds. 1979. *Education: Straightjacket or Opportunity?* (Special issue of *Social Problems*) New Brunswick, N.J.: Transaction Press.
Berg, Barbara S. 1978. *The Remembered Gate: Origins of American Feminism.* New York: Oxford University Press.
Berger, Marilyn. 1984. "Being Brooke Astor." *New York Times Magazine,* 20 May, p. 5.
Berger, Peter L., and Thomas Luckmann. 1967. *The Social Construction of Reality.* Garden City, N.Y.: Doubleday and Co.
Bergmann, Barbara R. 1986. *The Economic Emergence of Women.* New York: Basic Books.

Berk, Sarah Fenstermaker, ed. 1980. *Women and Household Labor.* Beverly Hills: Sage Publications.

Berle, Adolf, and Gardiner C. Means. [1932] 1968. *The Modern Corporation and Private Property.* New York: Harcourt, Brace and World, Inc.

Bernard, Jessie. 1981. *The Female World.* New York: Free Press.

Birmingham, Stephen. 1982. *The Grandes Dames.* New York: Simon and Schuster.

————. 1980. *California Rich.* New York: Simon and Schuster.

Blair, Karen. 1980. *The Clubwoman as Feminist.* New York: Holmes and Meier.

Boris, Elizabeth T., Patricia A. Unkle, and Carol A. Hooper. 1981. "1980 Trustee Report." Washington, D.C.: Council on Foundations, Inc., Mimeo.

Brumberg, Joan Jacobs. 1980. "Benevolent Beginnings: Volunteer Traditions among American Women, 1800–1860." In *Women, Volunteering and Health Policy.* 1980 Conference Papers of United Hospital Fund. New York: United Hospital Fund of New York.

Burke, Kenneth. 1954. *Permanence and Change.* Los Altos, Calif.: Hermes Publications.

Capek, Mary Ellen. 1984. "The Last Word." *Association of Governing Boards Reports* (Nov.–Dec.): 46–48.

————. 1986. "Women Trustees, or 'Would You Not Be More Comfortable on the Sofa?'" In *Women in Higher Education,* edited by Mariam Chamberlain. New York: Russell Sage Foundation.

Carlson, Norma Hynethia Downs. 1981. "Informal Adoption among Black Families in the Rural South." Ph.D. diss., Northwestern University, Evanston, Illinois.

Carnegie, Dale. 1936. *How to Win Friends and Influence People.* New York: Simon and Schuster.

Cartwright, Dorwin, ed. 1957. *Studies in Social Power.* Ann Arbor: University of Michigan Press.

Chambers, Clark A. 1963. *Seedtime of Reform.* Minneapolis: University of Minnesota Press.

Clusen, Ruth. 1979. "The League of Women Voters and Political Power." In *Women Organizing,* edited by Bernice Cummings and Victoria Schuck, 112–32. Metuchen, N.J.: The Scarecrow Press, Inc.

Cohen, Gaynor. 1979. "Symbiotic Relations: Male Decision-Makers, Female Support Groups in Britain and the United States." *Women's Studies International Quarterly* 2: 391–406.

Cohn, David Lewis. 1943. *Love in America.* New York: Simon and Schuster.

Coles, Robert. 1977. *Privileged Ones: The Well-Off and the Rich in America.* Boston: Little, Brown, and Company.

Conrad, William R., Jr., and William E. Glenn. 1983. *The Effective Voluntary Board of Directors.* Athens, Ohio: Swallow Press.

Cook, Alice, Val Lorwin, Arlene K. Daniels, eds. 1984. *Women and Trade*

Unions in Eleven Industrialized Countries. Philadelphia: Temple University Press.

Cookson, Peter W., Jr., and Carolilne Hodges Persell. 1985. *Preparing for Power: America's Elite Boarding Schools*. New York: Basic Books.

Coser, Rose Laub. 1975. "Stay Home Little Sheba: On Placement, Displacement and Social Change." *Social Problems* 22 (April): 470–79.

Cruse, Harold. 1967. *The Crisis of the Negro Intellectual*. New York: William Morrow and Co., Inc.

Cummings, Bernice, and Victoria Schuck, eds. 1979. *Women Organizing*. Metuchen, N.J.: The Scarecrow Press, Inc.

Daniels, Arlene K. 1987. "The Hidden Work of Constructing Class and Community: Women Volunteer Leaders in Social Philanthropy." In *Families and Work*, edited by Naomi Gerstl and Harriet Gross. Philadelphia: Temple University Press.

———. 1985. "Good Times and Good Works: The Place of Sociability in the Work of Women Volunteers." *Social Problems* 32 (April): 363–74.

———. 1983. "Self-Deception and Self-Discovery in Fieldwork." *Qualitative Sociology* 6 (Fall): 195–214.

———. 1980. "Getting In and Getting On: The Sociology of Infiltration and Ingratiation." Colloquium Proceeding, Sociology's Relations with the Community, University of Calgary, pp. 85–97.

———. 1979a. "Development of Feminist Networks in the Professions." In *Expanding the Role of Women in the Sciences*, vol. 323 of the *Annals of the New York Academy of Sciences*, edited by Anne M. Briscoe and Sheila M. Pfafflin, 215–27. New York: The New York Academy of Sciences.

———. 1979b. "W.E.A.L.: The Growth of a Feminist Organization." In *Women Organizing*, edited by Bernice Cummings and Victoria Schuck, 133–51. Metuchen, N.J.: The Scarecrow Press, Inc.

———. 1972. "A Sub-Specialty within a Professional Specialty: Military Psychiatry." In *Medical Men and Their Work*, edited by Eliot Freidson and Judith Lorber. Chicago: Aldine-Atherton Press.

———. 1966. "The Low-Caste Stranger in Social Research." In *Ethics, Politics, and Social Research*, edited by Gideon Sjoberg, 267–96. Cambridge, Mass.: Schenkman Publishing Co., Inc.

Daniels, Arlene K., and Richard R. Daniels. 1964. "The Social Function of the Career Fool." *Psychiatry* 27, no. 3 (August): 219–29.

Davidoff, Lenore. 1973. *The Best Circles*. Totowa, N.J.: Rowman and Littlefield.

Davis, Allison, Burleigh B. Gardner, and Mary R. Gardner. 1941. *Deep South*. Chicago: University of Chicago Press.

Davis, John P. 1905. *Corporations*, vol. 2. New York: The Knickerbocker Press.

Degler, Carl N. 1980. *At Odds*. Oxford: Oxford University Press.

DeVault, Marjorie L. 1984. "Women and Food: Housework and the Production of Family Life." Ph.D. diss., Northwestern University, Evanston, Illinois.

de Tocqueville, Alexis. [1840] 1954. *Democracy in America*, vol. 2. New York: Vintage Books.

Dimaggio, Paul. 1982. "Cultural Entrepreneurship in Nineteenth-Century Boston: The Creation of an Organizational Base for High Culture in America." *Media Culture and Society* 4: 33–50.

Dimaggio, Paul, and Michael Useem. 1978. "Social Class and Arts Consumption." *Theory and Society* 5: 141–61.

———. 1978. "Cultural Property and Public Policy: Emerging Tensions in Government Support for the Arts." *Social Research* 45 (Summer): 356–89.

Dobrofsky, Lynne, R. 1977. "Women's Power and Authority in the Context of War." *Sex Roles* 3: 141–57.

Domhoff, G. W. 1971. *The Higher Circles: The Governing Class in America.* New York: Vintage Books.

———. ed. 1980. *Power Structure Research.* Beverly Hills: Sage Publications.

Douglas, Ann. 1977. *The Feminization of American Culture.* New York: Alfred A. Knopf.

Douglas, Mary, and Baron Isherwood. 1978. *The World of Goods.* New York: Basic Books, Inc.

Drake, St. Clair, and Horace R. Cayton. 1945. *Black Metropolis.* New York: Harcourt, Brace and Company.

Durkheim, Emile. 1954. *The Elementary Forms of the Religious Life.* Glencoe, Illinois: The Free Press.

Duveneck, Josephine Whitney. 1978. *Life on Two Levels.* Los Altos, Calif.: William Kaufman, Inc.

Dye, Nancy Schrom. 1980. *As Equals and Sisters: Feminism, the Labor Movement, and the Women's Trade Union League of New York.* Columbia, Missouri: University of Missouri Press.

Eriksson-Joslyn, Kerstin. 1973–74. "A Nation of Volunteers: Participatory Democracy or Administrative Manipulation?" *Berkeley Journal of Sociology* 17: 159–81.

Ferree, Myra Marx. 1980. "Satisfaction with Housework: The Social Context." In *Women and Household Labor*, edited by Sarah Fenstermaker Berk, 89–112. Beverly Hills: Sage Publications.

Fowlkes, Martha R. 1980. *Behind Every Successful Man—Wives of Medicine and Academe.* New York: Columbia University Press.

Freeman, Jo. 1972–73. "The Tyranny of Structurelessness." *Berkeley Journal of Sociology* 17: 151–64.

French, John R. P., Jr., and Bertram Raven. 1957. "The Bases of Social Power." In *Studies in Social Power*, edited by Dorwin Cartwright, 150–67. Ann Arbor: University of Michigan Press.

Fussell, Paul. 1983. *Class.* New York: Summit Books.

Galaskiewicz, Joseph. 1985. *Social Organization of an Urban Grants Economy: A Study of Business Philanthropy and Nonprofit Organizations.* Orlando, Florida: Academic Press Inc.

Gans, Herbert J. 1967. *The Levittowners*. New York: Pantheon Books.

Gilligan, Carol. 1982. *In A Different Voice*. Cambridge: Harvard University Press.

Ginzberg, E., S. W. Ginsburg, S. Axelard, and J. L. Herma. 1951. *Occupational Choice: An Approach to a General Theory*. New York: Columbia University Press.

Gittell, Marilyn, and Nancy Naples. 1981. *Women Activists and Community Organization*. New York: Carnegie Foundation.

Gittell, Marilyn, and Teresa Shtob. 1981. "Changing Women's Roles in Political Volunteerism and Reform of the City." In *Woman and the American City*, edited by Catharine R. Stimpson et al., 64–75. Chicago: University of Chicago press.

Glanz, Rudolf, 1976. *The Jewish Woman in America*, vol. 2, *The German Jewish Woman*. New York: KTAV Publishing House, Inc., and the National Council of Jewish Women.

Gold, Doris. 1971. "Women and Volunteerism." In *Women in Sexist Society*, edited by Vivian Gornick and Barbara K. Moran, 533–54. New York: Basic Books.

Gross, Martin L. 1966. *The Doctors*. New York: Random House.

Hall, Oswald. 1948. "The Stages of a Medical Career." *American Journal of Sociology* 53: 327–36.

Hall, Roberta M., and Bernice R. Sandler. 1983. "Academic Mentoring for Women Students and Faculty: A New Look at an Old Way to Get Ahead." *Project on the Status and Education of Women*. Washington, D.C.: Association of American Colleges.

Harris, Richard. 1969. *A Sacred Trust*. Baltimore: Penguin Books.

Hausknecht, Murray. 1962. *The Joiners: A Sociological Description of Voluntary Association Membership in the United States*. New York: Bedminster Press.

Heimer, Carol. 1984. "Organizational and Individual Control of Career Development in Engineering Project Work." *Acta Sociologica* 27: 283–310.

Hochschild, Arlie Russell. 1975. "Inside the Clockwork of Male Careers." In *Woman and the Power to Change*, edited by F. Howe, 47–80. New York: McGraw Hill.

Huggins, Nathan Irvin. 1971. *Protestants Against Poverty: Boston Charities 1870–1900*. Westport, Conn.: Greenwood.

Hughes, Everett Cherrington. 1971. *The Sociological Eye*. Chicago: Aldine.

———. 1958. *Men and Their Work*. Glencoe, Ill.: The Free Press.

———. 1945. "Dilemmas and Contradictions of Status." *American Journal of Sociology* 50: 353–59.

Huizinga, Johan. 1950. *Homo Ludens: A Study of the Play Element in Culture*. Boston: Beacon Press.

Hunter, Floyd. 1963. *Community Power Structure*. Garden City, N.Y.: Anchor Books.

Independent Sector. 1981. *Americans Volunteer*. Washington, D.C.: Independent Sector.

Janeway, Elizabeth. 1980. *Powers of the Weak*. New York: Alfred A. Knopf.

Kahn-Hut, Rachel, Arlene Kaplan Daniels, Richard Colvard, eds. 1982. *Women and Work: Problems and Perspectives.* New York: Oxford University Press.

Kaminer, Wendy. 1984. *Women Volunteering.* Garden City, New York: Anchor Press Doubleday and Company, Inc.

Kanter, Rosabeth Moss. 1977. *Men and Women of the Corporation.* New York: Basic Books.

Keller, Suzanne. 1963. *Beyond the Ruling Class.* New York: Random House.

Kerbo, Harold R. 1983. *Social Stratification and Inequality.* New York: McGraw Hill.

Kessler-Harris, Alice. 1981. *Women Have Always Worked.* Old Westbury, N.Y.: The Feminist Press.

Kirstein, G. 1978. "Philanthropy: The Golden Crowbar." *The Nation* 16: 235–40.

Klapp, Orrin. 1962. *Heroes, Villains and Fools.* Englewood Cliffs, New Jersey: Prentice-Hall, Inc.

Lancashire, R. D. 1971. "Occupational Choice Theory and Occupational Guidance Practice." In *Psychology at Work,* edited by P. Warr. Harmondsworth: Penguin.

Lerner, Gerda. 1977. *The Female Experience.* Indianapolis: Bobbs-Merrill.

Levinson, Daniel. 1978. *The Seasons of Man's Life.* New York: Alfred A. Knopf.

Lipman-Blumen, Jean. 1972. "How Ideology Shapes Women's Lives." *Scientific American* 266: 34–42.

———. 1974. "The Development and Impact of Female Role Ideology." In *Women 1974: A Random House Annal.* New York: Random House.

———. 1984. *Gender Roles and Power.* New Jersey: Prentice Hall.

Loeser, Herta. 1974. *Women, Work, and Volunteering.* Boston: Beacon Press.

Lofland, Lyn H. 1975. "The 'Thereness' of Women: A Selective Review of Urban Sociology." In *Another Voice,* edited by Marcia Millman and Rosabeth Moss Kanter. Garden City, N.Y.: Anchor Books.

Lopata, Helena Znaniecki. 1971. *Occupation Housewife.* New York: Oxford University Press.

Lubove, Roy. 1965. *The Professional Altruist.* Cambridge, Mass.: Harvard University Press.

Luker, Kristin. 1984. *Abortion and the Politics of Motherhood.* Berkeley, Calif.: University of California Press.

Lyman, Elizabeth. 1982. Personal communication.

Lynd, Robert S., and Helen Merrill Lynd. 1929. *Middletown.* New York: Harcourt and Brace.

———. 1937. *Middletown in Transition.* New York: Harcourt and Brace.

Mace, Myles L. 1971. *Directors: Myth and Reality.* Boston: Graduate School of Business Administration, Harvard University.

Mannheim, Karl. 1961. *Ideology and Utopia.* New York: Harcourt and Brace.

Mansbridge, Jane J. 1980. *Beyond Adversary Democracy.* New York: Basic Books.

Margolis, Diane Rothbard. 1979. "The Invisible Hands: Sex Roles and the Division of Labor in Two Local Political Parties." *Social Problems* 26: 524–38.

Marwick, Arthur. 1980. *Class: Image and Reality in Britain, France, and the U.S.A. since 1930.* New York: Oxford University Press.

Marx, Karl, and Frederick Engels. 1976. *The German Ideology,* edited by C. J. Arthur. New York: International Publishers.

Mauss, Marcel. [1925] 1967. *The Gift.* New York: W. W. Norton.

McCarthy, Kathleen D. 1982. *Noblesse Oblige.* Chicago: University of Chicago Press.

McCourt, Kathleen. 1977. *Working-Class Women and Grass-Roots Politics.* Bloomington, Indiana: Indiana University Press.

McPherson, J. Miller, and Lynne Smith-Lovin. 1982. "Women and Weak Ties: Differences by Sex in the Size of Voluntary Organizations." *American Journal of Sociology* 87: 883–904.

Merton, Robert King, and Patricia L. Kendall. 1946. "The Focused Interview." *American Journal of Sociology* 51 (May): 541–47.

Miller, George A., Eugene Galanter, and Karl H. Pribram. 1960. *Plans and the Structure of Behavior.* New York: Holt, Rinehart and Winston.

Miller, Norman. 1950. "The Jewish Leadership in Lakeport." In *Studies in Leadership,* edited by Alvin W. Gouldner, 195–227. New York: Harper and Bros.

Millman, Marcia, and Rosabeth Moss Kanter. 1975. *Another Voice.* Garden City, N.Y.: Anchor Books.

Mills, C. Wright. 1956. *The Power Elite.* New York: Oxford University Press.

Moffatt, Francis. 1977. *Dancing on the Bank of the World.* New York: G. P. Putnam's Sons.

Moore, Joan W. 1961. "Patterns of Women's Participation in Voluntary Associations." *American Journal of Sociology* 66: 592–98.

Morris, Cerise. 1982. "No More Than Simple Justice: The Royal Commission of the Status of Women in Canada." Ph.D. diss., McGill University, Montreal, Canada.

Oakley, Ann. 1981. *Subject Women.* New York: Pantheon Books.

O'Connell, Brian. 1976. *Effective Leadership in Voluntary Organizations: How to Make the Greatest Use of Citizen Service and Influence.* New York: Association Press.

———. 1982. *Analysis of the Economic Recovery Program's Direct Significance for Philanthropic and Voluntary Organizations and the People They Serve.* Washington, D.C.: Independent Sector.

Ostrander, Susan A. 1980a. "Upper-Class Women: Class Consciousness as Conduct and Meaning." In *Power Structure Research,* edited by G. William Domhoff. Beverly Hills: Sage Publications.

———. 1980b. "Upper-Class Women: The Feminine Side of Privilege." *Qualitative Sociology* 3: 23–45.

———. 1984. *Women of the Upper Class.* Philadelphia: Temple University Press.

Parsons, Talcott. 1955. "The American Family: Its Relations to Personality and to the Social Structure." In *Family, Socialization, and Interaction Process,* edited by Talcott Parsons and Robert F. Bales, 3–34. Glencoe, Ill.: The Free Press.

Perlstadt, Harry. 1975. "Voluntary Association and the Community: The Case of Volunteer Ambulance Corps." *Journal of Volunteer Action Research* 4: 85–89.

Perrow, Charles. 1963. "Goals and Power Structures: A Historical Case Study." In *The Hospital in Modern Society,* edited by Eliot Freidson. New York: The Free Press.

Potter, David M. 1964. "American Women and the American Character." In *American Character and Culture,* edited by John A. Hague, 65–84. Deland, Fla.: Everett Edwards, Inc.

Rapp, Rayna. 1982. "Family and Class in Contemporary America." In *Rethinking the Family,* edited by Barrie Thorne, 168–87. New York: Longman, Inc.

Robinson, John P. 1980. "Housework Technology and Household Work." In *Women and Household Labor,* edited by Sarah Fenstermaker Berk, 53–68. Beverly Hills: Sage Publications.

Rohatyn, Felix. 1982. "New York and the Nation." *The New York Review of Books* 28: 26–28.

Rosaldo, Michelle Zimbalist, and Louise Lamphere, eds. 1974. *Women, Culture and Society.* Stanford, Calif.: Stanford University Press.

Rosen, Ruth, and Sue Davidson, eds. 1977. *The Maimie Papers.* Old Westbury, N.Y.: The Feminist Press.

Rosenfeld, Rachel. 1979. "Women's Occupational Careers: Individual and Structural Explanations." *Sociology of Work and Occupations* 6 (August): 283–311.

Ross, Aileen. 1968. "Philanthropy." In *International Encyclopedia of the Social Sciences,* vol. 12, edited by David Sills, 72–80. New York: MacMillan and The Free Press.

———. 1953. "The Social Control of Philanthropy." *American Journal of Sociology* 58: 451–60.

———. 1952. "Organized Philanthropy in an Urban Community." *Canadian Journal of Economics and Political Science* 18: 477–86.

Rossi, Alice. 1972. "Sex Equality: The Beginnings of Ideology." In *Toward a Sociology of Women,* edited by Constantina Safilios-Rothschild. Lexington, Mass.: Xerox College Publications.

Roth, Julius A. 1963. *Timetables: Structuring the Passage of Time in Hospital Treatment and Other Careers.* Indianapolis: Bobbs-Merrill.

Rubin, Lillian B. 1972. *Busing and Backlash.* Berkeley: University of California Press.

———. 1979. *Women of a Certain Age.* New York: Harper and Row.

———. 1976. *Worlds of Pain/Life in the Working-Class Family.* New York: Basic Books.

Ruddick, Sara, and Pamela Daniels, eds. 1977. *Working It Out*. New York: Pantheon Books.

Ryan, Mary P. 1981. *Cradle of the Middle Class: The Family in Oneida County, New York, 1790–1865*. Cambridge: Cambridge University Press.

Safilios-Rothschild, Constantina, ed. 1972. *Toward a Sociology of Women*. Lexington, Mass.: Xerox College Publications.

Sanday, Peggy. 1974. "Female Status in the Public Domain." In *Women, Culture and Society*, edited by Michelle Zimbalist Rosaldo and Louise Lamphere, 189–206. Stanford, Calif.: Stanford University Press.

Saraceno, Chiara. 1984a. "The Social Construction of Childhood: Child Care and Educational Policies in Italy and the U.S." *Social Problems* 31 (February): 351–63.

———. 1984b. "Shifts in Public and Private Boundaries: Women as Mothers and Service Workers in Italian Day Care." *Feminist Studies* 10 (Spring): 7–29.

Scott, Anne Firor. 1984. "A Case of Historical Invisibility." *The Journal of American History* 71: 7–21.

Sills, David. 1968. "Voluntary Association." In *International Encyclopedia of the Social Sciences*, vol. 16, edited by David Sills, 362–79. New York: MacMillan and Co., and The Free Press.

———. 1957. *The Volunteers: Means and Ends in a National Organization*. Glencoe, Ill.: The Free Press.

Simmel, Georg. 1950. *The Sociology of Georg Simmel*, edited by Kurt Wolf. Glencoe, Illinois: The Free Press.

Sjoberg, Gideon, ed. 1967. *Ethics, Politics, and Social Research*. Cambridge, Mass.: Schenkman Publishing.

Sklar, Kathryn Kish. [1973] 1976. *Catharine Beecher: A Study in American Domesticity*. New Haven: Yale University Press. Reprint. New York: W. W. Norton.

Slater, Carol. 1960. "Class Differences in Definition of Role and Membership in Voluntary Associations among Urban Married Women." *American Journal of Sociology* 55: 616–19.

Smith, Bonnie G. 1981. *Ladies of the Leisure Class*. Princeton: Princeton University Press.

Smith, Leticia M. 1975. "Women as Volunteers: The Double Subsidy." *Journal of Voluntary Action Research* 4: 119–36.

Smith, Ralph E., ed. 1979. *The Subtle Revolution: Women at Work*. Washington, D.C.: Urban Institute.

Stack, Carol B. 1974. *All Our Kin*. New York: Harper and Row.

Stall, Susan. 1982. "The Work Women Do in a Small Rural Town." Paper presented at the Midwest Sociological Association meetings, Des Moines, Iowa.

Starr, Paul. 1982. *The Social Transformation of American Medicine*. New York: Basic Books.

Stegner, Wallace. 1978. "Introduction." In *Life on Two Levels*, by Josephine Whitney Duveneck, ix–xiii. Los Altos, Calif.: William Kaufman.

Steinem, Gloria. 1986. "The Trouble with Rich Women." *Ms.* 14 (June): 41–43, 78–80.

Steinfels, Margaret O'Brian. 1980. "Women Volunteers from 1860 to the Present: A Historical Sketch and Modest Critique." In *Women, Volunteering, and Health Policy*, Conference Papers of the United Hospital Fund. New York: United Hospital Fund of New York.

Stigler, George J. 1963. "An Academic Episode." In *The Intellectual and the Market Place*, 1–7. New York: The Free Press of Glencoe and Macmillan.

Stimpson, Catharine R., Elsa Dixler, Martha J. Nelson, and Kathryn Yatrakis, eds. 1981. *Women and the American City*. Chicago: University of Chicago Press.

Stott, Mary. 1978. *Organization Women: The Story of the National Union of Townswomen's Guilds*. London: Heinemann.

Tax, Meredith. 1980. *The Rising of the Women: Feminist Solidarity and Class Conflict 1880–1917*. New York: Monthly Review Press.

Thorne, Barrie. 1975. "Protest and the Problem of Credibility: Uses of Knowledge and Risk-Taking in the Draft Resistance Movement of the 1960's." *Social Problems* 23: 111–23.

Toffler, Alvin. 1965. *The Culture Consumers: Art and Affluence in America*. Baltimore: Penguin Books.

Tuchman, Gaye. 1975. "Women and the Creation of Culture." In *Another Voice*, edited by Marcia Millman and Rosabeth Moss Kanter, 171–202. Garden City, New York: Anchor Books.

U.S. News and World Report. 1974. "Helping People, An American Custom on the Rise." *U.S. News and World Report* 77 (September 2): 29–32.

Useem, Michael. 1984. *The Inner Circle*. New York: Oxford University Press.

Vandepol, Ann. 1982. "Dependent Children, Child Custody, and the Mother's Pensions: The Transformation of State-Family Relations in the Early 20th Century." *Social Problems* 29: 221–35.

Vanek, Joann. 1974. "Time Spent in Housework." *Scientific American* 231: 116–20.

Van Maanen, John, ed. 1977. *Organizational Careers: Some New Perspectives*. London: John Wiley and Sons.

Veblen, Thorstein. [1899] 1953. *The Theory of the Leisure Class*. New York: New American Library.

Vidich, Arthur J., and Joseph Bensman. 1968. *Small Town in Mass Society*. Princeton: Princeton University Press.

Wadel, Cato. 1979. "The Hidden Work of Everyday Life." In *Social Anthropology of Work*, edited by Sandra Wallman, 365–84. New York: Academic press.

Wallman, Sandra. 1979. "Introduction." In *Social Anthropology of Work*, 1–24. New York: Academic Press.

Ware, Susan. 1981. *Beyond Suffrage: Women in the New Deal.* Cambridge, Mass: Harvard University Press.

Warner, W. Lloyd, J. O. Low, Paul S. Lunt, and Leo Srole. 1963. *Yankee City.* New Haven: Yale University Press.

Warner, W. Lloyd, and Paul S. Lunt. 1941. *The Social Life of a Modern Community.* New Haven: Yale University Press.

Webb, Eugene J., Donald T. Campbell, Richard D. Schwartz, and Lee Sechrest. 1966. *Unobtrusive Measures: Nonreactive Research in the Social Sciences.* Chicago: Rand McNally and Company.

Weber, Max. 1946. *The Theory of Social and Economic Organization.* New York: Oxford University Press.

Weitzman, Lenore. 1985. *The Divorce Revolution.* New York: Basic Books.

Whisler, Thomas L. 1984. *Rules of the Game: Inside the Corporate Boardroom.* Homewood, Ill.: Dow Jones.

————. 1982. "Corporate Governance and the Culture of the Boardroom." Comments given before the annual meeting of the Academy of Management, New York.

Whisler, Thomas L., and Paul M. Hirsch. 1979. "Reforming the Corporate Board: A Case of Mistaken Identity?" Chicago: Mimeograph.

Whyte, William Foote. 1937. *Informal Leadership and Group Structure in Street Corner Society.* Chicago: University of Chicago Press.

Wilensky, Harold L. 1961. "Orderly Careers and Social Participation: The Impact of Work History on Social Integration in the Middle Mass." *American Sociological Review* 26: 521–39.

Wood, Miriam Mason. 1985. *Trusteeship in the Private College.* Baltimore: The Johns Hopkins University Press.

Zald, Mayer N. 1969. "The Power and Functions of Boards of Directors: A Theoretical Synthesis." *American Journal of Sociology* 75: 97–111.

Zolberg, Vera L. 1984. "American Art Museums: Sanctuary or Free-for-All?" *Social Forces* 63: 377–92.

Index

297

Please remember that this is a library book,
and that it belongs only temporarily to each
person who uses it. Be considerate. Do
not write in this, or any, library book.